Criminal Markets and Mafia Proceeds

This book estimates the proceeds of crime and mafia revenues for different criminal markets such as sexual exploitation, drugs, illicit cigarettes, loan sharking, extortion racketeering, counterfeiting, illicit firearms, illegal gambling and illicit waste management. It is the first time that scholars have adopted detailed methodologies to ensure the highest reliability and validity of the estimation. Overall, estimated proceeds of crime amount to €22.8 billion: 1.5 per cent of the Italian GDP. Of this, up to €10.7 billion (0.7 per cent of the GDP) may be attributable to the Italian mafias. These figures are considerably lower than the ones most frequently circulated on the news, without any details about their methodology, which were defined by a UN study as 'gross overestimates'. Far from underestimating criminal revenues, the results of this study bring the issue of the proceeds of crime to an empirically based debate, providing support for improved future estimates and more effective policies.

The volume's contributions were inspired by a project awarded by the Italian Ministry of Interior to Transcrime, which produced the first report on mafia investments (www.investimentioc.it).

This book was originally published as a special issue of *Global Crime*.

Ernesto U. Savona is Director of Transcrime – Joint Research Centre on Transnational Crime of Università Cattolica del Sacro Cuore and University of Trento, Italy. He has worked at the US National Institute of Justice and was also President of the European Society of Criminology (2003) and Chair of the World Economic Forum's Global Agenda Council of Organized Crime (2011). He works on organised and economic crime with attention to opportunities created for these crimes by regulation (crime proofing).

Francesco Calderoni has been Assistant Professor at Università Cattolica del Sacro Cuore and Researcher at Transcrime – Joint Research Centre on Transnational Crime, Italy, since 2005. He has been an expert for the Council of Europe (2006–2007), the European Commission (2006), and the United Nations Office on Drugs and Crime (2012 and 2014). His research focuses on the mafias and organised crime, organised crime policies, illicit trade in tobacco products and network analysis of crime.

Criminal Markets and Mafia Proceeds

Edited by
Ernesto U. Savona and Francesco Calderoni

LONDON AND NEW YORK

First published 2015
by Routledge
2 Park Square, Milton Park, Abingdon, Oxon, OX14 4RN, UK

and by Routledge
711 Third Avenue, New York, NY 10017, USA

Routledge is an imprint of the Taylor & Francis Group, an informa business

© 2015 Taylor & Francis

All rights reserved. No part of this book may be reprinted or reproduced or utilised in any form or by any electronic, mechanical, or other means, now known or hereafter invented, including photocopying and recording, or in any information storage or retrieval system, without permission in writing from the publishers.

Trademark notice: Product or corporate names may be trademarks or registered trademarks, and are used only for identification and explanation without intent to infringe.

British Library Cataloguing in Publication Data
A catalogue record for this book is available from the British Library

ISBN 13: 978-1-138-82613-7

Typeset in Times New Roman
by RefineCatch Limited, Bungay, Suffolk

Publisher's Note
The publisher accepts responsibility for any inconsistencies that may have arisen during the conversion of this book from journal articles to book chapters, namely the possible inclusion of journal terminology.

Disclaimer
Every effort has been made to contact copyright holders for their permission to reprint material in this book. The publishers would be grateful to hear from any copyright holder who is not here acknowledged and will undertake to rectify any errors or omissions in future editions of this book.

Contents

Citation Information	vii
Notes on Contributors	ix
1. Introduction: Organised crime numbers Ernesto U. Savona	1
2. Estimating the revenues of sexual exploitation: applying a new methodology to the Italian context Marina Mancuso	10
3. The retail value of the illicit drug market in Italy: a consumption-based approach Luca Giommoni	27
4. A new method for estimating the illicit cigarette market at the subnational level and its application to Italy Francesco Calderoni	51
5. Estimating the size of the loan sharking market in Italy Attilio Scaglione	77
6. Proceeds from extortions: the case of Italian organised crime groups Maurizio Lisciandra	93
7. Counterfeiting, illegal firearms, gambling and waste management: an exploratory estimation of four criminal markets Francesco Calderoni, Serena Favarin, Lorella Garofalo and Federica Sarno	108
8. Mythical numbers and the proceeds of organised crime: estimating mafia proceeds in Italy Francesco Calderoni	138
Index	165

Citation Information

The chapters in this book were originally published in *Global Crime*, volume 15, issues 1–2 (February–May 2014). When citing this material, please use the original page numbering for each article, as follows:

Chapter 1
Introduction: Organised crime numbers
Ernesto U. Savona
Global Crime, volume 15, issues 1–2 (February–May 2014) pp. 1–9

Chapter 2
Estimating the revenues of sexual exploitation: applying a new methodology to the Italian context
Marina Mancuso
Global Crime, volume 15, issues 1–2 (February–May 2014) pp. 10–26

Chapter 3
The retail value of the illicit drug market in Italy: a consumption-based approach
Luca Giommoni
Global Crime, volume 15, issues 1–2 (February–May 2014) pp. 27–50

Chapter 4
A new method for estimating the illicit cigarette market at the subnational level and its application to Italy
Francesco Calderoni
Global Crime, volume 15, issues 1–2 (February–May 2014) pp. 51–76

Chapter 5
Estimating the size of the loan sharking market in Italy
Attilio Scaglione
Global Crime, volume 15, issues 1–2 (February–May 2014) pp. 77–92

Chapter 6
Proceeds from extortions: the case of Italian organised crime groups
Maurizio Lisciandra
Global Crime, volume 15, issues 1–2 (February–May 2014) pp. 93–107

CITATION INFORMATION

Chapter 7
Counterfeiting, illegal firearms, gambling and waste management: an exploratory estimation of four criminal markets
Francesco Calderoni, Serena Favarin, Lorella Garofalo and Federica Sarno
Global Crime, volume 15, issues 1–2 (February–May 2014) pp. 108–137

Chapter 8
Mythical numbers and the proceeds of organised crime: estimating mafia proceeds in Italy
Francesco Calderoni
Global Crime, volume 15, issues 1–2 (February–May 2014) pp. 138–163

Please direct any queries you may have about the citations to
clsuk.permissions@cengage.com

Notes on Contributors

Francesco Calderoni is Assistant Professor at Università Cattolica del Sacro Cuore of Milan, Italy and researcher at Transcrime – Joint Research Centre on Transnational Crime. He has been an expert for the Council of Europe (2006–2007), the European Commission (2006), and the United Nations Office on Drugs and Crime (2012 and 2014). His research focuses on the mafias and organised crime, organised crime policies, illicit trade in tobacco products and network analysis of crime.

Serena Favarin is a PhD candidate of the International PhD in Criminology at Università Cattolica del Sacro Cuore of Milan, Italy and researcher at Transcrime – Joint Research Centre on Transnational Crime. Her research interests include spatial analysis, urban security and illegal markets.

Lorella Garofalo works at the Joint Research Centre on Transnational Crime, Università Cattolica del Sacro Cuore of Milan, Italy and Transcrime – Joint Research Centre on Transnational Crime.

Luca Giommoni is a PhD candidate in Criminology at Università Cattolica del Sacro Cuore of Milan, Italy and researcher at Transcrime – Joint Research Centre on Transnational Crime. His areas of interest are the illicit drug market, drug policy, estimates of illicit markets and organised crime.

Maurizio Lisciandra is Assistant Professor in Economics at the University of Messina, Italy. His research interests mainly focus on economics of crime, crime costing, corruption, contract theory and economic history of property rights.

Marina Mancuso has a PhD in Criminology at Università Cattolica del Sacro Cuore of Milan, Italy and is researcher at Transcrime – Joint Research Centre on Transnational Crime. Her research interests include trafficking in human beings, sexual exploitation and organised crime.

Federica Sarno is a PhD candidate of the International PhD in Criminology at Università Cattolica del Sacro Cuore of Milan, Italy and researcher at Transcrime – Joint Research Centre on Transnational Crime. Her research interests include organised crime and mafia mobility.

Ernesto U. Savona is Director of Transcrime – Joint Research Centre on Transnational Crime of Università Cattolica del Sacro Cuore and University of Trento, Italy. He has worked at the US National Institute of Justice and was also President of the European Society of Criminology (2003) and Chair of the World Economic Forum's Global Agenda Council of Organized Crime (2011). He works on organised and economic crime with attention to opportunities created for these crimes by regulation (crime proofing).

NOTES ON CONTRIBUTORS

Attilio Scaglione is a Research Fellow in the Department of Law, Society and Sport at the University of Palermo, Italy. His research interests focus on organised crime, mafia and social network analysis. His PhD thesis has been published in the monograph *Reti mafiose* (2011).

INTRODUCTION
Organised crime numbers

Ernesto U. Savona

Università Cattolica del Sacro Cuore, Transcrime, Milan, Italy

This special issue of Global Crime is devoted to estimation of the proceeds of crime and mafia revenues in Italy. The articles in this special issue have been inspired by a study conducted by Transcrime for the Italian Ministry of Interior, which analysed the investments in the legal economy of the Italian mafias.[1] The study estimated the revenues from nine criminal activities: sexual exploitation of women, illicit firearms trafficking, drug trafficking, counterfeiting, the illicit cigarette trade, illicit gambling, illicit waste disposal, loan sharking and extortion racketeering. For this special issue, each estimation was revised and updated. Five of the following articles (Mancuso on sexual exploitation, Giommoni on drugs, Calderoni on illicit cigarettes, Lisciandra on extortion racketeering and Scaglione on loan sharking) focus on criminal activities for which the literature provided some previous attempts of estimation. The article by Calderoni, Favarin, Garofalo and Sarno presents exploratory estimations for counterfeiting, illicit waste trafficking, illegal gaming machines and illicit firearm trade. These estimations are exploratory because of the lack of previous experiences in the literature. The last article by Calderoni explores a possible methodology to attribute a share of the criminal revenues to the Italian mafias.

Overall, the articles in this special issue may contribute to the discussion on what to measure in regard to criminal activities and organised crime and how to do so. After considering how the need to measure organised crime has responded to different policy needs (Section 1), this article discusses the uncertainty of estimates (Section 2), analyses possible distortions in the numbers relative to the supply of and demand for organised crime activities and advocates better methodologies and better data collection procedures (Section 3). Section 4 concludes by introducing the next logical step: examination of the impact/harm of organised crime, a topic not covered by this special issue.

1. What to count and why

Traditionally, figures on organised crime have measured the number of groups/members/associates. 'How many organised criminals are there?' was for long the question addressed by policy and research reports during the 1980s and 1990s. This question proceeded in parallel with the problem of defining organised crime and its structure. Organised crime was initially synonymous with a large organisation in conceptual opposition to individual crime. The numbers provided were more imaginary than real. Used by law enforcement to attract more resources and/or by the media to highlight the severity of the problem for the general public, or used by policy-makers to legitimise their action against crime, these numbers were never explained in terms of the criteria used for their calculation. Information came from law enforcement investigations and political inquiries and committees, and law enforcement agencies made the calculations. The level of precision varied with the perimeter and structure of the criminal organisation concerned. When the organisation was located in one country and had a hierarchical structure, like La Cosa Nostra in the United States the calculation was less approximate than in other cases, such as Chinese or Russian organisations, less concentrated in a single country and comprising many different sub-organisations.

Subsequently, the attention slowly shifted from the number of members to the number of groups.[2] Answering the question 'how many organised crime groups are there?' yielded the necessary information on the level of complexity of organised crime in a given country, and on three other aspects: their level of fragmentation, competition and collusion. In the 1990s, discussion of the Colombian cartels was largely restricted to two of them – the Medellin and Cali cartels – even though they comprised a plurality of small organisations. Today, the number of cartels in Mexico is much larger; and because the geographical perimeter is the same, their number indicates the extent of organised crime in Mexico and also explains the violence among rival groups. In this case, numbers on groups contain more information than numbers on members. This may help law enforcement agencies in gauging the level of organised crime violence in local criminal markets, and in devising strategies, e.g. on whom should be arrested for reducing the fragmentation between groups and, indirectly, favouring the emerging of a monopolist one. The number of groups is less important for policy-makers because they do not help in identifying the right policies to address the phenomenon. If the focus is on crime control policies, one or more organised crime groups makes no difference. If the focus shifts towards opportunity reduction, in line with one of the prevailing approaches in Criminology, knowledge should rather focus on activities.[3] Knowing which activities organised criminals carry out and what are their economic benefits may allow policy-makers to pay attention to those opportunities available in the legitimate markets that could be exploited by organised crime.

2. What numbers?

What do we need to know today about illegal activities and/or organised crime? What are the numbers that yield better understanding of the problem and are useful for devising effective policies? If the approach to organised crime should be targeted more closely on reducing opportunities (prevention) and not consist solely in crime control policies, it is necessary to know where the opportunities for organised crime lie, what their economic magnitude is and how they impact on the legitimate economy. A recent example can clarify the point. The debate in favour of legalising marijuana ongoing in many countries, including Italy, has as its main argument the reduction of the opportunities offered by marijuana's illegality to organised crime. To test this argument, one should start by quantifying the criminal business generated by marijuana (turnover) and the profits of criminal organisations, then the impact of this legalisation on health, law enforcement and criminal justice should be assessed, and the harm measured. If this analysis is done correctly, it will help to focus on the costs and benefits of legalisation, thus assisting policy-makers and citizens to make appropriate choices and avoid ideological discussions.

These numbers are more important today as globalisation may increase the opportunities for legitimate enterprises and their criminal competitors. Regulation, a lack of controls and many other factors create opportunities for criminal exploitation. Various actors – organised crime groups or legitimate enterprises acting illegally – are attracted by these conditions and seek to transform the system's vulnerabilities into criminal opportunity, transferring the costs to institutions and individuals. The 'reducing opportunities' approach should focus not only on 'who' acts illegally, but also on 'what' their criminal activities are. The concept of illicit trade is broader than that of organised crime because it includes both criminal organisations producing, trafficking and selling drugs in violation of the law (in this case the UN and Regional Conventions against drugs) and legal enterprises trying to commercialise their products by avoiding taxes and/or breaching regulations (illicit fisheries). The concept of illicit trade covers the two areas of organised crime and economic crime, and the distinctions between them become less relevant.[4] This twofold focus on 'Who' and 'What' calls for data not only on the number of criminals and groups, but also on the revenues and profits from criminal activities, their economic size and their impact on the public and private sectors. This knowledge is of importance for the planning of crime prevention and crime control activities. What opportunities should be monitored? What vulnerabilities should be reduced? And what role can the private and public sectors play in reducing the harm caused by illicit trade?

Numbers become all the more important in this perspective because there is no limit to criminal creativity. Every day a new illicit trade is added to the long list of the ways in which persons are trafficked and commodities are illegally traded. When a new criminal activity is not well known, a new label is created, and an estimate is usually formulated to emphasise its seriousness. Frequently, this is a tactic to raise awareness and give the general public an idea of the scale of the problem. Nevertheless, these 'mythical numbers', accompanied by summary descriptions of the activities, are rarely the result of reliable data collection and transparently produced estimates. As a consequence, monitoring of the phenomena is difficult. International organisations, governments and businesses, which need to take action against illicit trade, are unable to determine how, where and on whom the illicit trade impacts.

Despite the above mentioned problems, reliable, valid and when possible comparable measures of the scale of illicit trades and their impact could contribute in orienting strategies and decisions. International organisations, governments and businesses can use these figures for various purposes. International organisations and governments may consider these estimates with the primary objective of monitoring illicit trade. They would thus be better informed on the scale, flow and trends, and therefore able to develop suitable countermeasures. The figures could be useful for businesses as well, familiarising them with potential victimisation and the risk of investments in a given market and/or country.

There is a demand for the collection of data that are more comparable (when they can be compared taking different definitions and sources into account), valid (when they measure the phenomenon without bias) and reliable (when data analysis can be repeated and yields the same results on different occasions). Consequently, the supply of transparent estimates is becoming an increasingly important issue for researchers and policy-makers at the public and private level. The academic literature expresses this demand, underlining the urgent policy needs at stake.[5] The special issue of this journal goes in this direction. Even if it is restricted to the proceeds of crime and mafia revenues for some criminal activities in Italy, the problems and methods adopted in the following articles could contribute to the international debate.

3. Markets, numbers and distortions

Data are needed to measure the revenues of illicit trade and its impacts. Both require a series of analyses ranging from very rough data, such as seizures, to more sophisticated ones on the demand for and supply of goods and commodities. The methodologies used to estimate the revenues from the criminal activities in Italy, and which are included in this special issue, vary according to the data available. The Italian exercise set out in this special issue is an example at basic level (impact is not considered) of what could and should be done internationally in defining criminal activities and measuring their revenues in a transparent and consistent way.

The measurement of the revenues and impacts of illicit trade does not go without problems. Distortions remain in the data collected and used for the estimates. They may produce a misrepresentation of the phenomenon which is either intentional or unintentional. The various articles included in this special issue consider the data collected for each activity and discuss their validity.

A number of factors on the quality, validity and reliability of data should be taken into account when estimates are made of the size and revenues of criminal activities and organised crime.

Law enforcement agencies are the main producers of data on illegal markets and organised crime from a supply side perspective. Their data are quantitative, e.g. reported crimes, and qualitative, e.g. evidence from investigations. The data may become official crime data when published in aggregated or disaggregated form according to the field concerned. Data are related to the crime committed and to the perpetrator. Both may be relevant and may be used as proxies for the size of the groups and their involvement in illegal activities. Other figures, such as those on homicides, may be used to assess the level of conflict among criminal organisations. Often, the data most frequently used for estimating illegal activities are those on seizures. If these are not interpreted and crossed with other data, as often happens, the information provided carries risks of distortion that may be unintentional or intentional.

Data on crimes reported can be attributed to organised crime when information is available on the perpetrators. More are these data on the perpetrator better is the possible qualification as an organised crime member. When data on crimes are not disaggregated by type of perpetrator, the attribution to organised crime carries the risk that, in a country known for a strong presence of organised crime, everything becomes organised crime. The opposite happens in the case of a country where organised crime is not perceived as a major issue. Both cases show distortions in the significance of the problem. When data on the perpetrator/s are not available, the assumption that the crime reported has been committed by organised crime is made by those who receive the report and enter the information into the system. If they have a clear protocol on how to classify the data that they receive, and if they are well trained in using this protocol, the risk of errors diminishes. Conversely, the risk of distortion increases.

When numbers represent the revenues from criminal activities, the risks of distortion increase. Law enforcement agencies produce data on seizures of all goods that are illegal, such as drugs and counterfeited goods, or which violate tax regulations, such as tobacco, alcohol and oil. Data are usually classified by quantities, which may be kilos or grams for drugs or by numbers and types for counterfeit merchandise. Seizures are also sometimes classified by the number of operations carried out. Data on seizures are influenced by many different factors. Seizures increase if the investigative capacity of the law enforcement organisation is high, and if they are allocated to transportation points (harbours, borders) where the likelihood of identification of the illegal goods is high because of their concentration. The origin of the cargo and other data requested by customs may help in understanding more about the scale of the activity during the importation phase.

Data on seizures of goods in the distribution phase are less helpful to measure the revenues from illicit activities. Seizures of drugs and counterfeited goods in certain locations may say more about the structure of the market at local level than about the scale of the activities.

Seizures may be used as proxies for the revenues from criminal activities if they are collected in a time series using both types of data (quantities and numbers of operations), if the points of transportation are mapped, they inform more about the supply of criminal activities in a given context. They do so even more if it is possible to add information on the perpetrators and facilitators, such as criminal groups operating in the areas involved (sending country and/or receiving country), and more if information can be added about the vulnerability of the point of importation (lack of controls and the presence of corruption). Indeed, these are the ways in which seizures have been used in some of the articles included in this special issue.

When seizures are considered solely as indicators of the revenues from criminal activities, because they are relatively easy to quantify and compare across countries, there is a greater risk of distortion. Also if these data could be easily comparable their distortion is high. Taken randomly, seizures on their own represent more the activity of law enforcement and customs agencies than the scale of the criminal activities.

Seizures and confiscations are also indicative of the assets of organised crime groups. Seizures may be proxies with which to quantify the proceeds from crime and investments of criminal groups because these assets may be confiscated only when there is strong evidence of a relation between these assets and the criminal characteristics of their owner. Law enforcement agencies usually produce figures on the assets seized and confiscated. The study by Transcrime which inspired all the essays in this special issue used the assets confiscated by the Italian authorities as proxies for the types of investment made by Italian organised crime.[6] This analysis opted in favour of confiscated assets instead of seizures data. Confiscation data may be more outdated, less frequently updated and less numerous, but they are better than seizures data because of the uncertainty of the latter.

These data are more distorted when they refer to the criminal organisation that has made the investments. Official data do not state the owners of investments, and it has been necessary to link assets to criminal groups through a series of secondary information, as detailed in the appendices to the Transcrime's report.

Data on the confiscation of organised crime assets vary from place to place. If they are not analysed in conjunction with other data, they more likely represent the activity of law enforcement agencies. The study by Transcrime used them as proxies and analysed them in conjunction with other variables, uncovering their potential for a better understanding of the investments of organised crime. Also, the study stressed the need for better data at country level, which, if standardised, could be useful for comparisons across countries and across the different economies of organised crime. Another project coordinated by Transcrime, project OC Portfolio funded under the DG HOME ISEC Programme, works in this direction.[7]

A variety of other, more qualitative, data derive from law enforcement investigations and criminal justice files. They range among the prices of drugs and other commodities at different market levels. Information is usually collected through convicted criminals. The case of data relative to smuggled or trafficked persons is relevant. More than counting the numbers of women trafficked for sexual exploitation or men for labour exploitation, surveys consider the different types of exploitation. Valid numbers may be provided when the prices paid by those who have been smuggled, trafficked or exploited is considered. Price is an essential component of a good estimate, but when data on demand are not reliable, the end result is poor because price on its own does not help. For this reason, better data on the demand side are needed.

Some data on the demand for criminal products are contained in crime statistics. More than the demand for these products, these statistics show the number of users that have been criminalised. Usually they gather a very low sample of the entire universe of drug users. For this reason, the demand represented by crime statistics says more about the criminalisation process than about the demand for criminal goods or services. If crime statistics on drug users or on persons who buy counterfeit goods are compared internationally, they may produce more distortion than information. Other official statistics, such as health statistics on the users of legal drugs like alcohol and tobacco, may help to quantify the demand for these goods. However, they should be treated with caution and never used alone, because they usually represent a specific segment of the population of users (those who go for treatment).

There is a need for other data which, merged with official ones, help to quantify the demand for illicit activities and thus shed light on the demand side of an illicit market. The area of drugs with significant health implications is populated by these surveys, which are well established at country and international level, where numbers of users by type of drug may be found. Giommoni's article in this special issue uses survey data to analyse the demand for different types of drugs and to estimate the size of the Italian drug trade. The 'health filter' helps in producing valid estimates. But this does not apply to other illegal markets such as counterfeiting, or dual markets such as alcohol, tobacco and gambling, where surveys on illegal users are in their infancy.

Counterfeiting is today a salient issue in the public debate on illicit markets for two reasons: its impact on businesses and the harm caused to health and security when pharmaceuticals, car or aircraft parts and food are involved. Rand Europe has conducted a literature review of studies proposing methodologies with which to estimate counterfeiting in various sectors.[8] The conclusion is as follows:

> It is clear from the review of the counterfeiting literature that, while numerous attempts to approximate the scale of the problem have been made, there has been little convergence on a preferred methodology and innovation in methods and forms of collecting data continues. Furthermore it is often difficult to assess the quality of specific studies in this literature, as there is frequently a lack of transparency about assumptions, data values or sources.[9]

The same conclusion is drawn by an OECD study[10] which, after estimates on counterfeiting and piracy, concludes that 'Many cited estimates of the scope and magnitude (and especially impact) of counterfeiting and piracy appear to be guesswork', adding that 'Governments and industry can help by maximizing the value of data by ensuring that it is systematically collected, comparable, comprehensive'.[11] The OECD study together with the Rand Europe report advocate involving private companies in the measurement process. The cooperation between public and private in fighting illicit trade should start from the data availability, a leitmotif heard at conferences but not put into practice. It seems that ignorance of the scale of the counterfeiting problem prevails over its real assessment. This lack of knowledge and the consequent distortions are useful for various reasons: private companies do not want to provide information on their victimisation because they fear that these data may be exploited by competitors. Some companies operating in the luxury apparel sector argue a single counterfeited item corresponds to the loss of production of the same legal item. That is to say, for every fake Rolex watch that enters the market there is a legal one that leaves it: a relation that does not exist, however, because the demand for fake watches is completely different from the demand for legal ones. Unfair competition may arise when the demand for car and aircraft parts or food are met by the counterfeiting industry when the customer is not aware and he/she pays the legal price.[12]

In some field, the contribution of the private sector to the measurement of the illicit trade is relevant. For example, since 2006, tobacco manufacturers have supported KPMG's Star Report which estimates the size of the illicit cigarette market in the Member States of the European Union.[13] This special issue includes an article by Calderoni which estimates the Italian illicit cigarette market based on the Star report, empty pack surveys and other data. Even if the quality of these data is questionable, the Star Report today is the only source of information on this illicit trade which provides annual estimates through a constant methodology. Is this a way to exert pressure to combat the illicit trade in tobacco products? Could it be part of the strategy of those companies to reduce the competition raised by the illegal markets? If this is the purpose, it is to be hoped that other industries will follow suit and provide data on the demand for and supply of illicit goods. Improvements can be made to data collection methods, but it is necessary to start from few data for gradually increasing their quantity and improving their quality. When this would be accomplished and data collected in a transparent way, it will possible to move ahead, assessing the impact of organised crime and measuring its harm to public and private sectors.

4. Introducing the next step: assessing the impact, measuring the harm

This special issue produces estimates of revenues from organised crime in Italy. Its value consists in the methodology used and adapted to the various criminal activities. Despite all the methodologies being applied to the Italian case, they call for better and more transparent methodologies that can be used in any country. This is the only antidote to the virus of the 'mythical numbers' that today form the content of the public discourse on organised crime in Italy and elsewhere (as discussed in the concluding article by Calderoni on mythical numbers and mafia revenues). Without valid numbers on the revenues side, it is not possible to conduct reliable analyses of the harm/cost by organised crime and its activities. Measurements of scale and impact inevitably go together.

Attempts have been made in the past to assess the cost of organised crime.[14] They use the paradigm developed by Brand and Price[15] and apply it to certain activities of organised crime.[16] The following are the costs considered in the literature originating from Brand and Price's work:

- Costs in anticipation of crime include defensive expenditure (for example, on chip and pin technology to help prevent credit card fraud) and precautionary behaviour; they are considered to be costs of crime because they are based on the risk of becoming a victim.
- Costs as a consequence of crime include the value of property stolen or damaged (for example, the value of plastic fraud), time costs of replacing property, documents and so on, the emotional and physical impact and reduced quality of life for victims and reduced effectiveness at work of people affected by crime. In cases where crime involves violence to the victim, health care costs fall on the health system and other health service providers.
- Costs in response to crime are numerous, and they generally relate to the criminal justice system. This includes costs of the police, criminal justice system, legal aid and non-legally aided defence costs and costs to the prison and probation services.

These cost items have been summarised in a recent report for the European Parliament as follows[17]:

- Private costs: these impact upon individuals directly connected to the victim;
- Parochial costs: these are born through community ties;
- Public costs: these occur when the impacts are shared among citizens not directly connected with each other.

The authors of the report to the European Parliament maintain that these categories are preferable to the Brand and Price paradigm because they are less static.[18] However, although they are less static, they cannot be operationalised as they should be.

If there are different categories for assessing the cost of organised crime, it is clear that harm and its costs should be extended to private business. To date, this issue has not been properly addressed because in the old perspective of crime control policies the main costs were direct ones related to victims, together with anticipation and response costs.

On shifting to a reduction-of-opportunity approach where organised and economic crime overlap, these cost categories should be widened and in some ways more closely focused. It is necessary more thoroughly to consider those factors that enable or facilitate the development of organised crime.[19] Money laundering and corruption are today among these costs because they produce unfair competition, thereby distorting the rules of the markets in which businesses operate. The impact of counterfeiting requires specific analysis of the various markets and related industries. There are similarities between counterfeit pharmaceuticals and counterfeit cigarettes also because both may damage the health of consumers and withdraw taxes from countries and income from producers. Differences should be considered when dealing with luxury products, in which case health is not an issue but the infringement of intellectual property rights causes damage to the legal manufacturers of luxury goods.

The debate on the measurement of organised crime has moved from the number of an organisation's members to identification and measurement of the opportunities exploited by criminal organisations. Concepts should be operationalised, indicators should be developed, proxies should be selected and data should be collected in order that the phenomena are analysed more accurately. The virtuous circle among more data, better methodologies, more impact assessment, harm analysis and focused public and private policies can be credible only if it is explained how the data have been collected and interpreted, so that everyone can control the process and repeat the analysis.

Notes

1. Transcrime, *Progetto PON Sicurezza 2007–2013*.
2. Europol, *EU Organised Crime Situation Report 1998*.
3. Bullock Clarke, and Tilley, *Situational Prevention of Organised Crimes*.
4. Ruggiero, *Organized and Corporate Crime in Europe*; and Di Nicola, *La Criminalità Economica Organizzata*.
5. Singer, "Vitality of Mythical Numbers"; Reuter, "(Continuing) Vitality of Mythical Numbers"; and Woodiwiss and Hobbs, "Organized Evil and the Atlantic Alliance."
6. Transcrime, *Progetto PON Sicurezza 2007–2013*.
7. For more information, see http://www.ocportfolio.eu/
8. Hoorens et al., *Measuring IPR Infringements*.
9. Ibid.
10. OECD, *Economic Impact of Counterfeiting and Piracy*.
11. Stryszowski, "Counterfeiting and Piracy," f. 12.

12. For a detailed analysis of the counterfeiting market see Favarini's contribution in the article 'Counterfeiting, illegal firearms, gambling and waste management: an exploratory estimation of four criminal markets' within this special issue.
13. KPMG, *Project Star 2010 Results*.
14. Savona and Vettori, "Evaluating the Cost of Organised Crime."
15. Brand and Price, *Economic and Social Costs*.
16. Home Office, *Organised Crime*.
17. Levi, Martin, and Gundur, *Economic, Financial & Social Impacts*.
18. Ibid., 71.
19. Global Agenda Council on Organized Crime, *Organized Crime Enablers*.

References

Brand, Sam, and Richard Price. *The Economic and Social Costs of Crime*. London: Home Office Research Study, 2000.
Bullock, Karen, Ronald V. Clarke, and Nick Tilley, eds. *Situational Prevention of Organised Crimes*. Cullompton, Devon: Willan Publishing, 2010.
Di Nicola, Andrea. *La Criminalità Economica Organizzata. Le Dinamiche Dei Fenomeni, Una Nuova Categoria Concettuale e Le Sue Implicazioni Di Policy*. Milano: Franco Angeli, 2006.
Europol. *EU Organised Crime Situation Report 1998*. The Hague: Europol, 2000.
Global Agenda Council on Organized Crime. *Organized Crime Enablers*. Geneve: World Economic Forum, 2012. Accessed December 18, 2013. http://www.weforum.org/reports/organized-crime-enablers
Home Office. *Organised Crime: Revenues, Economic and Social Costs, and Criminal Assets Available for Seizure*. London: Home Office, 2007.
Hoorens, Stijn, Hunt Priscillia, Malchiodi Alessandro, Pacula Rosalie Liccardo, Kadiyala Srikanth, Rabinovich Lila, and Barrie Irving. *Measuring IPR Infringements in the Internal Market. Development of a New Approach to Estimating the Impact of Infringements on Sales*. Brussels: RAND Europe, 2012.
KPMG. *Project Star 2010 Results*. Geneva: Philip Morris International, 2011. Accessed December 18, 2013. http://www.pmi.com/eng/tobacco_regulation/illicit_trade/documents/Project_Star_2010_Results.pdf
Levi, Michael, Innes Martin, and Rajeev V. Gundur. *The Economic, Financial & Social Impacts of Organised Crime in the EU*. Brussels: European Parliament, 2013.
OECD. *The Economic Impact of Counterfeiting and Piracy*. Paris: Organization for Economic Cooperation and Development, 2008.
Reuter, Peter. "The (Continuing) Vitality of Mythical Numbers." *Public Interest* 75 (1984): 135–147.
Ruggiero, Vincenzo. *Organized and Corporate Crime in Europe: Offers That Can't Be Refused*. Aldershot: Dartmouth, 1996.
Savona, Ernesto U., and Barbara Vettori. "Evaluating the Cost of Organised Crime from a Comparative Perspective." *European Journal on Criminal Policy and Research* 4, no. 15 (2009): 379–393.
Singer, Max. "The Vitality of Mythical Numbers." *Public Interest* 23 (1971): 3–9.
Stryszowski, Piotr. "Counterfeiting and Piracy: Statistics and Data Gathering." Paper presented at the OECD conference on illicit trade, Paris, April 2, 2013.
Transcrime. *Progetto PON Sicurezza 2007–2013. Gli Investimenti Delle Mafie*. Rapporto finale del progetto "I beni sequestrati e confiscati alle organizzazioni criminali nelle regioni dell'Obiettivo Convergenza: dalle strategie di investimento della criminalità all'impiego di fondi comunitari nel riutilizzo dei beni già destinati." Roma: Ministero dell'Interno. Accessed December 18, 2013. www.investimentioc.it
Woodiwiss, Michael, and Dick Hobbs. "Organized Evil and the Atlantic Alliance. Moral Panics and the Rhetoric of Organized Crime Policing in America and Britain." *British Journal of Criminology* 49, (2009): 106–128.

Estimating the revenues of sexual exploitation: applying a new methodology to the Italian context

Marina Mancuso

Transcrime Joint Research Centre on Transnational Crime, Università Cattolica del Sacro Cuore, Largo Gemelli, Milan, Italy

This article presents a methodology which allows to estimate the revenues of the sexual exploitation market, both outdoor and indoor, at subnational level. It is applied to the Italian context. The findings suggest that the revenues are not equally distributed across regions since they depend on different criminal opportunities and levels of demand.

Introduction

The sex market is a complex one because it is composed of different sub-markets, among them prostitution and sexual exploitation.[1] The former, defined as the 'exchange of sexual favours for money and/or other material benefits',[2] may be legal or illegal according to the legislation of the country concerned.[3] The latter is always considered an illegal market. It occurs when prostitutes lack autonomy and their activities and revenues are controlled by a third party.[4] In this case, people sexually exploited (mainly women, but also men and transgenders) are forced to prostitute themselves and to give the money earned to their exploiters. They are not free to decide their work schedules or to plan their movements because they are considered as a property by their exploiters. Like prostitution, sexual exploitation may take place outdoors or indoors (in private apartments or nightclubs).[5]

Considering the seriousness of this crime and the violation of human rights to which the victims are subject,[6] in recent years many studies on sexual exploitation have been carried out by international organisations and governments. These are studies at international and continental level, mainly on Europe and Africa, which are considered to be two key areas along the sex trafficking routes.[7] Indeed, this illicit market is often a transnational one which involves various countries: the origin countries in which the victims are recruited, transit countries, and destination countries in which there is high demand for sexual services.

Sexual exploitation is considered a crime which can generate high proceeds,[8] even though research on this issue is very limited. Therefore this study develops a methodology with which to estimate at subnational level the illicit revenues deriving from sexual exploitation, mainly of foreign women.[9] It applies the methodology to the Italian context because Italy is an interesting scenario in the sex trafficking market. Its strategic geographical position, increased affluence and the existence of a flourishing sex market have transformed it into a country of destination and transit for victims bound for the northern

EU countries.[10] With the entry into force of the so-called 'Merlin Law' (Law 75/1958), Italy adopted an abolitionism policy which replaced the regulation policy that had existed since 1861. According to this new legislation, prostitution in Italy is not illegal since only sexual exploitation constitutes a crime. Many scholars underline that this illicit practice in Italy mostly involves foreign women exploited by criminal groups mainly consisting of fellow countrymen.[11]

The article is divided into four main sections. The first section describes the characteristics of the sexual exploitation market and provides an overview of the available international and national estimates with their methodologies. The second section presents the methodology developed to produce estimates at regional level. The third section discusses the results, and the last one concludes.

The sexual exploitation market: characteristics and estimates

Demand and supply

As regards demand, some studies have sought to determine who the clients of prostitutes are, and their motives for paying for sexual services. They are based on information obtained from the analysis of self-selected samples of clients (e.g. online forums for clients and interviews with some of them). The results are very similar. Clients are rational consumers aware of the risks that they face in terms of health and reputation.[12] The main reasons for consuming sexual services by paying are: the desire to satisfy basic needs without having to invest in affection; being in a dominant position over women; the possibility to have particular sexual experiences; and varying people with whom to have these experiences. Besides these reasons, there are also the difficulty of finding stable partners and the possibility to forget personal problems and regain self-confidence.[13]

As regards supply, the literature has focused mainly on women exploited in the sex market. In general these women are from poor countries with high rates of poverty and unemployment (primarily countries in Northern and Western Africa and the Balkans). They are induced to move to economically more attractive countries (Italy, Spain, The Netherlands, Belgium, United Kingdom, Germany) by means of deception, force, threats or magic rituals according to their nationality.[14] The risk factors of the potential victims are connected with their status as women: greater vulnerability, higher susceptibility to manipulation, lower ability to protect themselves and defend their rights, lower levels of education and reduced employment prospects.[15] In recent years, a number of studies have underlined that some women are aware of the work that they will do in the destination country before they leave, even if they do not know the exploitation that they will suffer.[16] They agree to prostitute themselves mainly in order to support their families.[17]

Focusing on Italy, the arrival of foreign women has entailed a significant decrease in the prices of sexual services and a high mobility of prostitutes.[18] However, there are no precise data on the number of women victims of sexual exploitation in the total number of prostitutes.[19] One source reports that in 2004–2005 victims of prostitution ascribable to slavery accounted for 7–8% of total estimated adult prostitution, 14% if children were also included.[20]

The actors of sexual exploitation

According to the existing studies on the actors involved in sexual exploitation in Italy, foreign organised criminal groups are mainly responsible for commission of the crime.[21] In general, offenders have the same nationality as the victims. This facilitates recruitment and transportation, which require a common cultural and linguistic background if they are to be performed successfully. The extent and level of organisation of these groups vary according to the number of victims exploited and their relational and economic resources. There are very flexible and decentralised groups operating on a large scale, and more informal and restricted ones.[22] However, small criminal networks characterised by strong family and ethnic ties seem to be the most common.[23] They have a high level of internal cohesion and work autonomously without creating coalitions in order to gain monopoly on the market.[24]

Like criminals operating in other illicit markets, the members of these groups are rational actors who want to obtain high profits with few risks of being identified by law enforcement agencies, prosecuted and convicted. They are able to exploit criminal opportunities for enrichment connected with human migration and globalisation. Indeed, they present themselves as providers of services that satisfy the desire of the migrants to have better lives in another country.[25]

According to the literature, the Italian mafias have no direct interest in investing in sexual exploitation due to the traditional respect they feel for women.[26] They exercise only indirect control over the activities of foreign criminal groups.[27] In particular, as regards outdoor prostitution, they give authorisation to use certain streets in exchange for favours mainly linked with facilitations in purchasing drugs.[28] With regard to indoor prostitution, some recent cases of infiltration of nightclubs have been recorded. In these cases, mafias offered amounts of money and company shares until they gained economic control over the nightclubs.[29]

Estimates of the sexual exploitation market

All the estimates of the size of the sexual exploitation market have limitations. Many of them concern the high 'dark number' characterising this crime.[30] Because victims are completely subjugated by their exploiters, they are unlikely to report the crime to law enforcement agencies for fear of retaliation against them and their families. The physical and psychological submission hinders real awareness of their victim status, reinforcing dependence on their exploiters.[31] Other limitations concern the different methodologies used to collect and process data, as well as the difficulty of comparing the estimates due to different legislations and definitions of the crime.[32]

Despite these problems, some attempts have been made to estimate this illicit market in order to gain better understanding of its extent, and thereby identify adequate strategies to combat it. International organisations and governmental institutions have made estimates at international level. The International Labour Organisation (ILO), starting from reports of forced labour recognised under the ILO Convention N. 29 and 105, estimated that about 2.45 million people suffer a form of forced labour ascribable to human trafficking, 43% of whom are victims of sexual exploitation.[33] The US Department of State, on analysing data from American embassies, non-governmental offices and organisations, international organisations and other institutions, has estimated that 800,000 people are trafficked annually: 80% of them are women and children mainly involved in the sexual exploitation market.[34] Finally, the United Nations Office on Drugs and Crime (henceforth UNODC) produces periodic reports on trafficking in human beings presenting data on the global extent of sexual exploitation.[35] The last UNODC report was published in December 2012. The data contained in it referred to 132 countries and covered a two-year period, from August 2010 to August 2012. Some 88% of the data derived from national institutions, 5% from international governmental organisations and 7% from non-governmental organisations. They were collected from questionnaires distributed to governments, the results of the 'United Nations National Survey of Crime Trends and Operations of Criminal Justice Systems' and from official surveys in the public domain.[36] The findings showed that there had been a progressive reduction in victims of sexual exploitation between 2007 and 2011 (62% of victims whose exploitation was known in 2007 and 52% in 2011),[37] even though it was still the most frequent form of exploitation detected in Europe, Central Asia and the Americas.[38]

As regards the total amount of revenues produced by sexual exploitation, a study carried out by Belser provided a global estimate of almost 34 billion dollars.[39] This number was obtained by multiplying the average profits per victim by the estimated number of victims. In order to estimate the average profits per victim, some information was considered: the prices paid by clients according to the political, economic and social context of the geographical area concerned, the number of clients and the money withheld by victims. The prices of sexual services ranged from 15 to 16 dollars in Asia and Sub-Saharan regions to 100 dollars in the richer and more developed countries. They were defined according to different sources – not well-specified – including a tourist guide on the sex sector. The number of clients considered was 3 or 4 clients per day based on a large quantity of information collected from many sources, not well-specified either. With regard to the money withheld by victims, it was fixed at 30% of the total turnover according to an Interpol report published in 2002, which analysed the accounts of pimps in Finland.[40]

Some estimates of sexual exploitation market are available also at European level. In particular, UNODC has estimated from open sources that about 70,000 people are trafficked annually into Europe to be sexually exploited;[41] between 11,400 and 17,100 of them from West Africa.[42] The International Organization for Migration (IOM) has estimated that around 200,000 women and children are trafficked for sexual exploitation from Eastern Europe to the European Union.[43]

The only estimate on the revenues at European level has been made by UNODC. This estimated an annual turnover of 3 billion dollars[44] and a variable turnover between 152 and 228 million dollars resulting only from the sexual exploitation of West African women.[45] In this case the estimate was calculated by considering the stock of victims in Europe (about 140,000), 50 million sexual services provided annually, and 50 euros as the average price charged to clients.[46]

Some studies on specific European countries have produced estimates of the revenues arising from sexual exploitation. The methodology commonly used consists in estimating the average revenues per prostitute and multiplying the result by the total number of prostitutes.[47] In the United Kingdom, Dubourg and Prichard calculated the revenues produced by the sexual exploitation of trafficked women in specific indoor locations (i. e. flats, saunas and massage parlours, escort agencies and walk-ups). The total market size was the sum of the revenues identified in each of these locations both in London and in the rest of the UK. The revenues per location were obtained by multiplying the total number of exploited women in each location by the annual revenue per woman. The latter was calculated considering: number of sexual services provided in one day, price of the services, working days in a week and working weeks in a year. This information was gathered from a previous study published by Moffatt and Peters in 2004 on the UK prostitution industry. According to the method applied, the working days per week were multiplied by the working weeks. The result obtained was in turn multiplied by the number of sexual services per day and then by the price per service. According to the methodology adopted, the total market size in the UK was £277 million.[48]

Other studies on specific countries have shown the variables which affect the cost of sexual services (age of the woman, place in which the sexual service is consumed, the appearance of the woman, type of sexual service provided, duration of the encounter and geographical area),[49] and they have considered the relation between safe sex and the cost of sexual services.[50]

Italy

Most of the available estimates on the number of sexual exploitation victims in Italy have been produced by three research centres. These estimates refer to foreign women because they represent 90% of the prostitutes working on the street,[51] between 75% and 80% of women involved in indoor prostitution in the northern and central regions and between 40% and 50% of those in the southern regions.[52]

The first estimate was produced by PARSEC, a research centre in the district of Rome. It estimated the minimum and maximum number of foreign women involved in outdoor and indoor sexual exploitation at regional level. Data on sexual exploitation on the street referred to spring 2008–spring 2009. They were obtained from information collected by social workers providing assistance to women on the street. Data on indoor sexual exploitation referred to the period June 2004–June 2005. They derived from a coefficient representing the relation between indoor and outdoor prostitution, equal to 68.1%, identified by analysis of three studies on indoor prostitution.[53]

The second estimate on the yearly number of sexual exploitation victims in Italy was produced by Transcrime. The last one available dates to March 2003/March 2004. It was obtained on the basis of the number of victims contacting non-governmental organisations or law enforcement agencies, which was provided by the Italian Department for Equal Opportunities.[54]

The third estimate was produced in 1999/2000 by the European Institute for Crime Prevention and Control affiliated with the United Nations (HEUNI). In this case the methodology was not specified.[55]

Other estimates on the number of victims have been produced by organisations which come direct contact with women working on the street. However, they are local estimates for limited geographical areas, i.e. a city or certain districts of a city.[56]

Estimates on the revenues produced by the sexual exploitation market are also available. The only one at national level has been produced by SOS Impresa. By analysing Caritas dossiers, it estimated the revenues at 600 million euros in both 2008 and 2009.[57] Other estimates have been produced by local organisations, and they concern limited geographical contexts. In these cases, the information used for the estimates has been: the number of sexual services provided in one day, the cost of these services with or without a condom and the number of clients asking for unprotected sex. It has been collected from small samples of women involved in outdoor sexual exploitation and from analysis of advertisements relative to indoor sexual exploitation.[58]

All the estimates discussed have limitations. Those on the size of the market suffer from the already-mentioned dark number problem. Considering the perceptions of social workers is one way to remedy this shortcoming. It is also the only attempt to obtain regional estimates, even though it is affected by the reliability of data. On the other hand, estimates of revenues are very limited and do not furnish adequate figures at either national or regional level. This lack is all the more serious if the importance of data on revenues is considered. Indeed, they could be useful: (1) to understand the distribution of the crime across space; (2) to better identify the crime's 'hotspots' (i.e. regions in which exploiters invest); and (3) to investigate the vulnerabilities and criminal opportunities of each Italian region.

This study aims to fill this gap by developing a methodology which allows to estimate the regional revenues deriving from the outdoor and indoor sexual exploitation of foreign women at subnational level.

Methodology to estimate the sexual exploitation market

Based on the available research concerning the estimation of the revenues of sexual exploitation, two studies were considered as the main foundation for the development of a methodology at subnational level, due to their clear methodologies and the availability of data. They were the one produced by Belser and the one elaborated by Dubourg and Prichard, referring to the global and the UK context, respectively.[59] Table 1 summarises the data they used to produce the estimates.

Starting from the methods and the variables considered in these studies, the data used to estimate the revenues of the sexual exploitation market in Italy are presented in Table 2.

Estimates

This study estimates: (1) the volume of foreign women involved in sexual exploitation in some Italian regions for which data are lacking, and (2) the annual outdoor and indoor revenues of this market, respectively for the period 2008/2009 and 2004/2005, according to the availability of data.

Volume of the market in lacking regions

Data on the number of sexually exploited foreign women produced by PARSEC were used as the basis for the analysis. They were available for all the Italian regions with the exception of three: Trentino Alto Adige, Valle d'Aosta and Molise. Therefore the first step was to obtain missing estimates in order to include all regions in the analysis. The methodology used to calculate them was not the same for all the three regions because the available information was different. Indeed, the original data source indicated the total minimum and maximum number of women operating in a category called 'Others North' (Nprost other North$_{min}$ and Nprost other North$_{max}$). Because Trentino Alto Adige and

Table 1. Data for estimating the revenues of sexual exploitation market used in Belser and Dubourg and Prichard's studies.

	Variables	Disaggregation	Source
Belser's study	Prices paid by the clients	Macro-region	Literature and a tourist guide on the sex sector
	Number of clients per day	Global	Literature
	Money withheld by victims	Global	Literature
Dubourg and Prichard's study	Number of sexual services provided in one day	National	Literature
	Price per sexual service	National	Literature
	Working days in a week	National	Literature
	Working weeks in a year	National	Literature

Source: Author's elaboration.

Table 2. Data for estimating the revenues of sexual exploitation market in Italy.

Variable	Description	Disaggregation	Year	Source	Note
Number of women working outdoors	Minimum and maximum number of foreign women	Regional (excluding Trentino Alto Adige, Valle d'Aosta and Molise)	2008–2009	PARSEC	Total value distinct per nationality
Number of women working indoors	Minimum and maximum number of foreign women	Regional (excluding Trentino Alto Adige, Valle d'Aosta and Molise)	2004–2005	PARSEC	
Cost of sexual services per nationality	Minimum and maximum cost per sexual service	National	Unspecified	Literature and PIAM Onlus[60]	Available for Nigerian and East European women
Number of services per day	Minimum and maximum number of services per day	National	Unspecified	PIAM Onlus	Available for Nigerian and East European women
Number of working days in a year	Minimum and maximum number of working days in a year	National	Unspecified	Literature[61]	Maximum value: all days Minimum value: one rest day per week
Profits withheld by women	Percentage of profits withheld by women	National	Unspecified	Literature[62]	Percentages distinguished according to the location (indoor or outdoor)

Source: Author's elaboration.

Valle d'Aosta are the only northern regions without specific data, this number was used as the benchmark to obtain their regional estimates (NprostTAA$_{min}$ and NprostTAA$_{max}$, NprostVdA$_{min}$ and NprostVdA$_{max}$). It was multiplied by the percentage of the male population over the sum of the male population in the two regions indicated above (% popTAA$_{min}$ and %popTAA$_{max}$, %popVdA$_{min}$ and %popVdA$_{max}$). The result was divided by 100.

The formulas used to obtain the minimum and maximum number of foreign women in Trentino Alto Adige and Valle d'Aosta were:

$$\text{NprostTAA}_{min} = (\text{Nprost other North}_{min} \cdot \%\text{popTAA}_{min}) \div 100$$

$$\text{NprostTAA}_{max} = (\text{Nprost other North}_{max} \cdot \%\text{popTAA}_{max}) \div 100$$

$$\text{NprostVdA}_{\min} = (\text{Nprost other North}_{\min} \cdot \%\text{popVdA}_{\min}) \div 100$$

$$\text{NprostVdA}_{\max} = (\text{Nprost other North}_{\max} \cdot \%\text{popVdA}_{\max}) \div 100$$

As regards Molise, it was assumed that the rate of foreign women over the regional male population was the same as that of the adjacent regions (i.e. Lazio, Abruzzo, Campania and Apulia). Therefore the minimum and maximum rates of women over the average male population of these regions were calculated ($\text{RATEprostAR}_{\min}$ and $\text{RATEprostAR}_{\max}$). They were multiplied by the male population of Molise ($\text{PopMolise}_{\text{reg}}$) and divided by 100,000 in order to obtain the minimum and maximum number of foreign women in Molise ($\text{NprostMolise}_{\min}$ and $\text{NprostMolise}_{\max}$, respectively).

The formulas used to obtain the minimum and maximum number of foreign women in Molise were:

$$\text{NprostMolise}_{\min} = \text{RATEprostAR}_{\min} \left(\text{PopMolise}_{\text{reg}} \div 100000 \right)$$

$$\text{NprostMolise}_{\max} = \text{RATEprostAR}_{\max} \left(\text{PopMolise}_{\text{reg}} \div 100000 \right)$$

The same methodology used to estimate the foreign women in Molise was applied to Sicily ($\text{NprostSicily}_{\min}$ and $\text{NprostSicily}_{\max}$). Even though data on this region were already available in the PARSEC estimates, they were re-elaborated because they were unexpectedly identical to those of Sardinia. In this case, instead of considering the rates of the adjacent regions, all the Southern regions were taken into account ($\text{RATEprostSR}_{\min}$ and $\text{RATEprostSR}_{\max}$). The formulas below were applied:

$$\text{NprostSicily}_{\min} = \text{RATEprostSR}_{\min} \left(\text{PopSicily}_{\text{reg}} \div 100000 \right)$$

$$\text{NprostSicily}_{\max} = \text{RATEprostSR}_{\max} \left(\text{PopSicily}_{\text{reg}} \div 100000 \right)$$

The methodologies just described were applied in order to estimate foreign women operating both outdoors and indoors.

Annual revenues

The methodology developed to estimate the revenues of the sexual exploitation market was the same that was used to estimate the revenues from outdoor and indoor sexual exploitation. The only difference was that in the former case women were distinguished by nationality, while in the latter nationality was not considered owing to the lack of data disaggregated by this variable (see Table 2).[63] Therefore the available data on the cost of sexual services and the number of services per day per nationality were used only to estimate outdoor sexual exploitation. For indoor exploitation the average values were employed.

The regional revenues ($\text{SXrev}_{\text{reg}}$) were calculated by multiplying the number of women exploited (Wexp) by the revenue in one day (REVday) and by the working days in a year (WDyear).[64] The percentage of money held by women (%MW) was subtracted from the above results to obtain a more precise estimate of the revenues. As indicated in Table 2, the percentage was different per women involved in outdoor or indoor exploitation; more precisely it was higher for the women exploited indoors (40% against 20%). The formula used to calculate the annual revenues was:

$$SXrev_{reg} = \left(Wexp_{reg} \cdot REVday \cdot WDyear\right) - \%MW$$

The daily revenue (REVday) was obtained by multiplying the cost of a sexual service (Csex) by the number of sexual services provided in one day (Nsexday).

$$REVday = Csex \cdot Nsexday$$

The minimum estimates took into consideration all the minimum values of the variables. By contrast, all the maximum values were used to calculate the maximum estimates. After reviewing the literature,[65] the maximum revenues per sexual service were treated as equivalent to the daily revenue in indoor sexual exploitation.

$$SXrev_{maxreg} = \left(Wexp_{maxreg} \cdot REVday_{max} \cdot WDyear_{max}\right) - \%MW$$

$$SXrev_{minreg} = \left(Wexp_{minreg} \cdot REVday_{min} \cdot WDyear_{min}\right) - \%MW$$

The total size of the market was obtained by summing the regional revenues referring to outdoor and indoor exploitation, respectively.

Limitations

The methodology just discussed has three main limitations which future estimates should address. The first concerns the regional data used to calculate the volume of women involved in sexual exploitation market. These data were not updated and had been produced with an arguable methodology: the perceptions of social workers. However, they were chosen because they were the only estimates existing at regional level.

Second, the variables used to calculate the annual revenues (cost of sexual services, number of services per day, number of working days in a year) were considered as equal in all the regions owing to the lack of data distinguished by region. This may have been a risky assumption because differences among northern, central and southern regions were possible. However, it was the only solution adoptable considering the data available.

Third, the estimates referred to only one year. This means that it was not possible to investigate the trend in revenues over time, and thus understand whether this illicit market is always profitable to the same extent.

Results and discussion

Table 3 shows the revenues obtained by applying the methodology proposed. It includes the minimum and maximum values per region, distinguished between outdoor and indoor sexual exploitation and in total.[66]

As can be noted from the table, the highest minimum revenues are recorded by indoor exploitation (minimum value of 701.83 against the minimum value of 432.03 recorded by outdoor exploitation). As underlined in a previous study, the place in which sexual services are consumed is important for determining their cost.[67] Therefore the higher prices of indoor exploitation may be due to the comforts of having sex in apartments, nightclubs, etc.

By contrast, the highest maximum revenues correspond to outdoor exploitation (maximum value of 3254.59 against the maximum value of 1774.22 recorded by indoor exploitation). One reason for this may be the different methodology used to calculate the maximum estimates. As suggested by the literature,[68] the maximum cost of a sexual service was treated as daily revenue. This means that it was multiplied only one time by working days in a year and the maximum number of foreign women.

Focusing on the single regions, the largest revenues from both outdoor and indoor prostitution are registered in Lazio. Although this region does not have the largest regional population, it is a core region in which the capital city is located. The large flow of tourists and its centrality in the Italian peninsula probably explain the significant concentration of sexually exploited women, and consequently the high revenues.

The second region recording high levels of revenues is Lombardy. The explanation of this result may be that Lombardy is the most populated region in Italy and is one of the most economically developed regions in the country. The same reasons may explain the prominence of Veneto and Piedmont.

The southern regions present the lower values, with the exception of Campania and Sicily. This is due to: (1) the high number of men living in these regions and (2) the frequent 'backscratching' among local mafias (Camorra and Cosa Nostra, respectively) and criminal networks investing in sexual exploitation.

Table 3. Estimates of the minimum and maximum revenues (mln€) deriving from the sexual exploitation market by Italian region.

	Outdoor Exploitation (2008/2009) Min	Outdoor Exploitation (2008/2009) Max	Indooor Exploitation (2004/2005) Min	Indooor Exploitation (2004/2005) Max	Total Min	Total Max
Abruzzo	10.56	88.89	19.16	52.01	29.72	140.90
Basilicata	4.22	38.10	7.61	22.45	11.83	60.55
Calabria	6.33	50.79	7.61	22.45	13.94	73.24
Campania	21.12	152.39	30.71	82.13	51.83	234.52
Emilia Romagna	21.12	152.39	30.71	89.79	51.83	242.18
Friuli Venezia Giulia	21.12	177.78	38.31	104.57	59.43	282.35
Lazio	76.03	533.34	134.09	298.39	210.12	831.73
Liguria	19.01	165.08	30.71	89.79	49.72	254.87
Lombardia	73.91	507.95	115.22	260.61	189.13	768.56
Marche	14.78	114.29	26.76	67.34	41.54	181.63
Molise	2.35	17.06	4.02	9.67	6.37	26.73
Piemonte	33.79	253.97	57.47	134.14	91.26	388.11
Puglia	14.78	114.29	19.16	55.85	33.94	170.14
Sardegna	4.22	38.10	5.92	18.62	10.14	56.72
Sicilia	17.90	139.04	25.06	71.11	42.96	210.15
Toscana	23.23	177.78	34.65	96.91	57.88	274.69
Trentino Alto Adige	11.25	101.59	20.51	59.79	31.76	161.38
Umbria	16.89	139.69	30.71	82.13	47.60	221.82
Valle d'Aosta	1.41	12.70	2.59	7.55	4.00	20.25
Veneto	38.01	279.37	60.85	148.92	98.86	428.29
Total Italy	**432.03**	**3254.59**	**701.83**	**1774.22**	**1133.86**	**5028.81**

Source: Author's elaboration.

Conclusions

Considering the importance of knowing the amount of money revolving around the sexual exploitation market in order to identify the vulnerabilities of areas and remedy them, this article has proposed a methodology with which to estimate the revenues deriving from this market, both outdoor and indoor, at national and regional level. The methodology was applied to the Italian context because Italy is a crucial country given its geographical position and high demand for sexual services. It emerged from the literature review on the existing estimates that there are few studies dealing with revenues, and no study has tried to provide regional estimates. The difficulties of obtaining exhaustive information on the volume of the market complicate matters further.

The results show that some regions are more central than others in sexual exploitation. Interestingly, there is a correspondence between the two exploitation fields, outdoor and indoor: regions recording high values for the outdoor market have also high values for the indoor market, and vice versa. This suggests that exploiters are able to identify criminal opportunities in the various regions and also the areas in which the greatest demand is concentrated. Both opportunities and demand depend on many factors, e.g. possibility to establish good relations with local criminal organisations, the region's economic development and availability of a large potential target willing to pay for sexual services.

The methodology presented, and its application, could be improved and replaced if better data on which to base the analysis were produced. However, it may be employed in other contexts (1) to have a common methodological framework that allows comparison among results and (2) to gain better understanding of the dynamics of this illicit market across time and space.

Notes

1. Weitzer, "Sex Work," 1–45.
2. O'Connell Davidson, *La Prostituzione. Sesso, Soldi e Potere*, 21.
3. Prostitution is legal in countries where regulation or abolition policies are in force, whereas it is illegal in countries adopting prohibitionist or client criminalisation policies. Barbagli et al., *Sociologia Della Devianza*.
4. Batsyukova, "Prostitution and Human Trafficking," 46–50; Van Liemt, *Human Trafficking in Europe*; Weitzer, "Sex Work"; Weitzer and Ditmore, "Sex Trafficking," 325–46; Monzini, *Sex Traffic*; Monzini, *Il Mercato Delle Donne*.
5. Becucci and Garosi, *Corpi Globali*; Campbell, "Invisible Men," 155–71; Carchedi and Tola, *All'aperto e Al Chiuso*; Davidson, *La Prostituzione*; Becucci, "New Players in an Old Game," 57–69.
6. Abramson, "Beyond Consent," 473–502; Carchedi, *Prostituzione Migrante e Donne Trafficate*; Carling, *Migration, Human Smuggling and Trafficking*; Crowhurst, "The Provision of Protection" 217–28; Denisova, "Trafficking in Women and Children"; Farina and Ignazi, *Catene Invisibili*; Fitzgibbon, "Modern Day Slavery?" 81–9; Goodey, "Sex Trafficking in Women," 26–45.
7. UNODC, *Transnational Trafficking and the Rule*; UNODC, *Trafficking in Persons*; US Department of State, *Trafficking in Persons Report*; ILO, *Global Alliance Against Forced Labour*; UNODC, *The Globalization of Crime*; UNODC and SADC, *Situational Assessment of Human Trafficking*; UNODC, *Global Report on Trafficking*; UNODC, *Transnational Trafficking and the Rule of Law*.
8. UNODC, *The Globalization of Crime*.
9. The methodology was developed in a research project awarded by the Italian Ministry of Interior to Transcrime (*Joint Research Centre on Transnational Crime* of Università Cattolica del Sacro Cuore of Milan and Università di Trento). Transcrime, *Progetto PON Sicurezza 2007–2013*.
10. Europol, *OCTA 2011*; Monzini, *Il Mercato Delle Donne*; Savona et al., *Tratta Di Persone a Scopo*; van Moppes, *The African Migration Movement*.

11. Carchedi and Tola, *All'aperto e Al Chiuso*; Abbatecola, *L'altra Donna*; US Department of State, *Link Between Prostitution and Sex Trafficking*; Becucci and Garosi, *Corpi Globali*; Van Liemt, *Human Trafficking in Europe*.
12. Cameron and Collins, "Estimates of a Model of Male Participation," 271–88.
13. Brooks-Gordon, *The Price of Sex*; Di Nicola et al., *Prostitution and Human Trafficking*; Spizzichino, *La Prostituzione*; Leonini, *Sesso in Acquisto*; Pitts et al., "Who Pays for Sex and Why?" 353–8; Campbell, "Invisible Men"; Atchison et al., "Men Who Buy Sex," 172–03; Monto, "Prostitutes' Customers," 233–43; Jordan, "User Pays," 55–71.
14. Aronowitz, *Human Trafficking, Human Misery*; UNODC, *The Globalization of Crime*; UNODC, *Transnational Trafficking and the Rule*; Shelley, *Human Trafficking*.
15. UNICEF, UNOHCHR, and OSCE ODIHR, *Trafficking in Human Beings*; Wijers and Lap-Chew, *Trafficking in Women*.
16. Aronowitz, *Human Trafficking, Human Misery*; Oude Breuil et al., "Human Trafficking Revisited," 30–46.
17. Barbagli et al., *Sociologia Della Devianza*.
18. Becucci and Garosi, *Corpi Globali*; Becucci, "New Players in an Old Game."
19. Monzini, *Il Mercato Delle Donne*.
20. Carchedi and Tola, *All'aperto e Al Chiuso*, 101.
21. Becucci, "New Players in an Old Game"; UNODC and SADC, *Situational Assessment of Human Trafficking*; Europol, *OCTA 2011*; Savona et al., *Tratta Di Persone a Scopo*; Abbatecola, *L'altra Donna*; Picarelli, "Human Trafficking and Organized Crime," 115–135.
22. Aronowitz, *Human Trafficking, Human Misery*; Vermeulen et al., "Perceived Involvement of 'Organized Crime'," 247–73.
23. Schloenhardt, *Organised Crime and the Business*; Bosco et al., "Human Trafficking Patterns," 35–82; Savona et al., *Tratta Di Persone a Scopo*; Europol, *OCTA 2011*.
24. DIA, *Relazione Del Ministro dell'Interno*.
25. Vayrynen, *Illegal Immigration, Human Trafficking*; Danailova-Trainor and Belser, *Globalization and the Illicit Market*; Iselin, "Trafficking in Human Beings"; Becucci, *Criminalità Multietnica*; Becucci, "New Players in an Old Game."
26. Vermeulen et al., "Perceived Involvement of 'Organized Crime'"; Becucci and Garosi, *Corpi Globali*; UNICRI and Australian Institute of Criminology, *Human Smuggling and Trafficking*; Arlacchi, *Gli Uomini Del Disonore*; Becucci, "New Players in an Old Game."
27. DDA, *Relazione Sullo Stato*.
28. Macrì, *Conferenza Nazionale Sulla*; DIA, *Relazione Del Ministro dell'Interno*.
29. SOS Impresa, *Le Mani Della Criminalità*.
30. Savona and Stefanizzi, *Measuring Human Trafficking*.
31. Kelly, "You Can Find Anything You Want," 235–65.
32. IOM, *Guidelines for the Collection*; Laczko and Gramegna, "Developing Better Indicators," 179–94.
33. ILO, *A Global Alliance*, 10–14.
34. US Department of State, *Trafficking in Persons Report*, 7.
35. UNODC is the office responsible for implementing the UN 'Protocol to prevent, suppress and punish trafficking in persons, especially women and children'. This is the main international Protocol containing the first shared definition of human trafficking on which each signatory state should base the drafting of its national legislation.
36. UNODC, *Global Report on Trafficking*, 18.
37. Ibid., 37.
38. Ibid., 35.
39. Belser, *Forced Labour and Human Trafficking*.
40. Ibid.
41. UNODC, *The Globalization of Crime*, 16.
42. UNODC, *Transnational Trafficking and the Rule*, 41.
43. Lehti, *Trafficking in Women and Children*, 8.
44. See note 41 above.
45. See note 42 above.
46. UNODC, *The Globalization of Crime*, 49.
47. Dubourg and Prichard, "The Impact of Organized Crime."
48. Ibid., 18.

49. Moffatt and Peters, "Pricing Personal Services," 675–90.
50. Rao et al., "Sex Workers and the Cost," 585–603; Gertler et al., "Risky Business," 518–50.
51. Monzini, *Il Mercato Delle Donne*, 21.
52. Carchedi and Tola, *All'aperto e Al Chiuso*, 114.
53. Carchedi and Tola, *All'aperto e Al Chiuso*.
54. Di Nicola, *La Prostituzione nell'Unione Europea*, 85.
55. Lehti, *Trafficking in Women and Children*, 10; Morehouse, *Combating Human Trafficking*, 241–2.
56. Farina and Ignazi, *Catene Invisibili*.
57. SOS Impresa, *Le Mani Della Criminalità*, 7; SOS Impresa, *Le Mani Della Criminalità*, 6; UNODC, *Estimating Illicit Financial Flows*, 26.
58. Abele, *Dati Prostituzione (aggiornati Al Novembre 2008)*; Donadel and Martini, *Progetto West – La Prostituzione Invisibile*.
59. Belser, *Forced Labour and Human Trafficking*; Dubourg and Prichard, "The Impact of Organized Crime."
60. Carrisi, *La Fabbrica Delle Prostitute*; Da Pra Pocchiesa and Marchisella, *AAA tuttiacasa.it La Prostituzione Al Chiuso*; Donadel and Martini, *Progetto West – La Prostituzione Invisibile*; Abele, *Dati Prostituzione (aggiornati Al Novembre 2008)*.
61. Becucci and Garosi, *Corpi Globali. La Prostituzione in Italia*.
62. Di Nicola, *La Prostituzione nell'Unione Europea*.
63. UNICRI, *La Tratta Delle Minorenni*, 19.
64. As concerns the number of working days per year, in the maximum estimates 365 days have been considered, while in the minimum ones 313 (six working days per week).
65. Donadel and Martini, *Progetto West – La Prostituzione Invisibile*; Da Pra Pocchiesa and Marchisella, *AAA tuttiacasa.it La Prostituzione*.
66. The total minimum and maximum revenues per region have been obtained by summing up the equivalent minimum and maximum revenues in outdoor and indoor sexual exploitation, even though they are related to different years (2008/2009 and 2004/2005, respectively). The aim of this operation is just to have overall figures of this illicit market.
67. Moffatt and Peters, "Pricing Personal Services."
68. Donadel and Martini, *Progetto West – La Prostituzione Invisibile*; Da Pra Pocchiesa and Marchisella, *AAA tuttiacasa.it La Prostituzione Al Chiuso*.

Bibliography

Abbatecola, Emanuela. *L'altra Donna. Immigrazione e Prostituzione in Contesti Metropolitani*. Milano: Franco Angeli, 2006.

Abramson, Kara. "Beyond Consent: Toward Safeguarding Human Rights: Implementing the UN Trafficking Protocol." *Harvard International Law Journal* 44, no. 2 (2003): 473–502.

Arlacchi, Pino. *Gli Uomini Del Disonore*. Milano: Mondadori, 1992.

Aronowitz, Alexis. *Human Trafficking, Human Misery. The Global Trade in Human Beings*. Westport: Praeger, 2009.

Atchison, Chris, Laura Fraser, and John Lowman. "Men Who Buy Sex: Preliminary Findings of an Exploratory Study." In *Prostitution: On Whores, Hustlers and Johns*, edited by James E. Elias, Vern L. Bullough, Veronica Elias, and Gwen Brewer, 172–203. New York: Prometheus Books, 1998.

Barbagli, Marzio, Asher Colombo, and Ernesto Ugo Savona. *Sociologia Della Devianza*. Il Mulino: Bologna, 2003.

Batsyukova, Svitlana. "Prostitution and Human Trafficking for Sexual Exploitation." *Gender Issues* 24 (2007): 46–50.

Becucci, Stefano. *Criminalità Multietnica. I Mercati Illegali in Italia*. Bari: Editori Laterza, 2006.

Becucci, Stefano. "New Players in an Old Game: The Sex Market in Italy." In *Organized Crime: Culture, Markets and Policies*, edited by Siegel Dina and Hans Nelen, 57–69. New York: Springer, 2008.

Becucci, Stefano, and Eleonora Garosi. *Corpi Globali. La Prostituzione in Italia*. Firenze: Firenze University Press, 2008.

Belser, Patrick. *Forced Labour and Human Trafficking: Estimating the Profits*. Geneva: International Labour Office, 2005. http://www.ilo.org/wcmsp5/groups/public/—ed_norm/—declaration/documents/publication/wcms_081971.pdf

Bosco, Francesca, Vittoria Luda Di Cortemiglia, and Anvar Serojitdinov. "Human Trafficking Patterns." In *Strategies Against Human Trafficking: The Rule of the Security Sector*, edited by Cornelius Friesendorf, 35–82. Vienna: National Defence Academy and Austrian Ministry of Defence and Sports, 2009.

Brooks-Gordon, Belinda. *The Price of Sex. Prostitution, Policy and Society*. Devon: Willan, 2006.

Cameron, Samuel, and Alan Collins. "Estimates of a Model of Male Participation in the Market for Female Heterosexual Prostitution Services." *European Journal of Law and Economics* 16 (2003): 271–288.

Campbell, Rosie. "Invisible Men: Making Visible Male Clients of Female Prostitutes in Marseyside." In *Prostitution: On Whores, Hustlers and Johns*, edited by James E. Elias, Vern L. Bullough, Elias Veronica, and Gwen Brewer, 155–171. New York: Prometheus Books, 1998.

Carchedi, Francesco, ed. *Prostituzione Migrante e Donne Trafficate. Il Caso Delle Donne Albanesi, Moldave e Rumene*. Milano: Franco Angeli, 2004.

Carchedi, Francesco, and Vittoria Tola. *All'aperto e Al Chiuso. Prostituzione e Tratta: i Nuovi Dati Del Fenomeno, i Servizi Sociali, Le Normative Di Riferimento*. Roma: Ediesse, 2008.

Carling, Jørgen. *Migration, Human Smuggling and Trafficking from Nigeria to Europe*. Oslo: International Organization for Migration – International Peace Research Institute, 2004. http://iom.int/jahia/webdav/site/myjahiasite/shared/shared/mainsite/published_docs/serial_publications/mrs23.pdf

Carrisi, Giuseppe. *La Fabbrica Delle Prostitute. Un Viaggio Nel Mercato Criminale Del Sesso. Dai Villaggi Della Nigeria Ai Marciapiedi Italiani*. Roma: Newton Compton Editori, 2011.

Crowhurst, Isabel. "The Provision of Protection and Settlement Services for Migrants Women Trafficked for Sexual Purposes: The Case of Italy." In *Trafficking and the Global Sex Industry*, edited by Karen Beeks and Delila Amir, 217–228. Lanham: Lexington Books, 2006.

Da Pra Pocchiesa Mirta, and Simona Marchisella. *AAA tuttiacasa.it La Prostituzione Al Chiuso in Italia e in Europa. 2010: Come, Dove e Perché*. Torino: Pagine. il sociale da fare e pensare, 2010.

Danailova-Trainor, Gergana, and Patrick Belser. "Globalization and the Illicit Market for Human Trafficking: An Empirical Analysis of Supply and Demand." Working Paper No. 78. Geneva: Policy Integration Department – International Labour Office, 2006. Accessed December 17, 2013. http://www.ilo.org/wcmsp5/groups/public/—dgreports/—integration/documents/publication/wcms_081759.pdf

DDA (Direzione Distrettuale Antimafia). *Relazione Sullo Stato Della Criminalità Organizzata Nel Distretto Giudiziario Di Napoli*. Napoli: Direzione Distrettuale Antimafia, 2002.

Denisova, Tatyana A. "Trafficking in Women and Children for Purposes of Sexual Exploitation." Zaporizhie State University, 2004. http://www.childtrafficking.com/Docs/denisova__no_date___traffic.pdf

Di Nicola Andrea. *La Prostituzione nell'Unione Europea Tra Politiche e Tratta Degli Esseri Umani*. Milano: Franco Angeli, 2006.

Di Nicola Andrea, Cauduro Andrea, Lombardi Marco, and Paolo Ruspini. *Prostitution and Human Trafficking. Focus on Clients*. New York: Springer, 2009.

DIA (Direzione Investigativa Antimafia). *Relazione Del Ministro dell'Interno Al Parlamento Sull'attività Svolta e Sui Risultati Conseguiti Dalla Direzione Investigativa Antimafia*. Roma: Direzione Investigativa Antimafia, 2011. http://www.interno.it/dip_ps/dia/semestrali/sem/2011/1sem2011.pdf

DIA (Direzione Investigativa Antimafia). *Relazione Del Ministro dell'Interno Al Parlamento Sull'attività Svolta e Sui Risultati Conseguiti Dalla Direzione Investigativa Antimafia. 2° Semestre 2007*. Roma: Direzione Investigativa Antimafia, 2007. http://www.interno.gov.it/dip_ps/dia/semestrali/sem/2007/2sem2007.pdf

Donadel, Claudio, and Raffaello Martini. *Progetto West – La Prostituzione Invisibile*. Ravenna: WEST – Women East Smuggling Trafficking, 2005. http://www.regione.emilia-romagna.it/WEST/italiano/ricerche/prostituzione_invisibile/pdf/report_finale.pdf

Dubourg, Richard, and Stephen Prichard. "The Impact of Organized Crime in the UK: Revenues and Economic and Social Costs." In *Organised Crime: Revenues, Economic and Social Costs, and Criminal Assets Available for Seizure*, edited by Home Office, 1–51. London: Home Office, 2007. http://www.homeoffice.gov.uk/about-us/freedom-of-information/released-information1/foi-archive-crime/9886.pdf?view=Binary

Europol. *OCTA 2011. EU Organised Crime Threat Assessment*. The Hague: European Police Office, 2011. https://www.europol.europa.eu/sites/default/files/publications/octa_2011_1.pdf

Farina, Patrizia, and Sabrina Ignazi. *Catene Invisibili. Strumenti e Dati Per Comprendere La Prostituzione Straniera e Promuovere Percorsi Emancipativi*. Milano: Fondazione ISMU, 2011.

Fitzgibbon, Kathleen. "Modern Day Slavery? The Scope of Trafficking in Persons in Africa." *Africa Security Review* 12, no. 1 (2003): 81–89.

Gertler, Paul, Manisha Shah, and Stefano M. Bertozzi. "Risky Business: The Market for Unprotected Commercial Sex." *Journal of Political Economics* 113, no. 3 (2005): 518–550.

Goodey, Jo. "Sex Trafficking in Women from Central and East European Countries: Promoting a 'victim-centred' and a 'woman-centred' Approach to Criminal Justice Intervention." *Feminist Review* 76 (2004): 26–45.

Gruppo Abele. *Dati Prostituzione (aggiornati Al Novembre 2008)*. Torino: Gruppo Abele, 2008. http://www.gruppoabele.org/flex/cm/pages/ServeBLOB.php/L/IT/IDPagina/255

ILO (International Labour Office). *A Global Alliance Against Forced Labour. Global Report Under the Follow-up to the ILO Declaration on Fundamental Principles and Rights at Work 2005*. Geneva: International Labour Office, 2005. http://www.ilo.org/wcmsp5/groups/public/@ed_norm/@declaration/documents/publication/wcms_081882.pdf

IOM (International Organization for Migration). *Guidelines for the Collection of Data on Trafficking in Human Beings, Including Comparable Indicators*. Vienna: International Organization for Migration, 2009. http://publications.iom.int/bookstore/free/guidelines_collection_data_IOMVienna.pdf

Iselin, Brian. *Trafficking in Human Beings: New Patterns of an Old Phenomenon*. Colombia: Bogota, 2003.

Jordan, Jan. "User Pays: Why Men Buy Sex." *Australian and New Zealand Journal of Criminology* 30 (1997): 55–71.

Kelly, Liz. "'You Can Find Anything You Want': A Critical Reflection on Research on Trafficking in Persons Within and into Europe." In *Data and Research on Human Trafficking: a Global Survey*, edited by IOM, 235–265. Geneva: International Organization for Migration, 2005.

Laczko, Frank, and Marco A. Gramegna. "Developing Better Indicators of Human Trafficking." *Brown Journal of World Affairs* X, no. 1 (2003): 179–194.

Lehti, Martti. *Trafficking in Women and Children in Europe*. Helsinki: HEUNI – The European Institute for Crime Prevention and Control affiliated with the United Nations, 2003. http://www.heuni.fi/uploads/to30c6cjxyah11.pdf

Leonini, Luisa. *Sesso in Acquisto. Una Ricerca Sui Clienti Della Prostituzione*. Milano: Unicopli, 1999.

Macrì, Vincenzo. *Conferenza Nazionale Sulla 'Ndrangheta*. Roma: Direzione Nazionale Antimafia, 2004.

Moffatt, Peter G., and Simon A. Peters. "Pricing Personal Services: An Empirical Study of Earnings in the UK Prostitution Industry." *Scottish Journal of Political Economy* 51, no. 5 (2004): 675–690.

Monto, Martin M. "Prostitutes' Customers: Motives and Misconceptions." In *Sex for Sale: Prostitution, Pornography, and the Sex Industry*, edited by Ronald Weitzer, 233–243. New York: Routledge, 2010.

Monzini, Paola. *Il Mercato Delle Donne. Prostituzione, Tratta e Sfruttamento*. Roma: Donzelli, 2002.

Monzini, Paola. *Sex Traffic. Prostitution, Crime and Exploitation*. London and New York: Zed Books, 2005.

Morehouse, Christal. *Combating Human Trafficking. Policy Gaps and Hidden Political Agendas in the USA and Germany*. Wiesbaden: VS Verlag für Sozialwissenschaften, 2009.

O'Connell Davidson, Julia. *La Prostituzione. Sesso, Soldi e Potere*. Bari: Edizioni Dedalo, 2001.

Breuil Oude, Brenda Dina Siegel, Piet Van Reenen, Annemarieke Beijer, and Linda Roos. "Human Trafficking Revisited: Legal, Enforcement and Ethnographic Narratives on Sex Trafficking to Western Europe." *Trends in Organized Crime* 14 (2011): 30–46.

Picarelli, John. "Human Trafficking and Organized Crime in the US & Western Europe." In *Strategies Against Human Trafficking: The Rule of the Security Sector*, edited by Cornelius Friesendorf, 115–135. Vienna: National Defence Academy and Austrian Ministry of Defence and Sports, 2009.

Pitts, Marian K., Anthony M. Smith, Jeffrey G. Grierson, Mary O'Brien, and Sebastian Misson. "Who Pays for Sex and Why? An Analysis of Social and Motivational Factors Associated with Male Clients of Sex Workers." *Archives of Sexual Behavior* 33, no. 4 (2004): 353–358.

Rao, Vijayendra, Indrani Guptaa, Michael Lokshin, and Smarajit Jana. "Sex Workers and the Cost of Safe Sex: The Compensating Differential for Condom Use Among Calcutta Prostitutes." *Journal of Development Economics* 71 (2003): 585–603.

Savona, Ernesto, Roberta Belli, Federica Curtol, Silvia Decarli, and Andrea Di Nicola. *Tratta Di Persone a Scopo Di Sfruttamento e Traffico Di Migranti*. Trento: Transcrime, 2003. http://www.jus.unitn.it/users/dinicola/criminologia-ca/topics/materiale/dispensa_3_1.pdf

Savona, Ernesto, and Sonia Stefanizzi. *Measuring Human Trafficking. Complexities and Pitfalls*. New York: Springer, 2007.

Schloenhardt, Andreas. *Organised Crime and the Business of Migrant Trafficking. An Economic Analysis*. Canberra: Australian Institute of Criminology, 1999. http://www.cestim.it/argomenti/30traffico/30traffico_economia.pdf

Shelley, Louise. *Human Trafficking. A Global Perspective*. New York: Cambridge University Press, 2010.

SOS Impresa. *Le Mani Della Criminalità Sulle Imprese*. Roma: Confesercenti, 2008.

SOS Impresa. *Le Mani Della Criminalità Sulle Imprese*. Roma: Confesercenti, 2012.

Spizzichino, Laura. *La Prostituzione. Il Fenomeno e L'intervento Psicologico*. Roma: Carocci, 2005.

Transcrime. *Progetto PON Sicurezza 2007-2013: Gli Investimenti Delle Mafie. Rapporto Linea 1*. Milano: Ministero dell'Interno, 2013.

UNICEF, UNOHCHR, and OSCE ODIHR. *Trafficking in Human Beings in South Eastern Europe*. New York: United Nations Development Programme, 2005. http://www.unicef.org/ceecis/Trafficking.Report.2005.pdf

UNICRI. *La Tratta Delle Minorenni Nigeriane in Italia. I Dati, i Racconti, i Servizi Sociali*. Roma: United Nations Interregional Crime and Justice Research Institute, 2010. http://www.piemonteimmigrazione.it/site/images/stories/tratta/documenti/TrattaMinorenniNigeriaItalia_IT.pdf

UNICRI, and Australian Institute of Criminology. *Human Smuggling and Trafficking: A Desk Review on the Trafficking in Women from the Philippines*. Vienna: United Nations, 2000. http://www.childtrafficking.com/Docs/unicri_aic_2000_smuggling_.pdf

UNODC. *Estimating Illicit Financial Flows Resulting from Drug Trafficking and Other Transnational Organized Crimes*. Research Report. Vienna: United Nations Office on Drugs and Crime, 2011. http://www.unodc.org/documents/data-and-analysis/Studies/Illicit_financial_flows_2011_web.pdf

UNODC. *Global Report on Trafficking in Persons*. United Nation Office on Drugs and Crime, 2012. http://www.unodc.org/documents/data-and-analysis/glotip/Trafficking_in_Persons_2012_web.pdf

UNODC. *The Globalization of Crime. A Transnational Organized Crime Threat Assessment*. Vienna: United Nations Office on Drugs and Crime, 2010. http://www.unodc.org/documents/data-and-analysis/tocta/TOCTA_Report_2010_low_res.pdf

UNODC. *Trafficking in Persons: Global Patterns*. Vienna: United Nations Office on Drugs and Crime, 2006. http://www.state.gov/j/tip/rls/tiprpt/2011/

UNODC. *Transnational Trafficking and the Rule of Law in West Africa: A Threat Assessment*. Vienna: United Nation Office on Drugs and Crime, 2009. http://www.unodc.org/documents/data-and-analysis/Studies/West_Africa_Report_2009.pdf

UNODC, and SADC. *Situational Assessment of Human Trafficking. A 2005 Situational Assessment of Human Trafficking in the SADC Region. A Survey of South Africa, Zimbabwe and Mozambique*. Pretoria: United Nations Office on Drugs and Crime and Southern African Development Community, 2007. http://www.unodc.org/documents/human-trafficking/2005%20UNODC%20Situational%20Assessment.pdf

US Department of State. *The Link Between Prostitution and Sex Trafficking*. Lincoln: University of Nebraska – Department of State, 2004. http://digitalcommons.unl.edu/cgi/viewcontent.cgi?article=1037&context=humtraffdata

US Department of State. *Trafficking in Persons Report*. New York: Department of State – United States of America, 2008. http://www.state.gov/documents/organization/105501.pdf

Van Liemt, Gijsbert. *Human Trafficking in Europe: An Economic Perspective*. Geneva: International Labour Organization, 2004. http://digitalcommons.ilr.cornell.edu/cgi/viewcontent.cgi?article=1008&context=forcedlabor

Van Moppes, David. "The African Migration Movement: Routes to Europe." Working Paper Migration and Development Series – Report No. 5. Nijmegen: Radboud University, 2006.

Vayrynen, Raimo. *Illegal Immigration, Human Trafficking and Organized Crime*. Helsinki: United Nations University – World Institute for Development Economics Research, 2003. http://www.wider.unu.edu/publications/working-papers/discussion-papers/2003/en_GB/dp2003-072/_files/78091733799863273/default/dp2003-072.pdf.

Vermeulen, G., Y. Van Damme, and W. De Bondt. "Perceived Involvement of 'Organized Crime' in Human Trafficking and Smuggling." *International Review of Penal Law* 81 (2010): 247–273.

Weitzer, Ronald. "Sex Work: Paradigms and Policies." In *Sex for Sale. Prostitution, Pornography, and the Sex Industry*, edited by Ronald Weitzer, 1–45. New York: Routledge, 2010.

Weitzer, Ronald, and Melissa Ditmore. "Sex Trafficking: Facts and Fictions." In *Sex for Sale. Prostitution, Pornography, and the Sex Industry*, edited by Ronald Weitzer, 325–346. New York: Routledge, 2010.

Wijers, arjan, and Lin Lap-Chew. *Trafficking in Women, Forced Labour and Slavery-like Practices in Marriage, Domestic Labour and Prostitution*. Utrecht: STV, 1997.

The retail value of the illicit drug market in Italy: a consumption-based approach

Luca Giommoni

Università Cattolica del Sacro Cuore of Milan and Transcrime, Milan, Italy

This study estimates the retail value of the illicit drug market in Italy from a consumption-based approach. The illicit drugs considered in this analysis are heroin, cocaine, cannabis (herbal and resin), amphetamines and ecstasy. Results show that the value of the illicit drug market in Italy is much less than previously estimated and quantified at € 3.3 bn. Heroin and cocaine retain the biggest markets in terms of revenues, while cannabis is the most-consumed illicit drug. Synthetic illicit drugs account for roughly 10% of the illicit drug market. Conclusions offer some suggestions as to how uncertainties about estimates of the illicit drug market can be reduced.

Introduction

The supply and demand of illicit drugs

The United Nations Office on Drugs and Crime (UNODC) estimated that in 2011 between 3.6% and 6.9% of the world population aged 15–64, equal to 167–315 million people, has used illicit drugs in the previous year.[1] Cannabis is by far the most used illicit drug, with an annual prevalence between 2.6% and 5% in the adult population followed by amphetamines (0.3–1.2%) and opioids (0.6–0.8%). Approximately, between 13–21 million (equal to 0.3–0.4%) and 10.5–28 million (equal to 0.2–0.6%) people consumed, respectively, cocaine and ecstasy in the previous year.[2] Given the widespread diffusion and high prices that characterise illicit drugs, the combination of both of these factors makes the drug market the largest illicit market.[3]

The spread of the consumption of illicit drugs and the profits connected to its trafficking attract numerous criminal actors. Due to the involvement of complex criminal organisations, like the mafias, the supply chain of illicit drugs has often been portrayed as controlled by a few, big and very organised criminal organisations.[4] Despite this common view, numerous studies have shown that illicit drugs are supplied by many, small, loose criminal organisations acting in an open and non-monopolistic market.[5] The profits connected to the trafficking, the low barriers to entry, and the combined repression of law enforcement make the illicit drug market a competitive business with few opportunities to monopolise the supply.[6] Although some criminal groups can gain a certain control over some local market(s), they are more 'price takers rather than price givers.'[7] In this context the mafias are 'ones among the many' criminal organisations involved in the supply of illicit drugs.[8]

The usefulness of the estimates on the illicit drug market and previous attempts

Due to the large consumption, the violence involved in the trafficking and the consequences on health, the illicit drug market is the most studied illicit market. In recent years, governments, policymakers, national and international organisations acknowledged the relevance of the 'numbers' on illicit drugs market. This favoured the production of estimates on the size of the market (quantity of drug supplied or consumed) and the revenues connected to its trafficking (monetary value). Knowing the quantity of drugs consumed in a country is essential for understanding the impact that law enforcement can have on the market. As Kleiman pointed out, the effect of law enforcement does not depend on the volume of arrests (number of arrests), but on its intensity, namely, the number of arrests for drug sold.[9] Likewise, a seizure of 100 kilos of drug can be trivial in a market where the annual consumption is 100 tons, but critical in a market of 1 ton.[10] Estimates of the value of the drug market are also essential in understanding how criminal organisations finance themselves and to quantify their revenues. Any decision to regulate or legalise the drug market should consider the current value of the retail market and weigh costs and benefits of changing the current policy. As such, reliable estimates of the value of the drug market are essential for policymakers and for any decision that may have an impact on the drug market.

Along with studies trying to assess the value of the illicit drug market through a scientific method, there has been a growing production of figures often criticised because they are not based on scientific evidence.[11] The necessity to demonise drug trafficking has led to an exaggeration of these estimates in line with the interests of those advocating for a legalisation of the market or for a harsher enforcement of it.[12] Those supporting legalisation would say that in the face of such a huge problem, legalisation is the only solution. On the contrary, those supporting prohibition would highlight these values as a serious problem and require more efforts from law enforcement. Singer and, later, Reuter, defined these figures as 'mythical numbers,' namely, numbers that gain credibility and authority through repetition, but are not supported by any scientific evidence or detailed description of the methodology.[13]

In recent years, academics, international and national authorities provided numerous estimates of the value of the drug market nationally[14] and worldwide.[15] In 2003, the request by Eurostat to EU member states to provide some first estimates of the value of the illicit drug market triggered the production of estimates for Italy's illicit drug markets. Table 1 shows that from 2009 various scholars have provided estimates of the retail value of the illicit drug market in Italy.[16] Estimates range from € 6114 mn to € 23,904 mn. Differences are even greater when looking at single drug markets, with figures that differ even by a factor of 10. For example, the lower bound estimated for cocaine is € 1623 mn while the upper is equal to € 9771 mn; even larger is the range for cannabis (lower: € 793 mn; upper: € 9511 mn) and synthetic drugs (amphetamines and ecstasy). Although some of the differences can be due to the year of analysis, some ranges are still too wide. Hence, variation can be attributed to the different data, methods and assumptions employed in the analysis.[17] What is more concerning regarding these values is that previous studies showed how small changes in the underlying assumptions can produce remarkable variation in the final estimates[18]; the differences can be even larger.

Additionally, some of the above-mentioned figures seem too high when compared to other developed countries. For instance, Legleye et al.[19] and Pudney et al.[20] estimated the cannabis market for France and the United Kingdom, respectively, at € 789 mn and £ 1031 mn. This would be equal to an average annual expenditure per inhabitant of € 13 for France and € 20 for United Kingdom. Considering the study by Fabi, Ricci and Rossi,

Table 1. Previous estimates of the value of the illicit drug market in Italy.

Source	Year	Method	Heroin	Cocaine	Cannabis	Amphetamines	Ecstasy	Total
Canzonetti (2009)	2005	Demand	868	4096	4248	26	40	9278
	2005–2009	Supply	855	3963	4390	38	25	9271
Baldassarini and Corea (2009)	2005	Demand	2046	2774	793	533		6146
		Supply	887	3688	1516	23*		6114
Kilmer and Pacula (2009)	2005	Demand	2490	1623	2956	284**	639**	7991
Di Censi et al. (2010)	2008	Demand	1980	5413	3579	438***		11,410
Fabi, Ricci, and Rossi (2011)	2010	Demand	2453	9771	9511	2168***		23,904
Transcrime (2013)	2008	Demand	1842	1711**	3140**	367**	666**	7727
Rossi (2013)	2009	Demand-Supply		12,590				
Sallusti (2013)	2010	Demand	3340	10,266	7030			22,960
Caulkins, Kilmer and Graf (2013)	2008	Demand			1356			

*It includes also LSD; **Average between lower and upper bound; ***Classified as 'Other drugs.'

whose estimates are adopted by the Department of Antidrug Policy of the Italian Ministry of Interior, the spending per capita would be equal to € 157. The final figure estimated by the authors seems too high (€ 9511 mn), considering that a recent study assessed the EU cannabis market in a range from € 7 bn to € 10 bn for 2010.[21]

Journalists and other organisations have concurred to make the picture even more puzzling. Roberto Saviano, a well-known Italian writer and author of *Gomorrah*,[22] claimed that the cocaine trafficking is even bigger than oil and car markets.[23] SOS Impresa, an association against extortion racketeering based in Sicily, reported that drug trafficking in Italy is worth € 60 bn.[24]

Then, despite the relevance and usefulness of estimates on the monetary value of the drug market, there is still great uncertainty on the retail value of the illicit drug market in Italy. This uncertainty is particularly surprising, given the relevance of the organised crime sector in Italy, the notoriety of Italian mafia-like organisations (Cosa Nostra, Camorra and 'Ndrangheta) and their involvement in drug trafficking.[25]

The aim of this article is to estimate the retail value of the illicit drug market in Italy. The illicit drugs considered in this analysis are: heroin, cocaine, cannabis (herbal and resin cannabis), amphetamines and ecstasy.

This study is organised as follows. The next section presents the method employed to estimate the illicit drug market along with assumptions and data used. 'Results' and 'Discussion' sections show and discuss the results of the analysis. Conclusions assess the implications of the resulting estimates and how the current limits in the analysis can be addressed.

Methodology to estimate the illicit drug market

The illicit drug market can be estimated from the supply (supply-based approach) or the demand of drug (demand-based approach). The former includes estimates based on the production and those considering the amount of drug seized as proxy of the quantity of the drug available in the market. Estimates based on production start with the soil used to grow drug crops and quantify the drug available in the market considering production per hectare, seizures, drug imported/exported and average retail purity. Estimates based on seizures divide the quantity of drug seized by an assumed rate of drug seized on the total market (i.e., 10%). The demand-based approach includes estimates based on consumption and spending on the drug. Both start counting the number of users, but while the former multiplies by annual consumption (and then multiplies by the retail price), the latter considers the spending on the drug. Recently, Zuccato et al. settled a new method – so called wastewater analysis – that quantifies the amount of drug consumed in a community detecting the residues of the drug in the sewage system.[26]

Today the demand-side approach is the one most widely used. Estimates based on the production found its main application to estimate the global production of cocaine and heroin (whose production is concentrated in relatively few countries).[27] Seizure-based estimates are the easiest way to estimate the drug market, but many factors influence data on seizures beside the supply: law enforcement efforts, trafficking routes and dealers' cares.[28] Recently, Kilmer et al. acknowledged the limitations of the supply-side approach.[29] Seizure-based estimates are nearly circular with the seizure rate that has to be calculated starting from other approaches. Data on seizure can also be tricky, with an increase in the quantity of drugs seized that may mean an increase in the supply of drugs as well as an increase in drug law enforcement efforts. For production-based estimates, many doubts exists about yield and harvest per hectare of soil used to grow drug crops.

Moreover, it seems difficult to identify and assess drug routes in order to quantify the amount of cocaine nationally supplied starting from worldwide production.

The method employed in this article was developed in a research project awarded by the Italian Ministry of Interior to Transcrime[30] (Joint Research Centre on Transnational Crime of Università Cattolica del Sacro Cuore of Milan and Università di Trento) and updated according to some recent studies and data available.[31] This study estimates the Italian illicit drug market through a consumption-based method. Therefore, it first quantifies the national consumption of the drug and then multiplies this by the drug retail price per gram. Twenty-five per cent of the quantity of drug seized by law enforcement agencies is added to the total of drug consumed, assuming that 75% of the drug is seized at wholesale and the rest at retail.[32] Seizures at retail are considered in the estimates of the retail spending because, although users do not consume the drug seized, they spend money for its purchase. Then, the general formula to calculate the retail value of the illicit drug market (IDM) is

$$IDM = (\text{Drug consumed} + 25\% \text{ seizures}) * \text{price per gram}$$

The total consumption for heroin, cannabis (both herbal and resin), amphetamines and ecstasy is calculated by multiplying users by their annual consumption:

$$\text{Drug consumed} = \text{Users} * \text{AnnualConsumption}$$

User population can be estimated from multiple sources: arrests for drug dealing or use, population in treatment for drug abuse, respondents in surveys on household population, etc. In this article, information on the number of users was collected from the General Population Survey (GPS) and populations eligible for treatment for drug abuse. Cannabis, ecstasy and amphetamine users are estimated from the 2008 and 2012 GPS and adjusted according to an under-report rate considering that GPS may not be able to capture the whole population (further details are provided in the section 'Limitations'). For the same reasons, estimates of highly addictive drugs (heroin and cocaine) are based on alternative sources. Hence, heroin users are estimated considering people eligible for treatment for opioids use while cocaine consumption is estimated through data from wastewater analysis reported as the quantity of drug consumed per day per 1000 people.

According to the availability of the data, estimates refer to 2012 for cannabis and amphetamines, 2011 for heroin and cocaine and 2008 for ecstasy.

The following sections report assumptions and values used to estimate the market for each illicit drug. Table 2 presents data and sources used to estimate the illicit drug market in Italy.

Heroin

Heroin is, among the illicit drugs considered in this analysis, the most addictive. Its prevalence in the population is estimated through indirect methods that quantify the incidence of people eligible for treatment for opioid abuse. These are defined by the European Monitoring Centre for Drugs and Drug Addiction (EMCDDA) as problem drug users (PDU), namely, those who inject drugs or have a long duration of or regular use of opioids, cocaine and/or amphetamines. Since at least 95% of opioids users in Western Europe are estimated to consume heroin, it is assumed that opioid use coincides with heroin use.[33]

Table 2. Data and source for estimating the illicit drug market in Italy.

Dimension	Variable	Description	Disaggregation	Year	Source
Number of users	Heroin users	People eligible for treatment for opioids abuse	Regional	2011	Department of Antidrug Policy
	Cannabis and amphetamine users	Percentage of people in the population aged 15–64 that used cannabis or amphetamines in the previous year or month	National	2012	GPS – Department of Antidrug Policy
	Ecstasy users	Percentage of people in the population 15–64 that used ecstasy in the previous year	National	2008	GPS – Department of Antidrug Policy
	Under-reporting	Percentage of people who used drug but do not report their habit or people who are not captured by GPS (homeless)	n/a	n/a	Kilmer and Pacula[34]
	Share of cannabis products	Percentage of herbal/resin cannabis use	National	n/a	EMCDDA[35]
Drug consumption	Heroin consumption	Quantity of pure heroin used per year	Europe	n/a	Paoli Greenfiel and Reuter[36]
	Cocaine consumed	Quantity of pure cocaine consumed (mg) per day every 1000 people	17 Italian cities	2011	Zuccato and Castiglioni[37]
	Heroin and cocaine purity	Percentage of pure drug in a gram	National	2011	Italian forensic division of the Ministry of the Interior
	Frequency of cannabis consumption	Days used cannabis in the past month or year	National	National	GPS – Department of Antidrug Policy
	Quantity of cannabis consumed per day	Number of joints per day and grams of cannabis per joint	n/a	n/a	van Laar et al.[38]
	Amphetamine consumption	Days used amphetamines and grams per day	n/a	n/a	Frijns and van Laar[39]
	Ecstasy consumption	Days used ecstasy and tablets per day	n/a	n/a	Frijns and van Laar[40]
Seizures, prices and disaggregation over regions	Seizures	Quantity of drug seized by law enforcement authorities	Provincial	2012–2011–2008	Department of Public Security of the Ministry of the Interior
	Drug price	Price for a gram of drug at retail (heroin, cocaine, cannabis)	National	2011	Central Directorate for Anti-Drug Services (DCSA)
		Price for a tablet of ecstasy at retail	National	2008	Central Directorate for Anti-Drug Services (DCSA)
		Price for a gram of amphetamines at retail	National	2011	EMCDDA
	Problematic cocaine users	People eligible for treatment for cocaine abuse	Regional	2009	Mascioli and Rossi[41]

Heroin can be smoked or injected, yet much of the users consume heroin via injection. Quantifying the total consumption of heroin per user requires many assumptions (days of consumption per year, doses per day, grams per injection, etc.) with little changes in the values that can dramatically change the final estimates. For this reason, it is assumed that heroin users consume 30 grams of pure heroin per year, as estimated by Paoli, Greenfield and Reuter[42] and corroborated by other studies.[43] Pure heroin consumed is adjusted for average purity (22%). Finally, the total consumption of heroin is multiplied by the retail price of brown heroin, which is the most common form of heroin in Europe.[44]

Cocaine

Cocaine consumption in Italy is quantified through wastewater analysis. This method is based on the principle that the quantity of drug consumed is excreted as drug derivate via urine. Specific techniques (mass spectrometry) quantify the concentration of drug derivate in the wastewater. Considering the ratio of the drug excreted as derivate, the population served by the sewage system, and the water flow rate it is possible to quantify the amount of pure drug consumed every 1000 people.[45]

This approach is preferred to the classic approach that estimates consumption by multiplying users by pattern of consumption for many reasons. The primary reason is that very little is known about the quantity of cocaine consumed per user: days of consumption, lines per day and grams of cocaine per line. Given the high price of cocaine, small variations in these assumptions (i.e., 0.5 grams or 1 gram of cocaine per day) can critically alter the final estimates. Also, estimates of the users present drawbacks: household surveys often miss heavy users who are responsible for much of the consumption,[46] while estimates of people eligible for treatment for cocaine abuse are not as good as those for heroin.[47]

Wastewater analysis is not devoid of drawbacks and uncertainties,[48] but recent studies confirmed the validity of this approach to quantify the consumption of a drug.[49] Recently, Rossi pointed out that, compared to other approaches (survey and administrative data), wastewater analysis seems to underestimate the consumption of cocaine.[50] This conclusion is hard to verify since the author does not adjust drug consumption for purity and the comparison is heavily influenced by the assumptions made.

In 2011, the Mario Negri Institute[51] analysed concentration of drug residues in wastewater treatment plants for 17 Italian cities.[52] On average, the analysis shows that 337 mg of pure cocaine are consumed in Italy per day every 1000 inhabitants. Cocaine consumption in 2011 is quantified applying the following formula:

$$\text{Cocaine consumed} = \frac{337 \text{ Mg}/\%\text{Purity}}{1000} * \text{Inhabitants2011}$$

Cannabis

The estimate of cannabis users considers both users during the last month and the last year as reported by GPS 2012.[53] Users are divided among those consuming herbal and resin cannabis. EMCDDA estimates resin cannabis to account for 65–75% of the cannabis market in Italy with herbal cannabis representing the remaining 25–35%.[54] It is then assumed that 70% of users consume resin and the remaining 30% consume herbal cannabis. Last-month users are divided by daily, weekly and monthly users, considering

Table 3. Assumptions on cannabis consumption.

Class of user	Under-reporting (%)	Days of consumption	Joints per day of consumption	Grams per joint	Price discount (%)
Daily	40	312	3.93	0.265	25
Weekly	30	156	2.59	0.23	12.5
Monthly	20	36	1.65	0.166	0
Occasional	0	29.85	1.17	0.135	0

Source: Author's elaboration on GPS (2012), van Laar et al. (2013), Kilmer and Pacula (2009).

days of consumption in the last month. Last-year but not last-month users are identified as occasional users.

The under-reporting for cannabis use detected through surveys is estimated to range from 0% to 40%.[55] Since heavy users are more prone to under-report their habit, this range is adjusted according to intensity of use. Table 3 shows values and assumptions regarding under-reporting, days of consumption, joints per day and grams per joint for each class of user. Assumption about joints per day and grams per joint are from van Laar et al.[56] As Table 3 shows, cannabis consumption is positively correlated with frequency of consumption: the higher the number of days of consumption, the higher the quantity of cannabis consumed per day.

Then cannabis consumption in 2012 is estimated applying the formula:

$$\text{Cannabis Consumed} = \sum \text{Users}_u * (\text{DaysUsed}_u * \text{JointsperDay}_u * \text{GramsperJoint}_u)$$

where u identifies user's profile.

By multiplying grams of cannabis consumed by the retail price of cannabis two widely observed phenomena in the cannabis market are missed: quantity discount and cannabis received for free.[57] The former indicates that the price per gram varies according to the size of the purchase: the larger the purchase the less the price paid per gram. It is then assumed that daily and weekly users, who are the heaviest users, purchase cannabis in bulk. Since there are not specific studies about quantity discount in Italy, conservative measure is applied.[58] Then, daily and weekly users receive a discount of, respectively, 25% and 12.5% on the price per gram.[59]

The second factor that complicates estimates of retail spending in cannabis products is that cannabis is often exchanged between friends or relatives, who often do not pay for the cannabis consumed and receive it for free.[60] Due to the lack of studies on quantity discount in Italy, here, as well, a conservative measure is applied, assuming that occasional users receive 50% of the cannabis consumed as a gift.[61]

Amphetamines

Amphetamine users are estimated considering last year prevalence (LYP). Given the limited knowledge, the under-reporting for amphetamines is estimated between that of cannabis (20%) and cocaine (50%).[62] GPS does not allow any classification according to the frequency of consumption. Therefore, users are differentiated across three groups (infrequent, occasional and frequent) as reported in a recent study analysing users' answers on a web survey.[63]

Table 4. Assumptions on amphetamine consumption.

Class of user	Proportion of amphetamines users (%)	Days of consumption	Grams consumed per day
Infrequent	55	4.3	0.49
Occasional	26	25	0.64
Frequent	19	172	1.32

Source: Frijns and van Laar (2013).

Amphetamines are a synthetic product that can be in form of powder or tablets. This can be ingested, snorted and even injected. According to EMCDDA 'in the central and western parts of the European Union amphetamines are almost exclusively purchased in powder form.'[64] It is then assumed that amphetamines are consumed in powder form.

Alike distribution across classes of use, days of consumption and grams of amphetamines consumed per day are from Frijns and van Laar's study (Table 4).[65] As shown for cannabis, the higher the frequency of consumption, the higher the quantity of drug consumed per day.

Ecstasy

The Italian GPS reports that in 2012 the consumption of ecstasy was equal to 0. This result is quite surprising considering that LYP in 2008 was estimated in 0.7% of the population aged 15–64. Considering last-month prevalence (LMP), estimates for ecstasy users would not be very useful since ecstasy use is mainly associated with entertainment and party settings.[66] LMP would capture a handful of heavy users, while it would disregard a much more diffused phenomenon although less intensive in terms of consumption. For the mentioned reasons, ecstasy users are estimated considering LYP as reported in GPS 2008. As with amphetamines, ecstasy users are adjusted according to an under-reporting of 35%.[67]

Ecstasy is a synthetic drug also known as MDMA, although the former may include a larger set of substances. It is often diffused in form of tablets but can be available, although less commonly, in form of powder or capsules. Distribution of users across frequencies of consumption, days of consumption and tablets consumed are from Frijns and van Laar's study.[68] Table 5 presents data and assumptions. As can be seen, frequent users represent a minimum percentage of the user population, with most of the users who rarely consume ecstasy. This finding is consistent with the diffusion of ecstasy during concerts, music festivals or other places of entertainment.[69]

Table 5. Assumption on ecstasy consumption.

Class of user	Proportion of ecstasy users (%)	Days of consumption	Tablets consumed per day
Infrequent	67	4.7	1.51
Occasional	29	22.0	1.93
Frequent	5	133.0	2.83

Source: Frijns and van Laar (2013).

Subdivision across regions

The illicit drug market is estimated at the regional level. Little information used to estimate the retail value of the illicit drug market is available at the regional level. So, the consumption of the drug is distributed across regions according to the presence of people eligible for treatment for drug abuse (PDUs). In particular cocaine, amphetamines and ecstasy consumption is distributed according to the population eligible for cocaine abuse, while for cannabis, the total population eligible for cocaine and heroin abuse is considered.

$$\text{DrugConsumption}_{\text{Reg}} = \text{DrugConsumed}_{\text{National}} * \left(\frac{\text{PDUs}_{\text{Reg}}}{\text{PDUs}_{\text{National}}} \% \right)$$

For amphetamines and ecstasy, the sole PDUs for cocaine are considered because synthetic drugs are, in terms of effect, more similar to cocaine than heroin. Synthetic drugs and cocaine are in fact both stimulants.

Estimate of the heroin consumed does not need to be distributed because estimates are at regional level.

Limitations

This study is not exempt from limitations. These pertain to three main factors. The first one is the limited knowledge about patterns of consumption for illicit drugs and the sensibility of these analyses to changes in the assumptions. Previous studies showed how little changes can dramatically alter final figures. In this context, Kilmer et al. show how changing the amount of marijuana per joint from 0.43 to 0.3 gr. would cause a reduction in the baseline estimates by more than 30%.[70] This article applies a similar methodology to Transcrime's study but updates previous assumptions according to recent literature.[71] Although changes can seem trivial, they may have a remarkable impact on the final estimates.

The second factor is the tendency to under-report stigmatised behaviours (like drug consumption) and the inability of GPS to capture heavy users. In particular, GPS does not survey the homeless, institutionalised people, and non-native speakers. Although these groups are of particular interest because they may have a higher prevalence of drug consumption, they are excluded from these surveys for practical reasons (they can be hard to reach or identify and for budgetary reasons). In addition to those excluded from the sample frame, people with frenetic lifestyles may be excluded from the survey because they are never home. Beside those who are not captured in the survey, there may be people who do answer the questionnaires but lie or under-report their habit.[72] For all these reasons, users estimated through GPS (cannabis, amphetamines and ecstasy) are adjusted according to an under-reporting rate while cocaine and heroin are estimated through alternative approaches.

While some of the previous issues pertain to all the countries dealing with the estimates of the illicit drug market, others pertain specifically to Italy. In particular, Italy is one among the few European countries to collect data on drug prevalence thorough a mail survey. As a consequence, Italy has a relatively low response rate to GPS. This is usually between 32% and 37%, not considering GPS 2010 that received responses for approximately 15% of the questionnaires sent.[73] Although previous studies showed that non-respondents do not necessarily have a higher drug prevalence rate, future surveys should consider alternatives to increase the response rate.[74] Particularly interesting are the results of the GPS 2012 that shows a marked drop in the drug consumption prevalence compared to GPS 2008.[75] There are two hypotheses for this huge variation. The first one is an actual reduction in the number of consumers. This is supported by different sources that identified in the recent economic crisis and the effective strategies of supply and demand reduction measures the causes of this marked reduction.[76] Although these two explanations deserve further attention, these interpretations can be considered reasonable, and they may help to explain the lower values reported in the last GPS. The other hypothesis sustains that differences in the method of the survey affected the results. As reported by the EMCDDA: 'The most recent general population survey reported by Italy displays a wide variation in results compared with the previous surveys which may reflect methodological differences. […] given the lack of comparability between surveys should be treated with caution.'[77] Since little information is available on how the survey in 2008 was conducted, it is not possible to confirm to what extent this drop is due to methodological changes. Further details from the Department of Antidrug Policy would help at least to understand how changes could affect the prevalence rate and possibly, elaborate a scenario analysis. In view of these problems, the data from GPS 2012 is preferable (not for ecstasy, given the lack of data) for three reasons. First, there are no means to evaluate whether the reduction is due to the actual decline in the number of users or to methodological changes in the survey. Second, these data have been analysed and accepted by EMCDDA. Third, they are more recent.

The above-mentioned uncertainties suggest that estimates of the drug market have to be handled with caution. Values need to be considered as more of an approximation than a 'point value.' This study offers a best value instead of a range in order to provide the best results according to the methodology employed, but this does not mean the result is a 'point value.'

Given the large discrepancies between GPS 2008 and GPS 2012, the results of this study will certainly be lower than those reported in the research report 'Gli investimenti delle mafie' although it adopted a similar methodology.[78] It is here suggested to take caution when comparing these two studies, being aware that all the factors mentioned so far, although apparently trivial, can have remarkable consequences on the final estimates.

Results

Table 6 shows the monetary value of the illicit drug market across Italian regions. Values refer to 2011 for heroin and cocaine, 2012 for cannabis and amphetamines and 2008 for ecstasy. Cocaine and heroin are the largest markets with a total retail spending estimated at € 1170.9 mn for the former and at € 1152.7 mn for the latter. Much lower are the values for synthetic drugs, while cannabis products together reach a value of € 546.6 mn.[79]

Lombardy and Campania are, in terms of consumption and monetary value, the largest markets accounting for 32.5% of the national retail spending on illicit drugs. Although both regions have high revenues associated with illicit drugs, they have a different incidence in the legal economy. In fact, the total spending for drugs in Lombardy represents 0.21% on GDP while is the double in Campania (0.42%), the region with the highest incidence. Both regions are of interest for their relevance of the organised crime sector. Campania is the region of origin of the Camorra and the presence of the mafias there is a long-lasting phenomenon. On the contrary, the presence of mafia groups in Lombardy is a more recent phenomenon. Although organised crime groups in Lombardy

Table 6. Estimated annual retail expenditure (mn of €) for heroin, cocaine, cannabis (herbal and resin), amphetamine and ecstasy. Heroin and cocaine (2011), Cannabis and amphetamines (2012), ecstasy (2008).

Region	Heroin	Cocaine	Cannabis Herbal	Cannabis Resin	Amphetamines	Ecstasy	Total illicit drug market	Percentage on GDP
Abruzzo	33.7	13.7	3.0	8.3	2.5	3.0	64.1	0.22%
Basilicata	12.3	5.0	1.2	3.0	0.9	1.1	23.5	0.21%
Calabria	28.1	38.5	3.4	8.2	3.6	4.4	86.2	0.25%
Campania	150.1	131.1	17.7	48.0	23.8	29.0	399.8	0.42%
Emilia Romagna	93.8	73.4	10.5	28.4	13.1	15.9	235.3	0.17%
F.V. Giulia	23.6	8.7	2.0	5.6	1.6	1.9	43.4	0.12%
Lazio	78.2	101.0	15.0	28.5	17.4	21.2	261.4	0.15%
Liguria	48.4	53.3	4.3	11.9	4.9	6.0	128.7	0.29%
Lombardia	128.0	322.2	28.1	72.2	56.9	69.2	676.6	0.21%
Marche	40.5	14.4	4.9	9.3	2.6	3.2	74.9	0.18%
Molise	7.8	5.9	0.8	2.4	1.1	1.3	19.3	0.30%
Piemonte	69.2	112.0	32.9	29.4	18.9	23.0	285.5	0.41%
Puglia	77.0	57.3	8.3	23.0	10.4	12.6	188.7	0.55%
Sardegna	41.9	49.4	6.5	14.4	7.8	9.5	129.6	0.15%
Sicilia	76.7	60.1	8.9	23.5	10.9	13.2	193.3	0.18%
Toscana	95.3	35.3	8.0	22.7	6.5	7.8	175.6	0.52%
T.A. Adige	29.8	11.9	1.6	4.3	1.9	2.4	51.9	0.04%
Umbria	21.9	6.8	1.9	5.0	1.2	1.5	38.4	0.18%
V. Aosta	5.2	3.4	0.3	0.9	0.5	0.6	10.9	0.25%
Veneto	91.2	67.5	10.6	27.4	12.4	15.1	224.2	0.15%
Italy	1152.7	1170.9	170.1	376.5	199.1	241.9	3311.2	0.21%

Source: Author's elaboration.

Table 7. Spending and consumption of cannabis.

User profile	Annual spending (€) per user on cannabis		Cannabis consumed per group (Kg)		% Consumption	% Users
	Herbal	Resin	Herbal	Resin		
Daily	1991.0	2409.0	14,908	347,851	71	9
Weekly	664.3	803.8	3122	72,842	15	6
Monthly	80.6	97.5	1807	42,153	9	35
Less than monthly	19.3	23.3	1199	27,970	6	49

Source: Author's elaboration.

may not exert a territorial control like in the Southern territories, they can invest in legal and illegal markets facilitated by a better economic context.

Cannabis is the most widely diffused drug in Italy with an annual consumption estimated at 69.8 tons in 2012. The consumption for heroin (26.2 tons), cocaine (15.9 tons) and amphetamines (12.1 tons) is much less while the use of ecstasy is estimated at 12.5 mn of tablets in 2008.[80] Consumption of drug impacts with different intensity on users' finances according to the drug consumed. The average heroin user spends about € 5982 per year on heroin, while it varies according to frequency of consumption for amphetamines, ecstasy and cannabis.[81] The results for the cannabis market presented in Table 7 are interesting. On average resin users spend more than herbal users per year, but annual consumption and spending are correlated with intensity of use. The estimates show that daily users, although representing 9% of the user population, consume about 71% of cannabis available in Italy. This confirms previous studies showing that few users are responsible for much of the consumption.[82]

Discussion

The estimates for each illicit drug, although lower, lay within the range estimated in the report 'Gli investimenti delle mafie' (except for cannabis).[83] A few factors seem to contribute to this difference. The first is the reduction in the prevalence of drug consumption as reported by GPS 2012. As already mentioned, this can be due to an actual reduction in the number of users as well as to methodological changes in the survey. The second is the sensitivity of the analysis to changes in assumptions and data. As showed in the previous section, changes that appear trivial may dramatically affect the final figures. The third are the adjustments in the method and other assumptions according to the most recent literature and data (purity, price, type of product, etc.).

Considering all of these factors, it is not surprising that the estimates are lower than previously estimated. For example, allowing 0.4 grams of cannabis per joint for cannabis users, the value estimated in Kilmer and Pacula[84] and applied as best value in Transcrime's study, would cause an increase in the final estimate of € 353 mn (from € 547 mn to € 900 mn). Two other adjustments in the methodology seem to affect and reduce the estimates for cannabis. These are: (1) a higher percentage of cannabis users who use herbal instead resin cannabis (which is less expensive than resin), and (2) adjusting cannabis consumption according to quantity discount and cannabis exchanged for free. All these changes, made to refine and improve the previous analysis, combined with the reduction in the number of estimated users, cause a drastic reduction of the estimates for cannabis. Despite this, the figure estimated for cannabis in Italy is just slightly lower than that estimated for France in 2005 (€ 746–832 mn).[85]

The differences for heroin are due to the different products considered.[86] While in the previous study it was assumed that users consume in equal parts white and brown heroin, here, the quantity of heroin consumed at the national level is multiplied by the price of brown heroin that is more widespread and less expensive.[87] The results for cocaine are interesting in that, although estimated from a different approach, they show a value slightly lower but still in the range indicated in Transcrime's study. As already mentioned, the current economic crisis may have forced some users to quit the consumption of an expensive product like powder cocaine.[88] For synthetic drugs, differences in the results are explained with the caution approach undertaken in Transcrime's study. Ecstasy and amphetamines were in fact estimated considering 'the largest, but still defensible' range of consumption as estimated by Kilmer and Pacula.[89] In this study, values are updated considering the results of a recent research that differentiates users according to frequency of consumption.[90] Although this increases by far the quantity of drug consumed for frequent users, it also drastically reduces consumption for occasional users who represent the vast majority of the user population.

Along with differences compared to Transcrime's study, there are some remarkable discrepancies with estimates made by other authors.[91] In particular, differences are especially evident with regard to Italian authors,[92] while less marked in relation to international studies.[93] Indeed, estimated values for cocaine, amphetamines and ecstasy fall within the range estimated by Kilmer and Pacula.[94] The reasons for the lower values for cannabis are previously illustrated (less users and changes in the assumptions), while for heroin the main explanation can be found in the higher price considered by Kilmer and Pacula. This may reflect the different source used (Kilmer and Pacula collected data on price from UNODC) as well as a general decreasing in the price of illicit drugs.[95] Differences with Caulkins, Kilmer and Graf are traced to differences in the number of estimated users.[96] Given the year of the study and the unavailability of the results of GPS 2012, the authors based their estimates on GPS 2008. If updated according to the last GPS results, Caulkins, Kilmer and Graf's study would probably be close to those estimated here.

Particularly evident are the differences with Fabi, Ricci and Rossi,[97] Rossi[98] and Sallusti,[99] which refer approximately to the same years. There are two explanations for these discrepancies. First, the assumptions on higher drug consumption considered by these authors. For example, Fabi, Ricci and Rossi assume 2 grams of cocaine per day per 300 days of consumption in a year.[100] This would mean about 10 lines of cocaine per day, 600 grams of cocaine per year, and an average annual expenditure of €41,000 per capita. Sallusti assumes an annual consumption for frequent cocaine users between 225 and 195 grams.[101] This range is by far higher than the 128.92 grams recently estimated by Frijns and van Laar[102] and the 100 grams assumed by Kilmer and Pacula.[103] Similarly, assumptions for heroin seem overestimated when compared with the recent literature. Fabi, Ricci and Rossi assume 300 grams of heroin per year per user. Considering that heroin purity in Italy is around 21%, this value is by far higher than 30 grams estimated by Paoli, Greenfield and Reuter[104] and recently confirmed by Kilmer et al.[105] Interesting is the category 'other drugs' in Fabi Ricci and Rossi[106] and Di Censi et al.[107] Here the authors do not specifically state which illicit drugs are considered and assume the same pattern of consumption for the whole group 'other drugs.' As shown in the method section, each substance has specific patterns of consumption and thereby each drug should be considered individually.

The second explanation, which is mainly valid for cannabis, is the differences in the number of estimated users. Fabi, Ricci and Rossi,[108] Rossi,[109] Di Censi et al.[110] do not base their estimates on GPS but on alternative sources and methods. Although the methodology is not very detailed, the authors seem to apply a capture–recapture method to subjects identified by prefectures for possession of drug for 'personal use only' and results from surveys on the student population (SPS). Indirect methods, like capture–recapture methods, have gained a broad consensus for estimating heavy users or injecting drug users in last few years. On the contrary, they are rarely applied to estimate cannabis users. The main reason for this is that indirect estimates are influenced by the probability of being captured by routine statistics (in this case, police records).[111] In a market like cannabis, where product is often exchanged between friends and in closed settings, official statistics can hardly capture this phenomenon and produce accurate estimates.[112] Moreover, it is not clear how users are divided in the three classes of occasional, regular and problematic users. As already mentioned the distribution across these three groups can heavily influence the final estimates. It is then worth providing detailed information on how these groups are formed in order to allow users of these estimates to re-build the estimate process.

Recently, Carla Rossi from the University of Rome 'Tor Vergata,' appointed as an expert for Italy, provided the estimates on cannabis users for a report on the drug market for the European Commission. As the report states:

> The University of Rome applied an indirect estimate using registration data on cannabis dealers, which was used in for a capture-recapture analysis (Zelterman's estimate) to estimate the number of (active) cannabis dealers. These data were combined with data on a customer to seller ratio [...] 32 for cannabis.[113]

This method is as well applied in other studies by the same author.[114] Although promising, this approach has many limits. First, re-arrests are affected by law enforcement activities and dealers' skills.[115] It is not easy to figure out to what extent re-arrest distribution is influenced by these components. Second, as the very authors acknowledge, data on drug arrests in Italy are not available according to drug sold.[116] This means that the share of dealers for drug sold is based on some assumption not specified by the author. Third, the literature on customer–seller ratio is scant and the assumption of 32 users per dealer is based on a study carried out in 1995 in Montreal.[117] Given the differences between Italy and Montreal, this ratio can be different. For example, the study by Reuter and colleagues for Washington, DC, reports an average of 40 customers per dealer.[118]

Despite their limits, it is here maintained that GPSs are still the best instrument to estimate, at least, cannabis users. The limits of GPSs are well understood and examined in the literature.[119] This makes those who use their results aware of the possible problems. Alternative approaches to estimate users and drug market are useful and valued, but authors should acknowledge and make their limits clear.

Conclusion

This study applied a consumption-based approach to estimate the retail value of the illicit drug market in Italy. Heroin and cocaine are the largest markets in terms of revenues while cannabis is the most-consumed illicit drug. Lower is the consumption of synthetic drugs. In breaking-down estimates across regions, the illicit drug market turns out to be a phenomenon developed in Northern and richer regions as well as in Southern and less developed ones. Then, numerous factors seem to account for drug consumption.

This study applies methods, data and assumptions according to the most updated research. Nonetheless, some limitations are still affecting it. Estimates of the illicit drug market are not a mere calculus exercise as long as they provide a detailed methodology showing limits and weakness of this process. These are carefully described throughout the article, warning users of these estimates to use them with particular caution. In so doing, they are prevented from making an improper use of the estimates of the illicit drug market (such as the comparison with the legal economic sector) and perceptively applied for policy analysis.

The estimates show that the value of the illicit drug market is much lower than previously estimated. There are few possible explanations for this: (1) the reduction in the assumed pattern of consumption; (2) for only cannabis and amphetamines, the reduction in the number of estimated users due to methodological changes in the GPS 2012; and (3) an actual reduction in the consumption of drug.[120]

Estimating the quantity of drug consumed per user seems a major limitation for all countries dealing with estimates of the illicit drug market. Although not easily, these limits can be overcome by adding some further questions in GPSs about pattern of consumption (doses and grams consumed in a typical day of consumption and days of consumption in a year), and carrying out studies on drug consumption in specific population (arrestees, people in treatment services, etc.). Enlarging wastewater analysis over the national territory can produce near real-time results and be used for cross-checking estimates from other approaches.

Italian authorities may provide a solution to the low response rate to its GPS opting for a more expensive, but more effective, instrument like a face-to-face interview. The bigger investment made with face-to-face interviews can be compensated by reducing the frequency of GPS to every three to four years instead of the current two years. Caution is recommended when comparing results from different GPSs. It is particularly inaccurate to compare trends across years when GPSs differ in terms of methodology and adherence to the study advocating reduction in the drug prevalence consumption as a success of current drug policies.[121]

Values and figures often mentioned by politicians and media advocating for a change in the policy against illicit drugs, should be built with scientific rigour and not based on ideological purposes. Alternative drug policies, from legalisation to prohibition, should be based on non-partisan evidence, considering multiple factors: public expenditure, consequences and expenditure on health, law enforcement, job market, etc. As Goldstein pointed out more than 30 years ago, policing should focus on ends rather than the means.[122] Without considering the current situation (current consumption/spending) future scenarios can hardly be predicted. This would lead to elaborate policies without knowing what the possible outcomes can be.

Acknowledgements

I would like to thank Thomas Loughran, Theodore Wilson and Daren Fisher for their help and suggestions.

Notes

1. UNODC, *World Drug Report 2013*, 1.
2. UNODC, *World Drug Report 2012*.
3. Truman and Reuter, *Chasing Dirty Money*.
4. Paoli, "The Paradoxes of Organized Crime"; and Williams and Florez, "Transnational Criminal Organizations and Drug Trafficking."

5. Reuter, *Disorganized Crime*; Paoli, "The Paradoxes of Organized Crime"; Reuter and Haaga, *The Organization of High-Level Drug Markets*; and Paoli, *Illegal Drug Markets in Frankfurt and Milan*.
6. Pearsons and Hobbs, *Middle Market Drug Distribution*; and Kenney, "The Architecture of Drug Trafficking."
7. Paoli, "The Paradoxes of Organized Crime," 67.
8. Gambetta and Reuter, "Conspiracy Among the Many."
9. Kleiman, *When Brute Force Fails*.
10. Kilmer et al., "Bringing Perspective to Illicit Markets."
11. UNIDCP, *World Drug Report*; SOS Impresa, *Le mani della criminalità sulle imprese*, 2011; and Syal, "Drug Money Saved Banks."
12. Reuter, "The (continued) Vitality of Mythical Numbers"; and Woodiwiss and Hobbs, "Organized Evil and the Atlantic Alliance."
13. Singer, "The Vitality of Mythical Numbers"; and Reuter, "The (continued) Vitality of Mythical Numbers."
14. Pudney et al., "Estimating the Size of the UK Illicit Drug Market"; Bramley-Hanker, *Sizing the UK Market for Illicit Drugs*; Legleye, Lakhdar, and Spilka, "Two Ways of Estimating the Euro Value"; Casey et al., *Assessing the Scale and Impact*; Connolly, *The Illicit Drug Market in Ireland*; Center for the Study of Democracy, *Serious Organized Crime Threat Assessment. 2010–2011*; Moore et al., *Monograph No. 09*; Wilkins et al., *The Socio-Economic Impact*; Wilkins et al., "Estimating the Dollar Value"; ONDCP, *What America's Users Spend*; and Werb, Nosyk, and Kerr, "Estimating the Economic Value."
15. UNODC, *World Drug Report 2005*; Kilmer and Pacula, *Estimating the Size of the Illegal Drug Market*; UNODC, *Estimating Illicit Financial Flows*; and Trautmann, Kilmer, and Turnbull, *Further Insights into Aspects*.
16. Baldassarini and Corea, "How to Measure Illegal Drugs"; Canzonetti, "Il mercato"; Kilmer and Pacula, *Estimating the Size of the Illegal Drug Market*; Di Censi et al., *Il mercato illecito della droga*; Fabi, Ricci, and Rossi, "Segmentazione e valutazione del mercato"; Transcrime, *Gli investimenti delle mafie*; Sallusti, "Estimating Cocaine Market in Italy"; Rossi, "Monitoring the Size and Protagonists"; and Caulkins, Kilmer, and Graf, "Estimating the Size of the EU Cannabis Market."
17. For the sake of brevity methods, data and assumptions are not detailed in this article (just doing this would require a full length article). Those interested in the details of the analysis can make specific reference to the mentioned papers.
18. Kilmer et al., "Bringing Perspective to Illicit Markets"; and Kilmer and Pacula, *Estimating the Size of the Illegal Drug Market*.
19. Legleye, Lakhdar, and Spilka, "Two Ways of Estimating the Euro Value."
20. Pudney et al., "Estimating the Size of the UK Illicit Drug Market."
21. Caulkins, Kilmer, and Graf, "Estimating the Size of the EU Cannabis Market."
22. Saviano, *Gomorrah*.
23. Saviano, "Vi racconto l'impero della cocaina"; and Saviano, *Zero Zero Zero*.
24. SOS Impresa, *Le mani della criminalità sulle imprese*, 2009.
25. Santino, "Mafia and Mafia Type Organizations"; and Calderoni, "The Structure of Drug Trafficking Mafias."
26. Zuccato et al., "Cocaine in Surface Waters."
27. ONDCP, *Drug Availability Estimates in the United States*.
28. MacCoun and Reuter, *Drug War Heresis*.
29. See note 10 above.
30. Transcrime, *Gli investimenti delle mafie*.
31. Caulkins, Kilmer, and Graf, "Estimating the Size of the EU Cannabis Market"; van Laar et al., "Cannabis Market"; Frijns and van Laar, "Amphetamine, Ecstasy and Cocaine"; Trautmann, Kilmer, and Turnbull, *Further Insights into Aspects*; Rossi, "Monitoring the Size and Protagonists"; and Rossi, "New Methodological Tools," 201.
32. UNODC, *Estimating Illicit Financial Flows*.
33. Kilmer and Pacula, *Estimating the Size of the Illegal Drug Market*.
34. See note 33 above.
35. EMCDDA, *Cannabis Production and Markets in Europe*.
36. See note 56 above.

37. See note 51 above.
38. See note 56 above.
39. See note 63 above.
40. Ibid.
41. Mascioli and Rossi, "La stima delle popolazioni nascoste."
42. Paoli, Greenfield, and Reuter, *The World Heroin Market*.
43. Kilmer and Pacula, *Estimating the Size of the Illegal Drug Market*; and Kilmer et al., "Sizing National Heroin Markets."
44. EMCDDA, *Monitoring the Supply of Heroin to Europe*.
45. For example, benzoylecgonine (BEG) is the main derivate of cocaine consumption. About 45% of the cocaine consumed is excreted via urine as BEG. Concentration of BEG (nanograms/litre) are multiplied by the water flow rate (m^3/day). BEG load is than transformed in cocaine and reported on the population served by the sewage system in grams/day/1000 inhabitant.
46. Casey et al., *Assessing the Scale and Impact*.
47. EMCDDA reports values for overall problem drug users, injecting drug users and opioids drug users but not for cocaine.
48. These pertain the estimate of the population served by the sewage system, degradation of drug residues in the wastewater and back-calculation from residues to pure drug.
49. Thomas et al., "Comparing Illicit Drug Use"; and Reid et al., "Estimation of Cocaine Consumption."
50. Rossi, "New Methodological Tools."
51. Zuccato and Castiglioni, "Consumi di sostanze stupefacenti."
52. These are: Potenza, Gorizia, Merano, Pescara, Bari, Verona, Nuoro, Cagliari, Bologna, Terni, Palermo, Florence, Milan, Perugia, Turin, Naples, Rome
53. Last-year users consider those who consumed the drug in the previous 12 months but not in last month.
54. EMCDDA, *Cannabis Production and Markets in Europe*, 239.
55. Kilmer and Pacula, *Estimating the Size of the Illegal Drug Market*; Werb, Nosyk, and Kerr, "Estimating the Economic Value"; and Magura, "Validating Self-Reports of Illegal Drug."
56. van Laar et al., "Cannabis Market."
57. Clements, *Pricing and Packaging*; Caulkins and Padman, "Quantity Discounts and Quality Premia"; and Desimone, "The Relationship Between Illegal Drug Prices."
58. Caulkins and Paucula, "Marijuana Markets."
59. Clements, *Pricing and Packaging*; and Caulkins and Paucula, "Marijuana Markets."
60. Caulkins and Paucula, "Marijuana Markets"; and Kilmer and Pacula, *Estimating the Size of the Illegal Drug Market*.
61. Werb, Nosyk, and Kerr, "Estimating the Economic Value"; and Caulkins and Paucula, "Marijuana Markets."
62. See note 33 above.
63. Frijns and van Laar, "Amphetamine, Ecstasy and Cocaine."
64. EMCDDA, *Problem Amphetamine and Methamphetamine Use in Europe*, 18.
65. See note 63 above.
66. Ibid.
67. See note 33 above.
68. See note 63 above.
69. Ibid.
70. See note 10 above.
71. van Laar et al., "Cannabis Market"; and Frijns and van Laar, "Amphetamine, Ecstasy and Cocaine."
72. See note 21 above.
73. Other countries, i.e., Australia, have a response rate to survey on drug consumption similar to that reported for Italy.
74. Gfroerer, Lessler, and Parsley, "Studies of Nonresponse and Measurement Error"; Decorte et al., *Drug Use: An Overview*.
75. Given a response rate of approximately 13% and the fact that the EMCDDA has not accepted its results, the GPS 2010 is not considered in this analysis.

76. Zuccato et al., "Changes in Illicit Drug Consumption Patterns"; and EMCDDA and EUROPOL, *EU Drug Markets Report*.
77. EMCDDA, "EMCDDA Statistical Bulletin 2013."
78. See note 30 above.
79. The impact of retail seizure on the total quantity of drug available (drug consumed plus seizure) is residual: heroin (4%), cocaine (7%), cannabis (11%), amphetamines (0%), ecstasy (0.1%).
80. For amphetamines and ecstasy the average between the low and high values has been considered.
81. Information on annual spending cannot be estimated for cocaine since cocaine users have not been estimated.
82. Caulkins et al., *Marijuana Legalization*; Casey et al., *Assessing the Scale and Impact*; van Laar et al., "Cannabis Market"; and Frijns and van Laar, "Amphetamine, Ecstasy and Cocaine."
83. See note 30 above.
84. See note 33 above.
85. See note 19 above.
86. See note 44 above.
87. The retail price for white heroin in 2011 is € 63, while for brown heroin it is € 42.
88. Zuccato et al., "Changes in Illicit Drug Consumption Patterns."
89. Kilmer and Pacula, *Estimating the Size of the Illegal Drug Market*, 43.
90. See note 63 above.
91. Baldassarini and Corea, "How to Measure Illegal Drugs"; Canzonetti, "Il mercato: quantità, consumi, valori"; Kilmer and Pacula, *Estimating the Size of the Illegal Drug Market*; Di Censi et al., *Il mercato illecito della droga*; Fabi, Ricci, and Rossi, "Segmentazione e valutazione del mercato"; Transcrime, *Gli investimenti delle mafie*; Sallusti, "Estimating Cocaine Market in Italy"; Rossi, "Monitoring the Size and Protagonists"; and Caulkins, Kilmer, and Graf, "Estimating the Size of the EU Cannabis Market."
92. Fabi, Ricci, and Rossi, "Segmentazione e valutazione del mercato"; Rossi, "Monitoring the Size and Protagonists"; and Sallusti, "Estimating Cocaine Market in Italy."
93. See note 21 above.
94. Kilmer and Pacula, *Estimating the Size of the Illegal Drug Market*; and Caulkins, Kilmer, and Graf, "Estimating the Size of the EU Cannabis Market."
95. Costa Storti and De Grauwe, "Special Issue"; and Storti and De Grauwe, "Globalization and the Price Decline of Illicit Drugs."
96. See note 21 above.
97. Fabi, Ricci, and Rossi, "Segmentazione e valutazione del mercato."
98. Rossi, "Monitoring the Size and Protagonists."
99. Sallusti, "Estimating Cocaine Market in Italy."
100. See note 97 above.
101. See note 99 above.
102. See note 63 above.
103. See note 33 above.
104. See note 56 above.
105. Kilmer et al., "Sizing National Heroin Markets."
106. See note 97 above.
107. Di Censi et al., *Il mercato illecito della droga*.
108. See note 97 above.
109. See note 98 above.
110. See note 107 above.
111. Wiessing, Vicente, and Hickman, "Integrating Wastewater Analysis."
112. Caulkins and Paucula, "Marijuana Markets"; and Wiessing, Vicente, and Hickman, "Integrating Wastewater Analysis."
113. van Laar et al., "Cannabis Market," 153.
114. See note 98 above.
115. Bouchard and Tremblay, "Risks of Arrest Across Drug Markets."
116. Carla Rossi, "Epidemiological Indicators to Evaluate Drug."
117. Tremblay and Lacoste, "De L'insertion Sociale Des Marchés Urbains."

118. Reuter, MacCoun, and Murphy, *Money from Crime.*
119. Fendrich et al., "The Utility of Drug Testing"; Caulkins, Kilmer, and Graf, "Estimating the Size of the EU Cannabis Market"; and Kilmer and Pacula, *Estimating the Size of the Illegal Drug Market.*
120. EMCDDA and EUROPOL, *EU Drug Markets Report*; and Zuccato et al., "Changes in Illicit Drug Consumption Patterns."
121. *Relazione annuale al Parlamento sull'uso di sostanze stupefacenti anno 2011.*
122. Goldstein, "Improving Policing."

Bibliography

Baldassarini, Antonella, and Carolina Corea. "How to Measure Illegal Drugs in the National Accounts Framework. The Case of Italy." Presented at the Illicit Drug Market and Its Possible Regulatory Body, Roma, September 17, 2009.

Bouchard, Martin, and Pierre Tremblay. "Risks of Arrest Across Drug Markets: A Capture-Recapture Analysis of 'Hidden' Dealers and User Population." *Journal of Drug Issues* 35, no. 4 (2005): 733–754.

Bramley-Hanker, Edward. *Sizing the UK Market for Illicit Drugs.* London: Home Office, 2001.

Calderoni, Francesco. "The Structure of Drug Trafficking Mafias: The 'Ndrangheta and Cocaine." *Crime, Law and Social Change* 58, no. 3 (2012): 321–349.

Canzonetti, Alessio. "Il mercato: quantità, consumi, valori. Una stima delle dimensioni del mercato delle sostanze stupefacenti e della sua incidenza sul prodotto interno lordo nazionale, attraverso un approccio lato domanda e lato offerta." Presented at the Illicit Drug Market and its Possible Regulatory Body, Roma, September 17, 2009.

Casey, Jane, Hay Gordon, Christine Godfrey, and Steve Parrott. *Assessing the Scale and Impact of Illicit Drug Markets in Scotland.* Edinburgh: Scottish Government Social Research, 2009. Accessed May 28, 2012. http://www.scotland.gov.uk/Resource/Doc/287490/0087669.pdf

Caulkins, Jonathan P., Angela Hawken, Beau Kilmer, and Mark A. R. Kleiman. *Marijuana Legalization: What Everyone Needs to Know.* New York: Oxford University Press, 2012.

Caulkins, Jonathan P., Beau Kilmer, and Marlon Graf. "Estimating the Size of the EU Cannabis Market." In *Further Insights into Aspects of the Illicit EU Drugs Market*, edited by Franz Trautmann, Beau Kilmer, and Paul Turnbull. Luxembourg: Publications Office of the European Union, 2013. Accessed October 12. http://ec.europa.eu/justice/anti-drugs/files/eu_market_full.pdf

Caulkins, Jonathan P., and Rema Padman. "Quantity Discounts and Quality Premia for Illicit Drugs." *Journal of the American Statistical Association* 88, no. 423 (1993): 748–757.

Caulkins, Jonathan P., and Rosalie L. Paucula. "Marijuana Markets: Inferences from Reports by the Household Population." *Journal of Drug Issues* 36 (2006): 173–200.

Center for the Study of Democracy. *Serious Organized Crime Threat Assessment. 2010–2011.* Sofia: Center for the Study of Democracy, 2012.

Clements, Kenneth W. *Pricing and Packaging: The Case of Marijuana.* Economics Discussion/Working Paper. University of Western Australia, Department of Economics, 2004. Accessed July 28, 2013. http://econpapers.repec.org/paper/uwawpaper/04-03.htm

Connolly, Johnny. *The Illicit Drug Market in Ireland.* Dublin: Health Research Board, 2005. http://www.drugsandalcohol.ie/6018/1/HRB_Overview_2.pdf

Costa Storti, C., and P. De Grauwe. "The Cocaine and Heroin Markets in the Era of Globalisation and Drug Reduction Policies." *International Journal of Drug Policy* 20, no. 6 (November 2009): 488–496.

Decorte, Tom, Dimitri Mortelmans, Julie Tieberghien, and Sabrine De Moore. *Drug Use: An Overview of General Population Surveys in Europe.* Lisbon: European Monitoring Centre for

Drugs and Drug Addiction, 2009. http://www.emcdda.europa.eu/publications/thematic-papers/gps

Desimone, Jeff. "The Relationship Between Illegal Drug Prices at the Retail User and Seller Levels." *Contemporary Economic Policy* 24, no. 1 (2006): 64–73.

Di Censi, Luca, Roberto Ricci, Carla Rossi, Federico Sallusti, and E. Ventura. *Il mercato illecito della droga e le sue possibili regolamentazioni. Agire nel mercato per contrastare l'industria della droga.* Roma: Istituto Superiore di Sanità, 2010. Accessed June 20, 2012. http://www.illicitdrugmarket.net/view.php?idsec=comitato

EMCDDA. *Cannabis Production and Markets in Europe.* Lisbon: European Monitoring Centre for Drugs and Drug Addiction, 2012.

EMCDDA. "EMCDDA Statistical Bulletin 2013." 2013. Accessed November 11. http://www.emcdda.europa.eu/stats13#display:/stats13/gpstab5a

EMCDDA. *Monitoring the Supply of Heroin to Europe.* Lisbon: European Monitoring Centre for Drugs and Drug Addiction, 2008.

EMCDDA. *Problem Amphetamine and Methamphetamine Use in Europe.* Lisbon: EMCDDA – European Monitoring Centre for Drugs and Drug Addiction, 2010. Accessed July 27, 2013. http://www.emcdda.europa.eu/publications/selected-issues/problem-amphetamine

EMCDDA, and EUROPOL. *EU Drug Markets Report: A Strategic Analysis.* Lisbon: EMCDDA & EUROPOL, 2013.

Fabi, Francesco, Roberto Ricci, and Carla Rossi. "Segmentazione e valutazione del mercato dal lato della domanda." In *Il mercato delle droghe. Dimensione, protagonisti, politiche*, edited by Guido Mario Rey, Carla Rossi, and Alberto Zuliani. Venezia: Marsilio Editori, 2011.

Fendrich, Michael, Timothy P. Johnson, Joseph S. Wislar, Amy Hubbell, and Vina Spiehler. "The Utility of Drug Testing in Epidemiological Research: Results from a General Population Survey." *Addiction* 99, no. 2 (2004): 197–208.

Frijns, Tom, and Margriet van Laar. "Amphetamine, Ecstasy and Cocaine: Typology of Users, Availability and Consumption Estimates." In *Further Insights into Aspects of the EU Illicit Drugs Market*, edited by Franz Trautmann, Beau Kilmer, and Paul Turnbull. Luxembourg: Publications Office of the European Union, 2013. http://ec.europa.eu/justice/anti-drugs/files/eu_market_full.pdf

Gambetta, Diego, and Peter H. Reuter. "Conspiracy Among the Many: The Mafia in the Legitimate Industries." In *The Economics of Organized Crime*, edited by Gianluca Fiorentini and Sam Peltzman. Cambridge: Cambridge University Press, 1996. http://www.nuffield.ox.ac.uk/users/gambetta/Conspiracy%20among%20the%20many.pdf

Gfroerer, J., J. Lessler, and T. Parsley. "Studies of Nonresponse and Measurement Error in the National Household Survey on Drug Abuse." In *The Validity of Self-Reported Drug Use: Improving the Accuracy of Survey Estimates*, edited by Lana H. Harrison and Arthur Hughes, 273–295. NIDA Research Monograph 167. Rockville, MD: National Institute on Drug Abuse, 1997.

Goldstein, Herman. "Improving Policing: A Problem-Oriented Approach." *Crime & Delinquency* 25, no. 2 (1979): 236–258.

Kenney, Michael. "The Architecture of Drug Trafficking: Network Forms of Organisation in the Colombian Cocaine Trade." *Global Crime* 8, no. 3 (2007): 233–259.

Kilmer, Beau, Jonathan P. Caulkins, Rosalie Liccardo Pacula, and Peter H. Reuter. "Bringing Perspective to Illicit Markets: Estimating the Size of the U.S. Marijuana Market." *Drug and Alcohol Dependence* 119, no. 1–2 (2011): 153–160.

Kilmer, Beau, and Rosalie L. Pacula. *Estimating the Size of the Illegal Drug Market: A Demand-Side Approach.* Santa Monica, CA: RAND Corporation, 2009. http://www.rand.org/pubs/technical_reports/TR711

Kilmer, Beau, Jirka Taylor, Priscillia Hunt, and Peter McGee. "Sizing National Heroin Markets in the EU. Insights from Self-Reported Expenditures in the Czech Republic and England." In *Further Insights into Aspects of the EU Illicit Drugs Market*, edited by Franz Trautmann, Beau Kilmer, and Paul Turnbull. Luxembourg: Publications Office of the European Union, 2013. http://ec.europa.eu/justice/anti-drugs/files/eu_market_full.pdf

Kleiman, Mark. *When Brute Force Fails: How to Have Less Crime and Less Punishment.* Princeton, NJ: Princeton University Press, 2009.

Legleye, Stephane, Christian Ben Lakhdar, and Stanislas Spilka. "Two Ways of Estimating the Euro Value of the Illicit Market for Cannabis in France." *Drug and Alcohol Review* 27, no. 5 (2008): 466–472.

MacCoun, Robert, and Peter Reuter. *Drug War Heresis: Learning from Other, Vices, Times, & Places*. New York: Cambridge University Press, 2001.

Magura, Stephen. "Validating Self-Reports of Illegal Drug Use to Evaluate National Drug Control Policy: A Reanalysis and Critique." *Evaluation and Program Planning* 33, no. 3 (2010): 234–237.

Mascioli, Flavia, and Carla Rossi. "La stima delle popolazioni nascoste." In *Il mercato delle droghe. Dimensione, protagonisti, politiche*, edited by Guido Mario Rey, Carla Rossi, and Alberto Zuliani. Venezia: Marsilio Editori, 2011.

Moore, Timothy J., Jonathan P. Caulkins, Alison Ritter, Paul Dietze, Shannon Monagle, and Jonathon Pruden. *Monograph No. 09: Heroin Markets in Australia: Current Understandings and Future Possibilities*. DPMP Monograph Series. Fitzory: Turning Point Alcohol and Drug Centre, 2005.

ONDCP. *Drug Availability Estimates in the United States*. Washington, DC: Executive Office of the President – Office of National Drug Control Policy, 2012. http://www.whitehouse.gov/sites/default/files/page/files/daeus_report_final_1.pdf

ONDCP. *What America's Users Spend on Illegal Drugs*. Washington, DC: Office of National Drug Control Policy, 2012.

Paoli, Letizia. *Illegal Drug Markets in Frankfurt and Milan*. Lisbon: European Monitoring Centre for Drugs and Drug Addiction, 2000.

Paoli, Letizia. "The Paradoxes of Organized Crime." *Crime, Law and Social Change* 37 (2002): 51–97.

Paoli, Letizia, Victoria A. Greenfield, and Peter Reuter. *The World Heroin Market: Can Supply Be Cut?* Oxford: Oxford University Press, 2009.

Pearsons, Geoffrey, and Dick Hobbs. *Middle Market Drug Distribution*. London: Home Office, 2001.

Pudney, Stephen, Celia Badillo, Mark Bryan, Jon Burton, Gabriella Conti, and Maria Iacovou. "Estimating the Size of the UK Illicit Drug Market." In *Measuring Different Aspects of Problem Drug Use: Methodological Developments*. London: Home office, 2006.

Reid, Malcolm J., Katherine H. Langford, Merete Grung, Hallvard Gjerde, Ellen J. Amundsen, Jorg Morland, and Kevin V. Thomas. "Estimation of Cocaine Consumption in the Community: A Critical Comparison of the Results from Three Complimentary Techniques." *BMJ Open* 2, no. 6 (2012). Accessed November 12. http://bmjopen.bmj.com/content/2/6/e001637

Relazione annuale al Parlamento sull'uso di sostanze stupefacenti anno 2011. Rome, 2011. Accessed October 31, 2013. http://www.youtube.com/watch?v=5988nf3WN5M&feature=youtube_gdata_player

Reuter, Peter. *Disorganized Crime. The Economics of the Visible Hand*. Cambridge, MA: MIT Press, 1984.

Reuter, Peter. "The (continued) Vitality of Mythical Numbers." *Public Interest* 75 (1984): 135–149.

Reuter, Peter, and John Haaga. *The Organization of High-Level Drug Markets: An Exploratory Study*. Santa Monica, CA: RAND Corporation, 1989.

Reuter, Peter, Robert MacCoun, and Patrick Murphy. *Money from Crime. A Study of the Economics of Drug Dealing in Washington, D.C.* Santa Monica, CA: RAND Corporation, 1990.

Rossi, Carla. "Epidemiological Indicators to Evaluate Drug Supply Interventions: Estimating the Dealer Populations." Presented at the A compared assessment of European supply-control policies and interventions, Lisbon, February 7, 2013. Accessed November 6. http://www.drugpolicyevaluation.eu/web/workstream/4

Rossi, Carla. "Monitoring the Size and Protagonists of the Drug Market: Combining Supply and Demand Data Sources and Estimates." Presented at the Workstream 4: A compared assessment of European supply-control policies and interventions, Lisbon, February 7, 2013. Accessed October 11. http://www.drugpolicyevaluation.eu/web/workstream/4

Rossi, Carla. "New Methodological Tools for Policy and Programme Evaluation." Presented at the Workstream 1: Analysis of consumption and behavioural characteristics of consumers, Lisbon, February 7, 2013. Accessed October 11. http://www.drugpolicyevaluation.eu/web/workstream/9

Sallusti, Federico. "Estimating Cocaine Market in Italy: A National Accounts Framework." Presented at the Workstream 6: Evaluation of the economic impact of illicit drug market, Lisbon, February 8, 2013. http://www.drugpolicyevaluation.eu/web/workstream/6

Santino, Umberto. "Mafia and Mafia Type Organizations in Italy." In *Organized Crime: World Perspective*, edited by Jay S. Albanese, Dilip K. Das, and Arvind Verma. Upper Saddle River, NJ: Prentice Hall, 2003.

Saviano, Roberto. *Gomorrah: A Personal Journey into the Violent International Empire of Naples' Organized Crime System*. New York: Picador, 2008.

Saviano, Roberto. "Vi racconto l'impero della cocaina." *L'Espresso*, March 21, 2007. Accessed June 5, 2013. http://espresso.repubblica.it/dettaglio/vi-racconto-limpero-della-cocaina/1533128

Saviano, Roberto. *Zero Zero Zero*. Milano: Feltrinelli, 2013.

Singer, Max. "The Vitality of Mythical Numbers." *Public Interest*, no. 23 (1971): 3–9.

SOS Impresa. *Le mani della criminalità sulle imprese*. Roma: Confesercenti, 2009.

SOS Impresa. *Le mani della criminalità sulle imprese*. Roma: Confesercenti, 2011.

Storti, Claudia Costa, and Paul De Grauwe. "Globalization and the Price Decline of Illicit Drugs." *International Journal of Drug Policy* 22 (2011): 366–373.

Syal, Rajeev. "Drug Money Saved Banks in Global Crisis, Claims UN Advisor." *The Guardian*, December 13, 2009. Accessed October 24, 2013. http://www.theguardian.com/global/2009/dec/13/drug-money-banks-saved-un-cfief-claims

Thomas, Kevin V., Lubertus Bijlsma, Sara Castiglioni, Adrian Covaci, Erik Emke, Roman Grabic, F. Hernández, et al. "Comparing Illicit Drug Use in 19 European Cities Through Sewage Analysis." *Science of The Total Environment* 432 (2012): 432–439.

Transcrime. *Gli investimenti delle mafie*. Rome: Ministero dell'Interno, 2013. Accessed March 5. http://www.investimentioc.it/index.htm

Trautmann, Franz, Beau Kilmer, and Paul Turnbull. *Further Insights into Aspects of the EU Illicit Drugs Market*. Luxembourg: Publications Office of the European Union, 2013.

Tremblay, Pierre, and Julie Lacoste. "De L'insertion Sociale Des Marchés Urbains de Drogues Prohibées: Deux Cas de Figure Nord-Américains." *Déviance et Société* 23, no. 1 (1999): 41–58.

Truman, Edwin M., and Peter Reuter. *Chasing Dirty Money: Progress on Anti-Money Laundering*. Washington, DC: Peterson Institute, 2004.

UNIDCP. *World Drug Report*. Vienna: United Nations International Drug Control Programme, 1997.

UNODC. *Estimating Illicit Financial Flows: Resulting from Drug Trafficking and Other Transnational Organized Crimes*. Vienna: United Nations Office on Drugs and Crime, 2011. Accessed March 23, 2012. http://www.unodc.org/documents/data-and-analysis/Studies/Illicit_financial_flows_2011_web.pdf

UNODC. *World Drug Report 2005*. Vienna: United Nation Office on Drugs and Crime, 2005. Accessed March 22, 2012. http://www.unodc.org/pdf/WDR_2005/volume_1_web.pdf

UNODC. *World Drug Report 2012*. Vienna: United Nation Office on Drugs and Crime, 2012. Accessed June 27. http://www.unodc.org/documents/data-and-analysis/WDR2012/WDR_2012_web_small.pdf

UNODC. *World Drug Report 2013*. Vienna: United Nation Office on Drugs and Crime, 2013. Accessed July 22. http://www.unodc.org/unodc/secured/wdr/wdr2013/World_Drug_Report_2013.pdf

van Laar, Margriet, Tom Frijns, Franz Trautmann, and Linda Lombi. "Cannabis Market: User Types, Availability and Consumption Estimates." In *Further Insights into Aspects of the EU Illicit Drugs Market*, edited by Franz Trautmann, Beau Kilmer, and Paul Turnbull. Luxembourg: Publications Office of the European Union, 2013. http://ec.europa.eu/justice/anti-drugs/files/eu_market_full.pdf

Werb, Dan, Bohdan Nosyk, and Thomas Kerr. "Estimating the Economic Value of British Columbia's Domestic Cannabis Market: Implications for Provincial Cannabis Policy." *International Journal of Drug Policy* 20 (2009): 488–496.

Wiessing, Lucas, Julian Vicente, and Matthew Hickman. "Integrating Wastewater Analysis with Conventional Approaches to Measuring Drug Use." In *Assessing Illicit Drugs in Wastewater: Potential and Limitations of a New Monitoring Approach*, edited by Norbert Frost and Paul Griffiths. Lisbon: European Monitoring Centre on Drugs and Drug Addiction, 2008.

Wilkins, Chris, James Reilly, Emily Rose, Debashis Roy, Megan Pledger, and Arier Lee. *The Socio-Economic Impact of Amphetamine Type Stimulants in New Zealand*. Auckland: Centre for Social and Health Outcomes Research and Evaluation (SHORE), Massey University, 2004.

Wilkins, Chris, James L. Reilly, Megan Pledger, and Sally Casswell. "Estimating the Dollar Value of the Illicit Market for Cannabis in New Zealand." *Drug and Alcohol Review* 24, no. 3 (2005): 227–234.

Williams, P., and C. Florez. "Transnational Criminal Organizations and Drug Trafficking." *Bulletin on Narcotics* 46, no. 2 (1994): 9–24.

Woodiwiss, Michael, and Dick Hobbs. "Organized Evil and the Atlantic Alliance Moral Panics and the Rhetoric of Organized Crime Policing in America and Britain." *British Journal of Criminology* 49, no. 1 (2009): 106–128.

Zuccato, Ettore, and Sara Castiglioni. "Consumi di sostanze stupefacenti nelle città europee." *Ricerca E Pratica* 3, no. 28 (2012): 252–260.

Zuccato, Ettore, Sara Castiglioni, Mauro Tettamanti, Raffaela Olandese, Renzo Bagnati, Manuela Melis, and Roberto Fanelli. "Changes in Illicit Drug Consumption Patterns in 2009 Detected by Wastewater Analysis." *Drug and Alcohol Dependence* 118, no. 2–3 (2011): 464–469.

Zuccato, Ettore, Chiara Chiabrando, Sara Castiglioni, Davide Calamari, Renzo Bagnati, Silvia Schiarea, and Roberto Fanelli. "Cocaine in Surface Waters: A New Evidence-Based Tool to Monitor Community Drug Abuse." *Environmental Health* 4 (2005): 14.

A new method for estimating the illicit cigarette market at the subnational level and its application to Italy

Francesco Calderoni

Università Cattolica del Sacro Cuore and Transcrime, Milan, Italy

This study provides a methodology with which to estimate the volumes and revenues of the illicit cigarette market at the subnational level. It applies the methodology to Italy for a 4-year period (2009–2012), enabling assessment of the prevalence of the illicit trade across years and regions. Notwithstanding the alleged importance of mafias, the results provide a more complex picture of the Italian illicit tobacco market. The maximum total revenues from the illicit trade in tobacco products (ITTP) increased from €0.5 bn in 2009 to €1.2 bn in 2012. The prevalence of illicit cigarettes varies significantly across regions, because of the proximity to countries with cheaper cigarettes and the possible occurrence of other crime opportunities. Understanding of these factors is crucial for the development of appropriate policies against the ITTP. The methodology may be applicable to all other EU countries, providing detailed, yearly estimates of the illicit market at the subnational level.

Introduction

The illicit trade in tobacco products (hereinafter ITTP) comprises a variety of illegal activities, extending beyond the most popular categories of smuggling and counterfeiting. The most common definition of the ITTP (Article 1 of the Framework Convention on Tobacco Control of the World Health Organisation) is broad and somewhat tautological.[1] In fact, the ITTP encompasses different conducts, from criminal offences to administrative violations: namely, *contraband* (transport or sale of tobacco products from a country without paying taxes or violating laws that control the import and the export); *counterfeiting* (illegal production of goods with a trademark or a copy of the latter without the owners' permission); '*cheap whites*' or '*illicit whites*' (cigarettes produced in one country in order to be illegally exported to another country where the same products are not distributed in the legal market); '*unbranded*' tobacco (hand-rolled or semi-finished tobacco or also loose tobacco leaves with no labelling or health warning); *bootlegging* (the purchase of legal tobacco in low-tax countries for illegal resale in countries with higher taxes); and *illegal production* (products not declared to the tax authorities).[2] These different activities are inherently associated with the fact that tobacco products are legal commodities available in a market context.

The tobacco market is a dual market with a legal and illegal side.[3] The interaction between the two sides is due to numerous socio-economic, cultural and normative factors, including activities to combat trafficking.[4] In the legal market, tobacco products are subject to strict regulation and high taxation owing to their serious consequences for human health. Despite intensive regulation, the tobacco market is a truly global one, with multinational companies, centralised manufacturing (driven by economies of scale and the relatively easy transport of the products) and important import–export dynamics. The functioning of the legal tobacco market inevitably affects the illicit trade as well.

For the above-mentioned reasons, the ITTP is a problem in various respects. It affects tobacco control policies, supplying cheap and often uncontrolled tobacco products and jeopardising efforts to reduce smoking; it deprives governments of revenues from taxation; it impacts on the economy by unfairly competing with the sectors of tobacco manufacturing, wholesale and retail distribution.[5]

This study provides a methodology for the production of subnational (nuts-2[6] level) estimates of the volumes and revenues of the ITTP and particularly of illicit cigarettes.[7] It applies the estimation methodology to Italy, which is an interesting case study because of the traditional role of tobacco smuggling for the Italian mafias and the evolution of the ITTP in recent decades. The estimates for Italy show that the increase of the illicit market in the last 4 years is due to a generalised growth across all regions between 2009 and 2011. In 2012, the increase was mostly driven by three regions. Calculation of the revenues at the retail level from the ITTP point out that the allegation that the Italian mafias are earning up to €0.9 bn is unfounded.

The rest of the article is organised as follows: the first section briefly reviews the characteristics of the illicit trade in tobacco products and the existing estimates. The second section focuses on Italy, analysing the evolution of the ITTP in the past years and presenting qualitative and quantitative information available today. The third section outlines the methodology used for this study as well as its limitations, while the fourth section presents and discusses the results. The last section concludes the article.

The illicit trade in tobacco products: characteristics and estimates
Demand and supply

The demand for illicit tobacco products is associated with several factors. In particular, several studies have shown that the main factor determining the consumption of illicit tobacco is the price, which is significantly lower than that of the legitimate products. The price of illicit products may vary by country, product and other conditions of sale, and it ranges from 25% to 90% less than that of legitimate products.[8] In addition to price differentials, the literature has shown that smokers in low socio-economic conditions are more likely to consume illicit tobacco.[9] Furthermore, in some countries and areas where smuggling is a common practice, the consumption of illicit cigarettes may be regarded as a socially acceptable practice.[10]

Also the supply of illicit tobacco is strongly influenced by the dynamics of prices and taxes. Cigarettes are in fact the commodity with the highest tax value by weight, and the retail price is mainly determined by taxes, which may even exceed 70–80% of the same.[11] The illicit market aims to minimise or avoid taxes paid on products, and this makes it a business that can generate high profits.[12] Other factors favouring the development of the illicit tobacco market include the availability of cheap (including illegal) tobacco products, with areas close to cheaper cigarettes being more vulnerable to various forms of tax avoidance (both licit and illicit),[13] the dynamics and regulation of the legal market, for example the transit trade regime allowing the suspension of taxation for exported/ imported commodities transiting through third countries[14] illicit practices by some manufacturers, for example the supply of quantities of cigarettes exceeding the domestic demand to some countries from where the products are subsequently smuggled exploiting corruption and international trade schemes,[15] and the adoption of effective prevention policies and criminal enforcement actions.[16] Although a high level of taxation may be the initial incentive for the supply of illicit tobacco, these other factors are crucial for the development and maintenance of the illicit trade.

The actors of the ITTP

The literature has shown the presence of a variety of actors involved in the illicit tobacco market. First, the tobacco industry has been repeatedly reported for contributing to the smuggling of tobacco products. In many countries, governments have taken legal action for the fiscal losses caused by the industry's exploitation of transit trade, resulting in significant smuggling of tobacco products.[17] The pressure on the industry has led manufacturers to implement better controls on the supply chain and on the destination countries.[18] Another result was the signature of cooperation agreements with the authorities of various countries.[19] The agreements have improved the prevention and fight against large-scale tobacco smuggling, introducing systems to track and trace tobacco products and imposing payment on manufacturers in case the authorities seize products that are not counterfeit.[20]

Second, much of the criminological literature reports that those involved in the illicit tobacco trade are mainly small groups or independent criminal entrepreneurs.[21] These studies, primarily in the Netherlands, Germany, Greece and the United Kingdom, maintain that large organisations, structured and stable over time, should be considered exceptional in the illicit tobacco market. Even in the presence of quite extensive and organised criminal networks, as in the case of groups of Vietnamese origin in Berlin, there were no elements that suggested the creation of large coalitions or groups with an elaborate structure able to achieve monopoly on the illicit market by, for example, the frequent use of violence.[22]

Finally, several sources report the involvement of organised crime and terrorist groups in the illicit tobacco trade. These groups are attracted by the possibility of high profits with a low risk of identification and conviction. They take advantage of the international exchange networks already used, for example, to traffic drugs, arms and human beings.[23] According to various sources, stable and organised criminal groups, such as the Italian mafias, Eastern European or Asian criminal organisations, are present in different phases of the trade. These groups participate in the smuggling,[24] forgery,[25] storing and processing of illicit tobacco.[26] In regard to terrorist organisations, some studies have argued for their involvement in illicit tobacco.[27] However, these analyses are based on a limited number of cases and are often conducted on heterogeneous sources, such as official reports and articles in the media, which may over-emphasise the role of criminal and terrorist organisations. Some scholars have therefore argued that the involvement of terrorists and mafias is rare and that in any case they are unable to monopolise such a large illicit market.[28]

Estimates of the ITTP

Several studies have estimated the size of the illicit tobacco market at the global, continental and national level. The availability of studies is probably due to the impact that illicit trade can have on legitimate manufacturers and tobacco control policies and to the importance that taxes on tobacco products have for governments. This promotes estimations of the size and the fiscal impact of the illicit market to monitor and facilitate action against it. However, the agendas of the estimators may have an influence on the estimation process: manufacturers may prefer high figures to get more attention by the law enforcement agencies, policymakers may want to minimise the issue as this may indicate problems of efficiency or corruption, and tobacco control activist may either prefer higher, for example to point out the manufacturers' role in the ITTP, or lower numbers, for example to minimise the unwanted effects of tobacco control measures.[29]

Despite the abundance of estimations, there is no general consensus on the methodology. Existing studies are often based on various sources collected at irregular intervals. In particular, the approaches used have focused, for example, on the difference between exports and imports declared, or official/expert estimates, the link between sales and official prices in neighbouring countries, consumer surveys and observational data collection (inspection of packs and other products).[30] In addition to the above mentioned biases owing to the estimators' agendas, each of these methods has limitations with regard to the inclusion of various forms of trafficking and its reliability in the estimate.

At the global level, different studies have estimated the world illicit market at around 6% of total consumption in 1993, 8.5% in 1995, 10.7% in 2006 and 11.6% in 2007.[31] Although these estimates provide quite similar (and growing) values, they result from different approaches and different data of limited reliability. The only source providing yearly estimates of the illicit trade in tobacco products for a large number of countries (currently 80) is Euromonitor International (hereinafter EMI). EMI is a private company which publishes periodic reports on the global (and regional) illicit tobacco markets, estimating their size, revenues and related tax losses.[32] For 2011, EMI estimated illicit cigarettes at 571.8 billion units, corresponding to 9% of the world market (a figure that rises to 11.5% when excluding the main national market, China).[33] However, EMI does not provide detailed information on the methodology used, and several studies have challenged the reliability of its estimates.[34]

At the level of the European Union, Joossens and colleagues stated that the illicit market share was about 58 billion cigarettes in 2007 (8.5% of the total market).[35] Furthermore, a 2010 consumer survey on 17 EU countries and Albania reported that 3.4% of consumers purchased cigarettes 'from an individual selling cigarettes independently at local markets, delivery service, door-to-door, or just in the street', while 8.4% of smokers purchased from the same channels at least 1% of their consumption in the previous 30 days.[36] However, the authors acknowledged that the results may underestimate the size of the illicit market due to underreporting. To address this issue, the study also calculated a 'tax evasion score' based on the characteristics of the cigarette packs shown by the consumers surveyed.[37] The tax evasion score across all the countries was 8.1%.[38] The difference between the prevalence of smuggling reported by consumers and the tax evasion score further confirms the limited reliability of surveys for the measurement of the illicit trade. EMI provides national estimates of the ITTP for 25 out of 28 EU Member States, since there are no estimates for Luxembourg, Cyprus and Malta. The estimates of the illicit market, still with no detail on the methodology used to calculate them, amounted to 67.3 bn cigarettes in 2007 (8.8% of total consumption) and 77.3 bn in 2012 (12.2% of total consumption).[39]

Project Star provides a further estimate at the EU level. Since 2006, the project has provided annual estimates of the illicit tobacco market at a national and EU level, both in volume and as a percentage of the total market. Project Star is conducted by KPMG in furtherance of the agreements concluded among Philip Morris International, the European Commission, OLAF (the European Anti-Fraud Office) and the Member States to tackle the illicit trade.[40] The project is based on data on legal sales, consumer surveys and empty packs surveys (EPSs).[41] EPSs are contracted out by the main tobacco manufacturers to different market analysis companies. In each country, they periodically collect a sample of littered cigarette packs in a number of medium and large cities. The surveys aim to assess the market shares of manufacturers and brands and to measure the prevalence of non-domestic and counterfeit products. To this purpose, each pack is analysed to identify the manufacturer, brand, country variant and whether it is a counterfeit. According to the last issue of Project Star, in 2012, the ITTP amounted to 65.5 bn cigarettes, that is 11.1% of total consumption.

Some studies challenged the reliability of Project Star.[42] Joossens and colleagues questioned the results, arguing that 'the methodology for the collection of the empty packs in the report is insufficiently explained to judge its validity and that the report relies heavily on expertise and data provided by the tobacco industry'.[43] A study reviewing the methodology of Project Star argued that the study may 'provide a useful contribution to the debate', since 'its strength lies in the production of a useful model and providing estimates [...] independent of seizure data on which, despite their bias, such estimates are usually based'.[44] However, the authors pointed out a number of concerns about the methodology: lack of transparency and details on the data used in the model, overreliance on industry-produced data, risk of overestimation and the lack of external validation.[45]

Although most of the above concerns are important, Project Star still represents the best source of yearly estimates of the prevalence of the ITTP in the EU, enabling assessment of the evolution of the ITTP since 2006 through a constant methodology. With the exception of EMI's opaque estimations, there is no other source providing annual figures for each EU country. The criticisms about the industry-supported EPSs often overlook that such sources also provide some advantages. For example, EPSs are currently conducted by independent market analysis companies for the four main manufacturers. The sample size is large (more than 10,000 packs per wave in most EU countries). Identification of counterfeits is conducted in cooperation with the manufacturers because of their expertise in the identification of the security features designed in the packs, a practice also common whenever law enforcement agencies seize large quantities of cigarettes. EPSs' purpose is also to measure market shares, and this may reduce the risk of biases when they are jointly conducted for the four main manufacturers. Finally, in addition to possible industry biases, the lack of transparency about the methodology and results may also be due to other elements. For example, the data may disclose sensitive information, which both manufacturers and market research may be reluctant to share with potential competitors. This is also common in other industries (e.g. finance and insurance). At present, there is limited alternative to the use of industry data for the estimates, unless large-scale, independent data collection plans are enacted.

Alternative, independent estimates appear still unsatisfactory and are not conducted on a country-wide annual basis. Consumer surveys may be inadequate in evaluating illicit behaviours due to respondents' biases.[46] Independent pack collections, while providing more detail on the methodology, often rely on smaller samples.[47] For example, three industry-funded waves of EPSs in Poland gathered 34,000 packs in August–September 2011, 34,000 in October–November 2011 and 17,000 packs in March–April of 2012 (the sample for the capital Warsaw was between 2800 and 5600 packs per wave).[48] In September 2011, Stoklosa and Ross conducted an independent survey, collecting only 754 packs in Warsaw.[49] Overall, while the public and academic opinion should discuss its reliability and require full transparency on the methodology, there is little doubt that Project Star will most likely remain a point of reference for the estimation of the ITTP in the EU.

The past and present of the ITTP in Italy

The evolution of the illicit tobacco market in Italy

Historically, the Italian illicit tobacco market has been characterised by some special elements, which brought the ITTP to very high levels from the middle of the 1980s until the end of the 1990s.[50] First, cigarette smuggling played an important role in the evolution of the Italian mafias (Camorra, Cosa Nostra and the Sacra Corona Unita). After World War II, the illicit cigarette trade enabled Cosa Nostra and the Camorra to make considerable profits before the development of drug trafficking.[51] Later, also the Sacra Corona Unita and criminal organisations from Puglia region became involved in cigarette smuggling, opening new entry points for illicit tobacco on Italy's south-eastern coasts.[52]

Second, the business practices by tobacco manufacturers contributed to the illicit trade. These included, for example, the sale of products to some neighbouring countries in quantities largely exceeding the domestic demand for cigarettes.[53] The cigarettes were subsequently smuggled to Italy.

Third, the authorities of the neighbouring countries were actively involved in the smuggling schemes. For example, Montenegro (a part of the Federal Republic of Yugoslavia since 1992 and of the State Union of Serbia and Montenegro since 2003; an independent state since 3 June 2006) was one of the traditional destinations for cigarettes to be smuggled to Italy, which gained the country the nickname of 'the Tortuga of the Adriatic Sea'.[54] Since 1992, cigarettes were sold to broker companies based in a number of countries and delivered to Montenegro, where they paid a low tax. Allegedly, the revenues generated by cigarette smuggling made up to 60% of the Montenegrin domestic product.[55] The cigarettes were then smuggled to Italy with the cooperation of groups affiliated to the Sacra Corona Unita and the Camorra.[56] According to the Italian law enforcement and prosecution agencies, the authorities of Montenegro participated in the smuggling scheme, including the country's leading politician, both Prime Minister and President during those years.[57] However, Italian authorities eventually dropped the charges in March 2009 because of problems of diplomatic immunity.[58]

Since the middle of the 1990s, Italian authorities have adopted a number of measures to tackle cigarette smuggling. New legislation increased the penalties for cigarette smuggling and large scale law enforcement operations were launched, including the 2000 Operation *Primavera* (Springtime), which led to the arrest of more than 500 individuals.[59] Also, since 1991, the Italian government has increased its pressure on tobacco manufacturers, for example suspending the sales of a number of brands in 1991 and 1992. In 1992 and 1998, it entered into two agreements with Philip Morris, the leading manufacturer on the Italian market.[60] While the Antimafia Parliamentary Commission contended that these agreements were unsatisfactory, in 2001 Italy, first among EU countries, joined the lawsuit against PMI filed by the European Commission in New York, which resulted in the above mentioned 2004 agreement.[61] Finally, changes in international politics led to an end of the Montenegrin connection. In fact, according to the Italian Antimafia Parliamentary Commission, until the end of the 1990s, cigarette smuggling from Montenegro was tolerated for *realpolitik* reasons. Since 1996, Montenegrin authorities were opposing Slobodan Milosevic (President of Serbia until 1997, then President of the Federal Republic of Yugoslavia until 2000) in the period before the Kosovo War (February 1998–June 1999). After the war and the resignation of Milosevic in 2000, international support stopped, as demonstrated by the drop in the number of cases shipped to Montenegro (from 967,513 cases in 1998 to approximately 103,344 cases in 2000).[62] The combined effects of these measures induced a sharp decrease in the ITTP, to the point that Italy was considered a successful case at the international level.[63]

Information on the ITTP in Italy today

Today, according to law enforcement agencies, various criminal organisations, both domestic and foreign, dominate the ITTP in Italy. These groups would be the only ones able to organise the different phases of the complex smuggling operations. National and foreign organised criminals, often connected with the Italian mafias, would act as criminal enterprises, moving large quantities of cigarettes across seas and continents.[64] The media and other sources reported that mafia proceeds from illicit tobacco would be €0.9 bn in 2010.[65]

Although presently available qualitative information on the ITTP highlights the important role of the mafias and organised crime, quantitative sources suggest a more complex picture. Existing estimates show that the Italian illicit tobacco market passed from high levels until the 1990s to very low ones at the beginning of the 2000s. In the most recent years, however, estimates have started to grow again (Figure 1).

Several consumer surveys were conducted between 2005 and 2010. Reported purchases from illicit channels remained constantly below 1% and even 0% in 2010.[66] The 2010 survey also calculated the tax evasion score based on the features of the packs shown by the surveyed sample (1.5% of packs).[67] In 2011, Nomisma issued a report on cigarette counterfeiting in Italy.[68] The report estimated the illicit tobacco market for the years 2009–2010 at about 2.8 billion cigarettes per year (3.2% of total consumption), with 413 million (0.5%) and 2.4 billion units (2.7%) for counterfeits and contraband, respectively. The report also estimated the value of the national illegal market, which amounted to over 651 million euros, that is 3.6% of total market value.[69] The report, however, does not provide details on the methodology used.[70] Project Star assessed the illicit market share in 2012 at 8.5% of total consumption.[71] In the same year, EMI estimated the penetration of illicit tobacco at 5.8% of total consumption.[72]

A further proxy for the illicit trade may be the prevalence of non-domestic packs in Italian EPSs. Analysis of eight surveys conducted in the period 2009–2012 shows the national prevalence of non-domestic packs ranging from 3.7% in the second quarter of 2009 to 9.9 and 9.6% in the second and fourth quarters of 2012, respectively (Figure 2). The use of EPSs as proxies of the illicit trade is controversial. First, they measure the prevalence of non-domestic packs, which include both legal and illegal products. Further, the literature has pointed out a number of methodological uncertainties, also arguing that industry-sponsored EPSs may be biased by the industry's interest in inflating the estimates

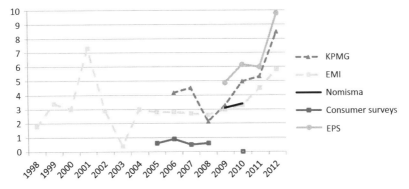

Figure 1. Estimates of the illicit trade in tobacco products in Italy. Share of total consumption (1998–2012).

Source: Author's elaboration.

Figure 2. Share of non-domestic packs out of total collected packs in empty packs surveys per region, quarter and year (2009–2012).

Source: Author's elaboration.

of the ITTP.[73] These concerns are important and further discussion of the reliability of the Italian EPSs is provided in the methodology section.

Despite the caution due to the mentioned criticisms, EPSs are the only source providing some information on the illicit market penetration at the local level. This is particularly important, since the recent increase in non-domestic packs at the national level does not correspond to a general growth in all regions. Figure 2 shows different evolution patterns. While in some regions the trend of the non-domestic share was decreasing (e.g. Liguria, Calabria, Puglia) or stable (e.g. Emilia-Romagna), other regions registered a striking increase (Friuli-Venezia Giulia and Campania). The data suggest that non-domestic packs may reflect the trend in the illicit market, since tourist numbers do not

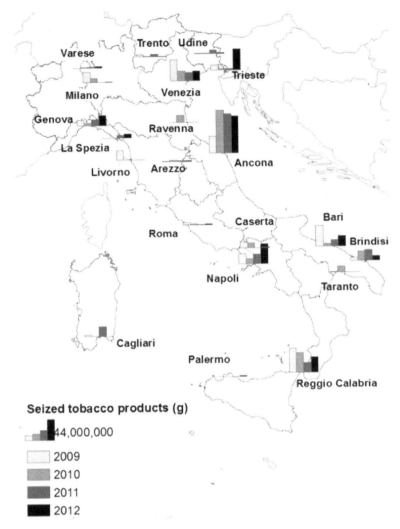

Figure 3. Seizures of tobacco products by the Guardia di Finanza per year and province of the seizure (grams) (2009–2012).

Source: Author's elaboration.

have such a degree of variation across years and do not concentrate in the regions with the highest non-domestic prevalence.[74]

Finally, seizure data do not reflect the penetration of the illicit trade in tobacco products. Data provided by the Guardia di Finanza (Italian financial police) for 2009–2012 show that seizures concentrate on land and sea borders (Figure 3). Furthermore, only a minority (between 28% and 35%) of the seized products are destined for Italy.[75]

The review of the available information on the Italian illicit tobacco market points out a complex situation. While the media and official sources highlight the significant involvement of Italian and foreign criminal organisations in the ITTP, arguing that domestic mafias would earn nearly €1 bn from illicit tobacco, the existing evidence is partially at odds with the picture of a criminal market monopolised by the mafias and organised crime. It is so for several reasons. First, the illicit market has undergone significant changes in the last two decades. From high levels during the 1990s, it dropped to low ones at the beginning of the 2000s; in recent years, most available estimates suggest a growth of illicit consumption. This is somewhat in contrast with the constant presence of organised crime in the country. Second, the existing data on seizures and non-domestic packs suggest that the levels of illicit trade may not relate only to a strong presence of the mafias and other criminal organisations. Data on seizures point out that the mafias are not the only actor at the wholesale distribution level. Most of the seizures in the last 3 years occurred in the port of Ancona, a city with low mafia presence. Conversely, ports where the mafias may have stronger control, such as in Naples, Bari and Reggio Calabria, show an irregular trend in the seizures. The data on empty packs point out that, at the retail level, the ITTP may reach high levels in areas with and without strong mafia control. While Campania (region of origin of the Camorra) has high levels of non-domestic packs, Calabria and Sicilia (origin of the 'Ndrangheta and Cosa Nostra, respectively) are below the national average. Finally, the data also show significant changes in the ITTP across time and regions. For example, the prevalence of non-domestic packs in Naples passed from 8% in the fourth quarter of 2011 to 46% and 50% in the second and fourth quarter of 2012, respectively; in Rome, it passed from 3.5% in the second quarter of 2009 to 10% in the last quarter of the same year.

The contrast between public opinion and empirical evidence is problematic and prevents better understanding of the functioning of the ITTP. There is a need for more studies on the factors driving the illicit market across time and space within the same country. However, such analyses require better estimates of the size of the illegal tobacco market, providing regional estimates of the volume and revenues generated by the ITTP. This study aims to fill this gap by developing a methodology with which to estimate the regional volumes and revenues from the illicit cigarette market and applying it to Italy for the period 2009–2012.

Methodology to estimate the illicit cigarette market
Data

The methodology used to estimate the illicit cigarette market was mainly based on the national estimate of the ITTP in Italy by KPMG's Project Star 2012 report, on EPSs data provided by Philip Morris International and on other publicly available data (Table 1).[76]

Table 1. Data for estimating the illicit trade in tobacco products in Italy.

Variable		Description	Disaggregation	Years	Source
Smokers	Sm	Persons >13 years old who declare to smoke per 100 residents with the same characteristics	Region	2009–2012	I.Stat, ISTAT
Inhabitants	Pop	Residents >13 years old at 31 December	Region	2009–2012	Geo Demo, ISTAT
Non-domestic packs	ND	Discarded packs of foreign origin	41 Italian cities	2009–2012	Empty packs surveys by MSIntelligence, provided by PMI
Illicit market	IM	Contraband and counterfeiting	National	2009–2012	KPMG[77]
Prices in illicit market	P	Price per pack	n/a	n/a	Press, open sources and contact with stakeholders

The estimates refer merely to the cigarette market and exclude hand rolling tobacco (HRT) owing to the lack of data.[78]

Given the above mentioned concerns about the use of industry-related sources, the choice of KPMG's Project Star and EPSs data was mainly due to the lack of comparable alternatives.

Despite the already mentioned criticisms to its methodology, Project Star is the only source of annual estimates of the ITTP in Italy through the application of the same model. Its usefulness was recently acknowledged even in the very critical review by Gilmore and colleagues.[79] The adoption of other estimates as a starting point would have yielded different results. However, alternative sources were discarded for several reasons: some estimates referred to a short time period and were outdated (e.g. Nomisma); the information available on the methodology used to obtain some estimates did not allow assessment of their reliability (e.g. EMI); consumer surveys are not available at subnational level and are unreliable on sensitive issues, such as the purchase of illicit products. The selection of Project Star's national figures as a starting point does not disregard the problems of the method proposed by KPMG. There is the need of alternative, independent and fully transparent estimates of the ITTP. Yet, until significant investments are made in this direction, Project Star is likely to remain the only available source. As the main goal of this study was to create a methodology providing annual estimates of the ITTP at the subnational level, future better estimates at the national level may replace Project Star's figures.

Industry-sponsored EPSs have a number of advantages and disadvantages. Among the advantages, EPSs have large samples and are repeated periodically. The Italian surveys gather and analyse a sample of 10,000 cigarettes packs from all the 41 cities with more than 100,000 inhabitants (covering 16 out of 20 regions) two times a year (every second and fourth quarter, thus avoiding the summertime, which may be biased by tourist in- and outflows). The collection plans are designed to cover different parts of the cities. Each city is divided into five sectors (North, South, East West, and Centre), and each sector is broken down into circular areas of 500 m radius. To ensure the statistical robustness of the sample, a sample of 30 packs is collected in each area.[80] For example, Figure 4 shows the collection areas for the city of Milan. The surveys cover most of the residential areas of the city, avoiding concentration in the city centre (where tourist presence may boost the prevalence of non-domestic packs) and areas of lower socio-economic conditions (where illicit consumption may be higher). Furthermore, EPSs are based on the actual packs and do not rely on consumers' perceptions and willingness to report. Currently, pack analysis enables identification of manufacturer, brand, country variant and whether the pack is counterfeit or an illicit white brand. This information enables some distinction among different types of illicit trade (contraband, counterfeit and illicit whites). Finally, the most important advantage is that EPSs are the only source providing insight into city and regional differences in the prevalence of non-domestic packs, which enable the elaboration of estimates at the subnational level.

The literature has pointed out several disadvantages of industry-sponsored EPSs.[81] First, the surveys measure the prevalence of non-domestic products, which inevitably include legitimately purchased cigarettes (e.g. by foreign tourists or nationals traveling abroad). Also, EPSs exclude illicit domestic products (e.g. contraband cigarettes of Italian variants), which may underestimate the illicit market. However, there seems to be no practicable method for a more precise identification of illicit products, as 'it is impossible to discriminate between smuggled goods, legal cross-border purchases and illegal cross-border purchases. The only possible distinction that can be made thanks to [pack surveys] is between counterfeit packs and others'.[82] Indeed, other independent surveys analysed

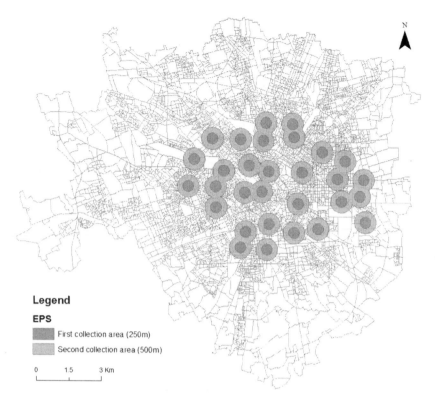

Figure 4. Collection points for the empty packs surveys in the city of Milan (2011–2012). *Source*: Author's elaboration.

whether packs bore tax stamps required for sale in the place of collection. This approach, however, focuses on tax avoidance (whether local taxes were paid or not), which may also be the result of legal purchases.[83] For this reason, the share non-domestic products should not be considered as a direct estimate of the illicit market, particularly in countries with high cigarette prices and regions bordering countries with lower prices.[84] Yet, notwithstanding these issues, the share of non-domestic products may be considered a good of approximation of the prevalence of illicit tobacco within the same country.

Second, the literature remarked that the information on the methodology is incomplete. The samples should be representative of the national population, while in some cases they may over-represent areas of particular interest for the manufacturers. Surveys are conducted only in large and medium cities, and there is insufficient information on the criteria for the selection of the streets. Some have contended that these methodological steps may be designed to inflate the prevalence of non-domestic packs, because of a higher presence of tourists, foreign students and people of lower socio-economic conditions.[85] While these concerns are important, the above exposed details on the methodology of the Italian EPSs suggest that the results should be reliable and also more robust than some independent surveys, where only a few packs where collected in some of the sampled city areas.[86] Inspection of the collection areas of industry-sponsored EPSs in the city of Milan showed a preference towards residential, non-peripheral and non-tourist areas (Figure 4). Furthermore, most of the limitations of current surveys are also due to their costs in terms of money and time. According to PMI, each EPSs wave costs more than € 70,000. Coverage of rural areas and more detailed analyses on packs may significantly increase the costs of the surveys.

Third, EPSs exclude other tobacco products such as HRT, and do not include homes and workplaces. These limitations are likely due to feasibility and cost constraints.

Finally, the use of industry-sponsored sources may inadvertently support the policy agenda of tobacco manufacturers, accused of exploiting the issue of illicit trade for their commercial purposes.[87] However, the Italian EPSs are collected using a specifically designed methodology, which does not appear aimed at inflating the prevalence of non-domestic products, for example by focusing on specific hotspot cities, tourist areas or neighbourhoods with low socio-economic conditions. Although the industry should be more transparent on the methodology of the EPSs and should improve the quality of the data, the surveys are currently the only available annual source on the consumption of non-domestic cigarettes.

The above considerations suggest that EPSs data should be treated with caution and that further efforts are needed to refine their methodologies. Yet, the available information on the Italian EPSs point out that these data can be used as a proxy of the regional prevalence of the illicit market. As already argued, this study has adopted EPSs because of the lack of better alternatives. If new, independent and more reliable proxies become available, they may be integrated in the methodology with limited effort.

Estimates

This study estimated the volumes and revenues of the illicit cigarette market for the period 2009–2012 owing to the availability of data for these years.

For every year, the national illicit market (IM_{nat}) as estimated by KPMG was divided among the Italian regions in proportion to the number of smokers, in turn obtained by multiplying the percentage of smokers (Sm_{reg}) by the population >13 years old in each region (Pop_{reg}).

$$IM_{reg} = \frac{IM_{nat} \cdot Sm_{reg} \cdot Pop_{reg}}{Sm_{nat} \cdot Pop_{nat}}$$

The resulting IM_{reg} estimated the regional size of the ITTP, assuming that all regions have the same prevalence of illicit tobacco consumption. This assumption, however, appears implausible: the analysis of the Italian EPSs presented in Figure 2 highlighted that non-domestic packs are distributed unequally across the country, which may suggest that illicit consumption may be concentrated unevenly.

The IM_{reg} was adjusted to account for these differences in the regional illicit consumption. The proxy for the regional levels of illicit trade was the regional share of 'non-domestic' packs collected by EPSs (ND_{reg}). The regional share was the average of the non-domestic share in the two surveys per year (one in the second quarter and one in the last quarter). The non-domestic share was the ratio between the sum of non-domestic packs and the sum of the total packs collected in all the cities in a region.[88]

The regional illicit markets were weighted for the ratio between the ND in the region and the average of the regional ND share. To return the sum of the regional illicit markets to the national total, the values were divided by their sum and multiplied by IM_{nat}, obtaining the regional illicit markets adjusted ($IMadj_{reg}$).[89]

$$\text{IMadj}_{\text{reg}} = \text{IM}_{\text{reg}} \times \frac{\text{ND}_{\text{reg}}}{\text{avg.ND}_{\text{reg}}} \times \frac{\text{IM}_{\text{nat}}}{\sum \text{IM}_{\text{reg}} \frac{\text{ND}_{\text{reg}}}{\text{ND}_{\text{nat}}}}$$

Regional revenues from the illicit trade in tobacco products (IMrev$_{\text{reg}}$) were obtained by dividing the values of IMadj$_{\text{reg}}$ by 20 (the most sold pack size in Italy) and multiplying the result by the price of an illicit 20-cigarette pack. After reviewing open sources and press releases and after interviewing stakeholders (law enforcement, prosecution and industry experts), the study adopted a minimum illicit price of €2.75 and a maximum one of €3.5 per 20-cigarette pack. The selection of these prices is reasonable, since they are below the prices of the most popular brands in Italy. During the same period, the price of a 20-cigarette pack of Marlboro (the most sold brand in Italy) rose from €4.3 (2008) to €5 (end 2012).[90] This is also in line with the range of prices of illicit cigarettes identified by Joossens and colleagues.[91]

$$\text{IMrev}_{\text{reg}_{\text{max}}} = \frac{\text{IMadj}_{\text{reg}}}{20} \cdot €3.5$$

$$\text{IMrev}_{\text{reg}_{\text{min}}} = \frac{\text{IMadj}_{\text{reg}}}{20} \cdot €2.75$$

Results and discussion

Table 2 shows the regional estimates of the volumes and revenues of the ITTP for the period 2009–2012. The national revenues from the ITTP increased by nearly 2.5 times during the period observed, rising from €532 mn in 2009 (max estimate) to €1275mn in 2012 (max estimate). The estimated volumes of the illicit market correspond to significant tax losses. The revenue loss for the Italian government in the period was approximately €423 mn in 2009, €650 mn in 2010, €739 mn in 2011 and €1184 mn in 2012, totaling €2995 mn.[92] Considering that the total tax collected in Italy on cigarettes is in the range of €14,000 mn per year, the ITTP may have an impact of up to approximately 8.5% of the total revenues from cigarettes.[93]

Over the years, the largest regional illicit markets changed among the most populated Italian regions (Lazio in 2009, Lombardia in 2010 and 2011, Campania in 2012) (Figure 5, left map). The values were normalised by the smoking population to take the different sizes of the regions into account (Figure 5, right map). At the national level, the illicit trade rose from an equivalent of 12.6 20-cigarette packs per smoker in 2009 to 32.2 in 2012.[94] Among the regions, in the 4 years considered, only Friuli-Venezia Giulia always recorded normalised volumes higher than the national ones. Three other regions had higher values in three out of 4 years (Campania, Marche and Veneto). In part, the estimates for Friuli-Venezia Giulia and Marche may be due to the data, since the EPSs for these regions surveyed only the regional capitals of Trieste and Ancona, which are located on the coast and close to countries with lower cigarette prices.

These figures suggest that the regional prevalence of the ITTP is mostly related to the availability of illicit tobacco because of the proximity to countries with lower prices or to the presence of large transport infrastructures. Friuli-Venezia Giulia and Veneto are close to Slovenia, where cigarettes are cheaper.[95] While consumers may legitimately purchase cigarettes in the neighbouring country, the easy access provides also an opportunity for the development of small scale contraband or bootlegging. The removal of border controls between Italy and Slovenia (owing to the European Union policies) may have further

Table 2. Estimates of the volume (mn sticks) and minimum/maximum revenues (mn€) of the illicit tobacco market by Italian region (2009–2012).

	2009			2010			2011			2012		
	Volume	Revenue		Volume	Revenue		Volume	Revenue		Volume	Revenue	
	IMadj	IMrev$_{min}$	IMrev$_{max}$	IMadj	IMrev$_{min}$	IMrev$_{max}$	IMadj	IMrev$_{min}$	IMrev$_{max}$	IMadj	IMrev$_{min}$	IMrev$_{max}$
Abruzzo	141.5	19.5	24.8	58.7	8.1	10.3	52.0	7.2	9.1	166.2	22.9	29.1
Basilicata	22.6	3.1	4.0	43.8	6.0	7.7	42.4	5.8	7.4	31.7	4.4	5.5
Calabria	46.9	6.5	8.2	109.3	15.0	19.1	80.5	11.1	14.1	84.2	11.6	14.7
Campania	310.4	42.7	54.3	470.6	64.7	82.4	637.2	87.6	111.5	2085.7	286.8	365.0
Emilia-Romagna	261.7	36.0	45.8	259.1	35.6	45.4	247.3	34.0	43.3	325.3	44.7	56.9
Friuli-Venezia Giulia	125.7	17.3	22.0	95.7	13.2	16.7	127.8	17.6	22.4	370.8	51.0	64.9
Lazio	397.8	54.7	69.6	286.6	39.4	50.2	307.5	42.3	53.8	416.3	57.2	72.9
Liguria	101.4	13.9	17.7	122.4	16.8	21.4	107.6	14.8	18.8	85.3	11.7	14.9
Lombardia	365.0	50.2	63.9	1107.0	152.2	193.7	1143.0	157.2	200.0	1124.3	154.6	196.8
Marche	90.9	12.5	15.9	123.5	17.0	21.6	194.2	26.7	34.0	116.7	16.0	20.4
Molise	18.8	2.6	3.3	19.7	2.7	3.5	18.5	2.5	3.2	25.6	3.5	4.5
Piemonte	204.2	28.1	35.7	348.8	48.0	61.0	437.7	60.2	76.6	412.0	56.7	72.1
Puglia	123.5	17.0	21.6	429.6	59.1	75.2	208.6	28.7	36.5	225.3	31.0	39.4
Sardegna	95.3	13.1	16.7	115.2	15.8	20.2	118.3	16.3	20.7	174.1	23.9	30.5
Sicilia	139.3	19.2	24.4	261.6	36.0	45.8	197.9	27.2	34.6	466.7	64.2	81.7
Toscana	218.1	30.0	38.2	282.5	38.8	49.4	195.8	26.9	34.3	327.6	45.0	57.3
Trentino-Alto Adige	30.1	4.1	5.3	77.0	10.6	13.5	131.1	18.0	22.9	94.2	13.0	16.5
Umbria	75.5	10.4	13.2	70.0	9.6	12.2	90.7	12.5	15.9	63.9	8.8	11.2
Valle d'Aosta	4.8	0.7	0.8	8.9	1.2	1.6	8.9	1.2	1.6	8.7	1.2	1.5
Veneto	266.5	36.6	46.6	259.8	35.7	45.5	463.0	63.7	81.0	685.4	94.2	119.9
Italy	3040	418.0	532.0	4550	625.6	796.3	4810	661.4	841.7	7290	1002.4	1275.8

Source: Author's calculations.

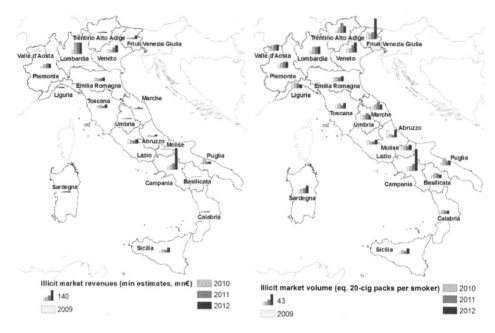

Figure 5. Illicit cigarette market per region in value (minimum estimates, mn€) and equivalent 20-cigarette packs per smoker (2009–2012).

Source: Author's calculations.

reduced the risks for individuals willing to engage in the ITTP. For example, it may be possible to drive a car across the border, fill it with cigarette cartons, and re-enter Italy with a very low risk of being controlled. Furthermore, all the above-mentioned four regions have important ports (Trieste, Venice, Ancona and Naples), which may function as important gateways for the entry of illicit tobacco into Italy. This may also make illicit products more available in the port cities.

The findings also suggest that the mafias may be an important driver of the ITTP, although not the only one. In Campania, the significant growth of the illicit trade in 2012 suggests a correlation with the strong presence of the Camorra, a mafia with a consolidated expertise in cigarette smuggling. The sudden increase in a single year, however, points out that mafia control alone is not a sufficient condition. More probably, the Camorra has been able to exploit its traditional expertise in cigarette smuggling, but also some criminal opportunities which have occurred in 2012. For example, new methods of smuggling may have been adopted in the port of Naples, as signalled by an increase of the seizures, although inferior to the increase of the estimated prevalence of illicit cigarettes. Other regions with a traditionally strong presence of the mafias (Sicily, Calabria and Puglia) did not show a similar growth pattern. Also the seizures in the main ports of these regions had irregular trends, despite the strong mafia control over the cities of Palermo and Reggio Calabria. These differences across traditional mafia regions may further confirm that the mafias are not a sufficient condition for the development of large illicit markets.[96]

The estimates of the ITTP were high also in regions with a very low presence of the mafias. Contrary to Campania, Friuli-Venezia Giulia, Veneto and Marche had a very low presence of mafias, but high estimates of the ITTP.[97] This confirms that the presence of the mafias is not only insufficient, but unnecessary for the development of the ITTP at the regional level. As discussed earlier, the causes of the consumption of illicit cigarettes in these regions may be due to the proximity to Slovenia.

Another significant characteristic is the growth pattern of the ITTP across the years. From 2009 to 2011, the regional values were concentrated around the average (average packs per smoker 13.99, 18.54 and 20.89, with st. dev of 5.69, 4.39 and 8.41, respectively). This reveals a general increase in most regions. In 2012, the growth was significant, mainly due to three earlier mentioned regions: Friuli-Venezia Giulia and Campania exceeded 80 packs per smoker, while Veneto went up to 41 (2012 regional average was 29.35, st. dev 19.67). Without these regions, the national increase would have been in the range of approximately 1 pack per smoker.

The estimation of the revenue generated by the ITTP does not provide support to the claim that in 2010 the mafias would have gained up to €0.9 bn from illicit cigarettes.[98] The total estimated revenues at the retail level for the same year range between €625 mn and €796 mn, well below the alleged mafia revenues. Furthermore, not all such revenues should be attributed to the mafias, given the variety of actors which may be involved in the different stages of the illicit market.

Overall, the application of the proposed methodology to Italy call for the adoption of different policy measures for the prevention and control of the ITTP. In the regions close to Slovenia, better controls may be implemented to ensure that cheaper foreign cigarettes are not smuggled into the country. Probably, this may require more efforts in the cooperation between Italian and Slovenian authorities. In Campania, further analyses should identify the opportunities that triggered the boom of the illicit market in 2012. For example, the implementation of new tracking systems within the port of Naples may contribute to effectively reduce the risk of smuggling. Also, further research should assess whether the illicit trade in the region is controlled, at least in part, by the Camorra, given the solid expertise of this mafia in the smuggling of cigarettes.

Conclusions

This study has described a methodology for the estimation of the illicit cigarette market at the subnational level. The methodology is based mainly on data produced with the financial support of the tobacco industry. The review of available alternatives highlighted that independent sources do not allow estimation of the regional prevalence across different years and have problems of reliability (e.g. consumers survey are likely to underestimate illicit consumption, due to respondents' underreporting). Concerns about possible biases by the tobacco industry are legitimate and should not be underestimated. The tobacco industry should be more transparent on the methodologies adopted in the study it supports, which would also contribute to its attempts to present itself as a reliable partner in the fight against illicit tobacco. Since the development of independent measurements with a level of detail comparable to that of industry-supported sources appears far to come, at present the latter ones provide the only possibility to estimate the prevalence of the ITTP at the subnational level across different years and countries.

Notwithstanding the possible limitations of the data, the proposed estimation method requires a relatively limited number of sources. The starting points were Project Star's national estimates of the illicit trade (currently available for 27 EU Member States), which may be replaced by other, independent assessments whenever they will be developed. Data for the regional estimation are the smoking population and non-domestic packs found by EPSs. The former data are normally available, while the EPSs are conducted by the tobacco manufacturers in a number of countries and disseminated through media and reports, but often in aggregated form. Also EPSs data may be replaced with better data, if available. The limited requirements in terms of data may allow application of the method to other countries, which may provide insight into the regional prevalence of the illicit cigarette market across time and space.

Application of the method to Italian regions from 2009 to 2012 yielded insight into the chronological and spatial evolution of the ITTP. Indeed, while most publicly available estimates are at the national level, the regional estimates for Italy reveal that the illicit trade varies significantly across time and regions. The results show that the increase at the national level was driven by a general growth across most regions in the first three years and by an increase concentrated in only three regions in 2012. Also, the analysis points out that a strong presence of the mafias in a region is not a sufficient condition for the growth of the ITTP. This contrasts with the opinion of the media and public agencies, which frequently attributes the illicit tobacco trade to organised crime. It also demonstrates that illicit cigarettes have a complex market, which is influenced by a number of factors.

Notes

1. Article 1 FCTC, Use of terms.
   'For the purposes of this Convention:
   (a) "illicit trade" means any practice or conduct prohibited by law and which relates to production, shipment, receipt, possession, distribution, sale or purchase including any practice or conduct intended to facilitate such activity.
   [...]
   (f) "tobacco products" means products entirely or partly made of the leaf tobacco as raw material, which are manufactured to be used for smoking, sucking, chewing or snuffing'.
2. Allen, *The Illicit Trade in Tobacco Products*; von Lampe, "The Illegal Cigarette Trade," 201; and Joossens and Raw, "From Cigarette Smuggling to Illicit Tobacco Trade."
3. Calderoni, Savona, and Solmi, *Crime Proofing the Policy Options*.
4. Transcrime, *Plain Packaging and Illicit Trade*; and The European House Ambrosetti, *Studio strategico: I nuovi provvedimenti*.
5. Joossens et al., "Issues in the Smuggling of Tobacco Products."
6. Nuts is an acronym for *Nomenclature des unités territoriales statistiques* (Nomenclature of Units for Territorial Statistics). It is the geocode standard for referencing the subdivisions of countries for statistical purposes within the European Union. As of December 2013, there are 270 nuts-2 regions in the EU.
7. The methodology was developed as part of a research project awarded by the Italian Ministry of Interior to Transcrime (*Joint Research Centre on Transnational Crime* of Università Cattolica del Sacro Cuore of Milan and Università di Trento). Transcrime, *Progetto PON Sicurezza 2007–2013*.
8. Joossens et al., *How Eliminating the Global Illicit Cigarette Trade*, 13.
9. Joossens et al., "Illicit Cigarettes and Hand-Rolled Tobacco"; Siggens, Murray, and Walters, *West Midlands Regional Illicit Tobacco Survey*; and NEMS Market Research, *North of England Illicit Tobacco Survey*.
10. Ciecierski, "The Market for Legal and Illegal Cigarettes"; Zatonski, "Democracy and Health"; and Wiltshire et al., "They're Doing People a Service."
11. Joossens and Raw, "Cigarette Smuggling in Europe," 149–50; and Levinson, *An Inquiry into the Nature, Causes and Impacts*, 21.
12. According to experts, for instance, the counterfeiting of cigarettes yields profits equal to 40 times the capital invested: van Heuckelom, "The Counterfeiting Phenomenon and Its Scale"; and Gutauskas, "Lithuania," 72. See also van Duyne, "Organizing Cigarette Smuggling and Policy Making"; von Lampe, "Assessing Organized Crime"; von Lampe, "Explaining the Emergence of the Cigarette"; and Reidy and Walsh, *Economics of Tobacco: Modelling the Market*.

13. Lakhdar, Lermienier, and Vaillant, *Estimation Des Achats Transfrontaliers de Cigarettes 2004–2007*; Merriman, "The Micro-Geography of Tax Avoidance"; and Lakhdar, "Quantitative and Qualitative Estimates of Cross-Border."
14. Joossens et al., "Issues in the Smuggling of Tobacco Products," 328.
15. OCCRP, "Big Trouble at Big Tobacco."
16. Joossens and Raw, "Cigarette Smuggling in Europe"; Joossens et al., "Issues in the Smuggling of Tobacco Products"; Blecher, "A Mountain or a Molehill"; and OCCRP, "Big Trouble at Big Tobacco."
17. Joossens and Raw, "Cigarette Smuggling in Europe"; Beelman et al., "Tobacco Companies Linked to Criminal Organizations"; Beelman et al., "Major Tobacco Multinational Implicated"; Beare, "Organized Corporate Criminality: Corporate Complicity"; and von Lampe, "The Cigarette Black Market."
18. However, in 2011, an investigative report alleged the involvement of Japan Tobacco International in repeated smuggling activities in Middle East. See OCCRP, "Big Trouble at Big Tobacco."
19. For instance, since 2004, the four major tobacco companies (Philip Morris International, Japan Tobacco International, British American Tobacco and Imperial Tobacco) have signed agreements with the EU Commission and the Member States aimed at cooperation in the fight against the illicit trade and counterfeiting of tobacco. The agreements stipulate, among other things, the commitment of companies to prevent the illegal tobacco trade with all necessary steps, including the monitoring of exports, which must be proportionate to the demand for tobacco in the destination countries.
20. Joossens and Raw, "Progress in Combating Cigarette Smuggling."
21. van Duyne, "Organizing Cigarette Smuggling and Policy Making"; von Lampe, "The Cigarette Black Market"; Antonopoulos, "Cigarette Smugglers"; Hornsby and Hobbs, "A Zone of Ambiguity"; and von Lampe, "The Illegal Cigarette Trade."
22. von Lampe, "The Trafficking in Untaxed Cigarettes in Germany."
23. Coker, "Smoking May Not Only Be Hazardous to Your Health"; and Seely, *Cross Border Shopping and Smuggling*.
24. van Duyne, von Lampe, and Passas, *Upperworld and Underworld in Cross-Border Crime*.
25. von Lampe, "Explaining the Emergence of the Cigarette."
26. Kegö, Leijonmarck, and Molcean, *Organized Crime and the Financial Crisis*.
27. Shelley and Melzer, "The Nexus of Organized Crime and Terrorism"; Shelley and Picarelli, "Methods Not Motives"; Coker, "Smoking May Not Only Be Hazardous to Your Health"; and Allen, *The Illicit Trade in Tobacco Products*.
28. Shen, Antonopoulos, and von Lampe, "The Dragon Breathes Smoke"; and von Lampe, "The Illegal Cigarette Trade."
29. Chaloupka and Tauras, *The Demand for Cigarettes in Ireland*, 19; Niwserwis, *Nielegalny Rynek Wyrobów Akcyzowych w Polsce*, 6; Gilmore et al., "Towards a Greater Understanding"; Caneppele, Savona, and Aziani, *Crime Proofing of the New Tobacco Products Directive*; and Fooks, Peeters, and Evans-Reeves, "Illicit Trade, Tobacco Industry-Funded Studies."
30. Merriman, Yurekli, and Chaloupka, "How Big Is the Worldwide Cigarette-Smuggling Problem?," 371–82; and Gallus et al., *PPACTE, WP2: European Survey on Smoking. Final Report*, 20–21.
31. Merriman, Yurekli, and Chaloupka, "How Big Is the Worldwide Cigarette-Smuggling Problem?"; and Shafey et al., *The Tobacco Atlas*.
32. Euromonitor International, "Illicit Trade in Tobacco Products 2012."
33. Ibid., 23–5.
34. Blecher, "A Mountain or a Molehill"; Lencucha and Callard, "Lost Revenue Estimates from the Illicit Trade of Cigarettes," 319; and Blecher et al., "Euromonitor Data on the Illicit Trade in Cigarettes."
35. Joossens et al., *How Eliminating the Global Illicit Cigarette Trade*, 9–11.
36. Gallus et al., *PPACTE, WP2: European Survey on Smoking. Final Report*, 30.
37. Ibid., 26.
38. Ibid., 5.
39. Euromonitor International, "Data on the Penetration of the Illicit Tobacco."
40. KPMG, *Project Star 2012 Results*.

41. The estimation methodology starts from legal domestic sales. The share of legal sales exported is estimated on the basis of EPSs in all Member States. The difference between legal sales and exports provides an estimate of the legal domestic consumption. The consumption of non-domestic cigarettes, also estimated on the basis of EPSs, is added to the legal domestic consumption. The non-domestic consumption is divided between non-domestic legal consumption (estimated on the basis of surveys of consumers' purchases abroad) and contraband & counterfeiting (the difference between the total non-domestic consumption and domestic non-legal consumption). Ibid., 203 and ff.
42. Joossens et al., "Illicit Cigarettes and Hand-Rolled Tobacco"; Gilmore et al., "Towards a Greater Understanding"; and Stoklosa and Ross, "Contrasting Academic and Tobacco Industry."
43. Joossens et al., "Illicit Cigarettes and Hand-Rolled Tobacco," 5.
44. Gilmore et al., "Towards a Greater Understanding," 7–8.
45. Ibid.
46. Gallus et al., *PPACTE, WP2*: European Survey on Smoking. Final Report; and Joossens et al., "Illicit Cigarettes and Hand-Rolled Tobacco."
47. Stoklosa and Ross, "Contrasting Academic and Tobacco Industry"; Chernick and Merriman, "Using Littered Pack Data"; Merriman, "The Micro-Geography of Tax Avoidance"; and Ben Lakhdar, "Quantitative and Qualitative Estimates of Cross-Border."
48. Almares, *Poland Market Survey: Empty Discarded Pack Collection, August–September 2011*; Almares, *Poland Market Survey: Empty Discarded Pack Collection, October–November 2011*; and Almares, *Poland Market Survey: Empty Discarded Pack Collection March – April 2012*.
49. Stoklosa and Ross, "Contrasting Academic and Tobacco Industry," 2. The authors grossly misinterpreted the data on the industry-EPSs of 2011. They argued that 'despite the original sampling target of 34,000 packs, the study collected 694,547 discarded cigarette packs [...]. The reason this sample size changed so dramatically remains unclear' (Ibid.). In fact, the 2011 report by Almares points out that 694,547 are the number of sticks and not the number of packs (Almares, *Poland Market Survey: Empty Discarded Pack Collection, August–September 2011*, 7).
50. Gallus et al., "Price and Consumption of Tobacco in Italy over the Last Three Decades," 334–5; Calderoni et al., *Italy*, 68.
51. CPA, *Relazione sul traffico mafioso*; Arlacchi, *Gli uomini del disonore*; Arlacchi, *Addio Cosa Nostra*; Massari, *La Sacra Corona Unita*; CPA, *Relazione sullo stato della*; CPA, *Relazione sul fenomeno criminale*, 70–74; and Paoli, "Mafia and Organised Crime in Italy."
52. CPA, *Relazione sullo stato della*.
53. CPA, *Relazione sul fenomeno criminale*, 88.
54. DIA, *Esito Attività Di Indagine Svolta*, 14; Ivanovic, "Speedboats, Cigarettes, Mafia and Montenegrin Democracy"; Sisti, "The Montenegro Connection: Love, Tobacco, and the Mafia."
55. Ivanovic, "Speedboats, Cigarettes, Mafia and Montenegrin Democracy."
56. Ibid.
57. Sisti, "The Montenegro Connection: Love, Tobacco, and the Mafia."
58. Ibid.
59. CPA, *Relazione sul fenomeno criminale*, 80–88; Calderoni et al., *Italy*, 69.
60. CPA, *Relazione sul fenomeno criminale*, 89–91.
61. Ibid., 88–96.
62. Ibid., 41.
63. Joossens and Raw, "Progress in Combating Cigarette Smuggling"; DNA, *Relazione annuale 2006*, 284.
64. DNA, *Relazione annuale sulle attività*, 377–83; Russo, Interview with Giovanni Russo, Direzione Nazionale Antimafia; Di Lucia, Interview with Massimiliano Di Lucia, Guardia di Finanza.
65. SOS Impresa, *Le mani della criminalità sulle imprese*.
66. Gallus et al., "Cigarette Smuggling in Italy, 2005–8"; Gallus et al., *PPACTE, WP2: European Survey on Smoking*.
67. Gallus et al., *PPACTE, WP2: European Survey on Smoking*. 67.
68. Nomisma, *La contraffazione delle sigarette in* Italia *primo rapporto nomisma*.
69. Ibid., 80.

70. Correspondence with the authors of the Nomisma estimates revealed that these were calculated using an 'econometric model' based on seizures and on the possibility to check incoming loads and those circulating in the area (e-mail from Silvia Zucconi, 31 May 2012, h. 13:34).
71. KPMG, *Project Star 2012 Results*, 118.
72. Euromonitor International, "Data on the Penetration of the Illicit Tobacco."
73. See note 42 above.
74. Data available from the data warehouse of the Italian National Institute of Statistics, entry Services and Tourism, ISTAT, "I.Stat: Movimento dei clienti negli esercizi ricettivi."
75. Formisano and Vico, *Commissione parlamentare d'inchiesta sui fenomeni*.
76. KPMG, *Project Star 2012 Results*; EPSs data were provided in the context of the project the Factbook on the Illicit Trade in Tobacco products, conducted by Transcrime with the financial contribution of PMI. See Calderoni et al., *Italy*.
77. KPMG, *Project Star 2012 Results*.
78. Remarkably, in some countries, HRT shows high levels of illicit products and this suggest that future estimates should include it (see e.g. Calderoni et al., *United Kingdom*).
79. Gilmore et al., "Towards a Greater Understanding."
80. Within every area, two collection routes are defined: one within a 250 m radius and one within a 500 m radius from the centre. Collectors are unaware of the total number of packs to be collected in the area and therefore they walk through the whole first route. Subsequently, a supervisor checks the number of packs collected; if the number is less than 30, a second collection through the second route is conducted. If the number is still insufficient, the collection starts again from the first route. If more than 30 packs are collected, the supervisor randomly removes the packs. The packs are collected either from the streets or from the top of trash bins, without rummaging.
81. See note 42 above.
82. Lakhdar, "Quantitative and Qualitative Estimates of Cross-Border," 16.
83. Merriman, "The Micro-Geography of Tax Avoidance"; Chernick and Merriman, "Using Littered Pack Data"; Stoklosa and Ross, "Contrasting Academic and Tobacco Industry."
84. Gilmore et al., "Towards a Greater Understanding."
85. Ibid., 3.
86. Chernick and Merriman, "Using Littered Pack Data," 641; Ibid., 81.
87. Fooks, Peeters, and Evans-Reeves, "Illicit Trade, Tobacco Industry-funded Studies"; Stoklosa and Ross, "Contrasting Academic and Tobacco Industry."
88. The surveys did not include any city from the three smallest regions (Basilicata, Molise and Valle d'Aosta) and Sardinia. The missing values were imputed by calculating the average of the regional shares of neighbouring regions (for Sardinia, an island, the national value was used). In 2012, the EPS for the city of Naples were outliers, because of exceptionally high shares of non-domestic packs (46% and 50% for Q2 and Q4, respectively). To prevent bias in the estimates, the regional share for Naples's region, Campania, was reduced to the level of the second highest region (North-Eastern Friuli-Venezia-Giulia), passing from 39.9% to 23.7%. Moreover, Campania was not included in the neighbouring regions for the purpose of imputing missing values in 2012.
89. This passage was due to the fact that the adjustment for the illicit consumption was done using percentage variables. These could not take into account the differences among the regions in terms of absolute values. This would have resulted in the sum of the regional illicit markets being different from the estimate by KPMG, which would have contrasted with the assumption of Project Star's results as the starting point of the estimation.
90. KPMG, *Project Star 2010 Results*; KPMG, *Project Star 2012 Results*; and WHO, "WHO Report on the Global Tobacco Epidemic, 2011, Country Profile Italy."
91. Joossens et al., *How Eliminating the Global Illicit Cigarette Trade*, 15.
92. The illicit market volumes were converted into equivalent legal market values. The calculation considered the average price of the most popular price category for 2009–2010 and the weighted average price of all consumed cigarettes for 2011–2012. The total tax as a share of the mentioned price was applied to the legal market values (taxes remained relatively constant at approximately 75% of the final retail prices in the period). Data on prices and taxes are at July of each year (See European Commission, "Manufactured Tobacco: Excise Duty Rates – European Commission"). The figures may actually underestimate the tax evasion due to the ITTP, since the calculations for 2009 and 2010 are based on the most popular price

category, which is generally cheap products, while those for 2011 and 2012 are based on the actual composition of legal sales in Italy. Both approaches are based on pack prices, which may be lower than the products trafficked most often (frequently medium and premium brands). If based on Marlboro prices, estimated total tax loss from 2009 to 2012 would have reached €3.4bn (+16% compared to the figures in the text).
93. The European House Ambrosetti, *Studio strategico: I nuovi provvedimenti*, 34. For a more accurate measurement of the tax losses caused by the ITTP, it should be considered that in theory the removal of illicit cigarettes would result in a general increase of the market price and, in turn, to a reduction of consumption.
94. Regional IMadj volumes were divided by 20 and by Sm.
95. In July 2012, the cheapest brand price was €2.8 in Slovenia and 4.3€ in Italy. See Calderoni et al., *Italy*, 75, 85.
96. Paoli, "The Paradoxes of Organized Crime."
97. Transcrime, *Progetto PON Sicurezza 2007–2013*.
98. SOS Impresa, *Le mani della criminalità sulle imprese*.

Bibliography

Allen, Elizabeth. *The Illicit Trade in Tobacco Products and How to Tackle It*. Washington, DC: International Tax and Investment Center, 2011.
Almares. *Poland Market Survey: Empty Discarded Pack Collection, August–September 2011*. Warsaw: Almares Institute for Consulting and Market Research, 2011a. http://www.bat.com.pl/group/sites/bat_84bcnd.nsf/vwPagesWebLive/DO84BJH5/$FILE/medMD8S8KF7.pdf
Almares. *Poland Market Survey: Empty Discarded Pack Collection, October–November 2011*. Warsaw: Almares Institute for Consulting and Market Research, 2011b.
Almares. *Poland Market Survey: Empty Discarded Pack Collection March–April 2012*. Warsaw: Almares Institute for Consulting and Market Research, 2012.
Antonopoulos, Georgios A. "Cigarette Smugglers: A Note on Four 'Unusual Suspects'." *Global Crime* 8, no. 4 (2007): 393.
Arlacchi, Pino. *Addio Cosa Nostra: La vita di Tommaso Buscetta*. Milano: Rizzoli, 1994.
Arlacchi, Pino. *Gli uomini del disonore: La mafia siciliana nella vita del grande pentito Antonino Calderone*. Milano: Mondadori, 1992.
Beare, Margaret E. "Organized Corporate Criminality: Corporate Complicity in Tobacco Smuggling." In *Critical Reflections on Transnational Organized Crime, Money Laundering and Corruption*, edited by Margaret E. Beare, 183–206. Toronto: University of Toronto Press, 2003.
Beelman, Maud S., Bill Birnbauer, Duncan Campbell, William Marsden, Erik Schelzig, and Leo Sisti. "Tobacco Companies Linked to Criminal Organizations in Lucrative Cigarette Smuggling." *The Center for Public Integrity*. Accessed March 3, 2001. http://projects.publicintegrity.org/Content.aspx?context=article&id=351
Beelman, Maud S., Duncan Campbell, Maria Teresa Ronderos, and Erik Schelzig. "Major Tobacco Multinational Implicated in Cigarette Smuggling, Tax Evasion, Documents Show." *The Center for Public Integrity*. Accessed January 31, 2000. http://projects.publicintegrity.org/report.aspx?aid=335
Blecher, Evan. "A Mountain or a Molehill: Is the Illicit Trade in Cigarettes Undermining Tobacco Control Policy in South Africa?." *Trends in Organized Crime* 13, no. 4 (April 30, 2010): 299–315.
Blecher, Evan, Alex Liber, Hana Ross, and Johanna Birckmayer. "Euromonitor Data on the Illicit Trade in Cigarettes." *Tobacco Control* (June 21, 2013). doi:10.1136/tobaccocontrol-2013-051034
CPA. *Relazione sul traffico mafioso di tabacchi e stupefacenti nonché sui rapporti tra mafia e gangsterismo italo-americano (Relatore Zuccalà)*. Roma: Commissione Parlamentare di inchiesta sul fenomeno della mafia in Sicilia, February 4, 1976.
CPA. *Relazione sullo stato della lotta alla criminalità organizzata nella provincia di Brindisi (Rel. Del Turco)*. Roma: Commissione Parlamentare di inchiesta sul fenomeno mafia e delle altre associazioni criminali similari, Luglio 1999.

CPA. *Relazione sul fenomeno criminale del contrabbando di tabacchi lavorati esteri in Italia e in Europa – Relatore On. Alfredo Mantovano*. Roma: Commissione parlamentare di inchiesta sul fenomeno della Mafia e delle altre associazioni criminali similari, March 6, 2001.

Calderoni, Francesco, Monica Angelini, Marco De Simoni, Serena Favarin, and Martina Rotondi. *Italy. The Factbook on the Illicit Trade in Tobacco Products 2*. Trento: Transcrime – Università degli Studi di Trento, 2013. http://transcrime.cs.unitn.it/tc/1132.php

Calderoni, Francesco, Monica Angelini, Marco De Simoni, Serena Favarin, and Martina Rotondi. *Italy. The Factbook on the Illicit Trade in Tobacco Products 2*. The Factbook. Trento: Transcrime – Università degli Studi di Trento, 2013.

Calderoni, Francesco, Serena Favarin, Ombretta Ingrascì, and Anne Smit. *United Kingdom. The Factbook on the Illicit Trade in Tobacco Products 1*. Trento: Transcrime – Università degli Studi di Trento, 2013. http://transcrime.cs.unitn.it/tc/1104.php

Calderoni, Francesco, Ernesto U. Savona, and Serena Solmi. *Crime Proofing the Policy Options for the Revision of the Tobacco Products Directive: Proofing the Policy Options Under Consideration for the Revision of EU Directive 2001/37/EC Against the Risks of Unintended Criminal Opportunities*. Trento: Transcrime – Joint Research Centre on Transnational Crime, 2012.

Caneppele, Stefano, Ernesto U. Savona, and Alberto Aziani. *Crime Proofing of the New Tobacco Products Directive*. Trento: Transcrime – Joint Research Centre on Transnational Crime, September 2013.

Chaloupka, Frank J., and John A. Tauras. *The Demand for Cigarettes in Ireland*. Dublin: HSE National Tobacoo Control Office, August 2011.

Chernick, Howard, and David Merriman. "Using Littered Pack Data to Estimate Cigarette Tax Avoidance in NYC." *National Tax Journal* 66, no. 3 (September 2013): 635–668.

Ciecierski, Christina. "The Market for Legal and Illegal Cigarettes in Poland: A Closer Look at Demand and Supply-Side Characteristics." Northeastern Illinois University, University of Illinois at Chicago, 2007. http://r4d.dfid.gov.uk/PDF/Outputs/RITC/Grant_223_Smuggling_in_PL_Manuscrip.pdf

Coker, Dale. "Smoking May Not Only Be Hazardous to Your Health, but Also to World Political Stability: The European Union's Fight Against Cigarette Smuggling Rings That Benefit Terrorism." *European Journal of Crime, Criminal Law and Criminal Justice* 11 (2003): 350.

DIA. *Esito Attività Di Indagine Svolta Sul Conto Di Djukanovic Milo+ 4. N. 125/BA/2°SN. 125/BA/2°Sett. Inv. Giud./H5. 148-1/1379 Di Prot.ett. Inv. Giud./H5. 148-1/1379 Di Prot.* Bari: Direzione Investigativa Antimafia – Centro operativo di Bari, February 2, 2005.

DNA. *Relazione annuale sulle attività svolte dal Procuratore nazionale antimafia e dalla Direzione nazionale antimafia nonché sulle dinamiche e strategie della criminalità organizzata di tipo mafioso nel periodo 1° luglio 2005–30 giugno 2006*. Roma: Direzione Nazionale Antimafia, 2006.

DNA. *Relazione annuale sulle attività svolte dal Procuratore nazionale antimafia e dalla Direzione nazionale antimafia nonché sulle dinamiche e strategie della criminalità organizata di tipo mafioso nel periodo 1° luglio 2011–30 giugno 2012*. Roma: Direzione Nazionale Antimafia, Dicembre 2012.

Di Lucia, Massimiliano. Interview with Massimiliano Di Lucia, Guardia di Finanza. Phone call, June 24, 2013.

Euromonitor International. "Data on the Penetration of the Illicit Tobacco." *Euromonitor International*, 2013.

Euromonitor International. "Illicit Trade in Tobacco Products 2012: Will the New Protocol Prove Effective?" Passport. Euromonitor International, 2013.

European Commission. "Manufactured Tobacco: Excise Duty Rates – European Commission." *Taxation and Customs Union*. Accessed July 4, 2013. http://ec.europa.eu/taxation_customs/taxation/excise_duties/tobacco_products/rates/index_en.htm

The European House Ambrosetti. *Studio strategico: I nuovi provvedimenti per il settore del tabacco: i fattori di rischio economici e sociali*. Roma: The European House Ambrosetti, 2011.

Fooks, Gary Jonas, Silvy Peeters, and Karen Evans-Reeves. "Illicit Trade, Tobacco Industry-Funded Studies and Policy Influence in the EU and UK." *Tobacco Control* 23, no. 1 (January 1, 2014): 81–83. doi:10.1136/tobaccocontrol-2012-050788

Formisano, Anna Teresa, and Ludovico Vico. *Commissione parlamentare d'inchiesta sui fenomeni della contraffazione e della pirateria in campo commerciale-Relazione sulla contraffazione nel settore del tabacco*. Camera dei deputati, settembre 2012.

Gallus, Silvano, Esteve Fernandez, Joanne Townsend, Anna Schiaffino, and Carlo La Vecchia. "Price and Consumption of Tobacco in Italy over the Last Three Decades." *European Journal of Cancer Prevention* 12, no. 4 (2003): 333–337.

Gallus, Silvano, Alessandra Lugo, Carlo La Vecchia, Paolo Boffetta, Frank J. Chaloupka, Paolo Colombo, Laura Currie, et al. *PPACTE, WP2: European Survey on Smoking. Final Report.* Dublin: PPACTE Consortium, 2012. http://www.ppacte.eu/index.php?option=com_docman&task=doc_download&gid=185&Itemid=29

Gallus, Silvano, Irene Tramacere, Piergiorgio Zuccaro, Paolo Colombo, and Carlo La Vecchia. "Cigarette Smuggling in Italy, 2005–8." *Tobacco Control* 18 (2009): 159–160.

Gilmore, Anna B., Andy Rowell, Silvano Gallus, Alessandra Lugo, Luk Joossens, and Michelle Sims. "Towards a Greater Understanding of the Illicit Tobacco Trade in Europe: a Review of the PMI Funded 'Project Star' Report." *Tobacco Control* (December 11, 2013). doi:10.1136/tobaccocontrol-2013-051240

Gutauskas, Aurelijus. "Lithuania." In *Organized Crime and the Financial Crisis Recent Trends in the Baltic Sea Region*, edited by Walter Kegö, Erik Leijonmarck, and Alexandru Molcean, 59–83. Stockholm: Institute for Security and Development Policy, 2011.

Hornsby, Rob, and Dick Hobbs. "A Zone of Ambiguity: The Political Economy of Cigarette Bootlegging." *British Journal of Criminology* 47, no. 4 (July 1, 2007): 551–571.

ISTAT. "I.Stat: Movimento dei clienti negli esercizi ricettivi – dati annuali nazionali, ripartizionali e provinciali." *ISTAT.IT*, 2013. Accessed January 27, 2014. http://dati.istat.it/

Ivanovic, Zeljko. "Speedboats, Cigarettes, Mafia and Montenegrin Democracy." *Institute for War and Peace Reporting.* Accessed November 10, 2005. http://iwpr.net/report-news/speedboats-cigarettes-mafia-and-montenegrin-democracy

Joossens, Luk, Frank J. Chaloupka, David Merriman, and Ayda Yurekli. "Issues in the Smuggling of Tobacco Products." In *Tobacco Control in Developing Countries*, edited by Frank J. Chaloupka and Prabhat Jha, 393–406. Oxford: Oxford University Press, 2000.

Joossens, Luk, Alessandra Lugo, Carlo La Vecchia, Anna B. Gilmore, Luke Clancy, and Silvano Gallus. "Illicit Cigarettes and Hand-Rolled Tobacco in 18 European Countries: a Cross-sectional Survey." *Tobacco Control* (December 10, 2012). doi:10.1136/tobaccocontrol-2012-050644

Joossens, Luk, David Merriman, Hana Ross, and Martin Raw. *How Eliminating the Global Illicit Cigarette Trade Would Increase Tax Revenue and Save Lives.* Paris: International Union Against Tuberculosis and Lung Disease (The Union), 2009.

Joossens, Luk, and Martin Raw. "Cigarette Smuggling in Europe: Who Really Benefits?." *Tobacco Control* 7, no. 1 (March 1, 1998): 66–71.

Joossens, Luk, and Martin Raw. "From Cigarette Smuggling to Illicit Tobacco Trade." *Tobacco Control* 21, no. 2 (March 1, 2012): 230–234. doi:10.1136/tobaccocontrol-2011-050205

Joossens, Luk, and Martin Raw. "Progress in Combating Cigarette Smuggling: Controlling the Supply Chain." *Tobacco Control* 17, no. 6 (November 2008): 399–404.

Kegö, Walter, Erik Leijonmarck, and Alexandru Molcean, eds. *Organized Crime and the Financial Crisis Recent Trends in the Baltic Sea Region.* Stockholm-Nacka: Institute for Security & Development Policy, 2011. http://www.isdp.eu/images/stories/isdp-main-pdf/2011_kego-leijonmarck-molcean_organized-crime-and-the-financial-crisis.pdf

KPMG. *Project Star 2010 Results.* KPMG. Accessed August 22, 2011. http://www.pmi.com/eng/tobacco_regulation/illicit_trade/documents/Project_Star_2010_Results.pdf

KPMG. *Project Star 2012 Results.* Project Star. KPMG, 2013. Accessed January 27, 2014. http://www.pmi.com/eng/media_center/media_kit/Documents/Project_Star_2012_Final_Report.pdf

Lakhdar, Christian Ben. "Quantitative and Qualitative Estimates of Cross-Border Tobacco Shopping and Tobacco Smuggling in France." *Tobacco Control* 17, no. 1 (February 2008): 12–16. doi:10.1136/tc.2007.020891

Lakhdar, Christian Ben, Aurélie Lermienier, and Nicolas Vaillant. *Estimation Des Achats Transfrontaliers de Cigarettes 2004–2007.* Tendances. OFDT, March 2011.

Lencucha, R., and C. Callard. "Lost Revenue Estimates from the Illicit Trade of Cigarettes: A 12-country Analysis." *Tobacco Control* 20, no. 4 (February 17, 2011): 318–320.

Levinson, Bruce. *An Inquiry into the Nature, Causes and Impacts of Contraband Cigarettes.* Washington, DC: Center for Regulatory Effectiveness, January, 2011.

Massari, Monica. *La Sacra Corona Unita: Potere E Segreto.* Saggi Tascabili Laterza 221. Roma: Laterza, 1998.

Merriman, David. "The Micro-Geography of Tax Avoidance: Evidence from Littered Cigarette Packs in Chicago." *American Economic Journal: Economic Policy* 2 (2010): 61–84.

Merriman, David, Ayda Yurekli, and Frank J. Chaloupka. "How Big Is the Worldwide Cigarette-Smuggling Problem?." In *Tobacco Control in Developing Countries*, edited by Frank J. Chaloupka and Prabhat Jha, 365–392. Oxford: Oxford University Press, 2000.

NEMS Market Research. *North of England Illicit Tobacco Survey*. Billingham: NEMS Market Research, 2009.

Niwserwis. *Nielegalny Rynek Wyrobów Akcyzowych w Polsce*. Warsaw, Poland, 2011. Accessed January 27, 2014. http://niwserwis.pl/artykuly/nielegalny-rynek-wyrobow-akcyzowych-w-polsce.html

Nomisma. *La contraffazione delle sigarette in Italia primo rapporto nomisma*. Bologna: Nomisma Società di Studi Economici S.p.A, 2011.

OCCRP. "Big Trouble at Big Tobacco." *Organized Crime and Corruption Reporting Project*. Accessed November 3, 2011. http://www.reportingproject.net/troubles_with_big_tobacco/

Paoli, Letizia. "Mafia and Organised Crime in Italy: The Unacknowledged Successes of Law Enforcement." *West European Politics* 30, no. 4 (2007): 854.

Paoli, Letizia. "The Paradoxes of Organized Crime." *Crime, Law and Social Change* 37 (2002): 51–97.

Reidy, Padraic, and Keith Walsh. *Economics of Tobacco: Modelling the Market for Cigarettes in Ireland*. Dublin: The Office of the Revenue Commissioners, February 2011.

Russo, Giovanni. Interview with Giovanni Russo, Direzione Nazionale Antimafia. Corrispondenza elettronica, June 17, 2013.

Seely, Antony. *Cross Border Shopping and Smuggling*. Great Britain, Parliament, House of Commons, Library, 2002.

Shafey, Omar, Michael Eriksen, Hana Ross, and Judith Mackay. *The Tobacco Atlas*. 3rd ed. Atlanta: American Cancer Society, 2009.

Shelley, Louise I., and Sharon A. Melzer. "The Nexus of Organized Crime and Terrorism: Two Case Studies in Cigarette Smuggling." *The International Journal of Comparative and Applied Criminal Justice* 32, no. 1 (2008): 43–65.

Shelley, Louise I., and John T. Picarelli. "Methods Not Motives: Implications of the Convergence of International Organized Crime and Terrorism." *Police Practice and Research: An International Journal* 3, no. 4 (2002): 305.

Shen, Anqi, Georgios A. Antonopoulos, and Klaus von Lampe. "The Dragon Breathes Smoke." *British Journal of Criminology* 50, no. 2 (March 1, 2010): 239–258.

Siggens, Geoff, Paul Murray, and Sean Walters. *West Midlands Regional Illicit Tobacco Survey*. Billingham: NEMS Market Research, 2010.

Sisti, Leo. "The Montenegro Connection: Love, Tobacco, and the Mafia." *The Center for Public Integrity*. Accessed June 2, 2009. http://www.publicintegrity.org/2009/06/02/2854/montenegro-connection

SOS Impresa. *Le mani della criminalità sulle imprese*. Roma: Confesercenti, 2012.

Stoklosa, Michal, and Hana Ross. "Contrasting Academic and Tobacco Industry Estimates of Illicit Cigarette Trade: Evidence from Warsaw, Poland." *Tobacco Control* (August 13, 2013). doi:10.1136/tobaccocontrol-2013-051099

Transcrime. *Plain Packaging and Illicit Trade in the UK: Study on the Risks of Illicit Trade in Tobacco Products as Unintended Consequences of the Introduction of Plain Packaging in the UK*. Milano: Transcrime – Joint Research Centre on Transnational Crime, 2012.

Transcrime. *Progetto PON Sicurezza 2007-2013: Gli investimenti delle mafie. Rapporto Linea 1.* Milano: Ministero dell'Interno, 2013. www.investimentioc.it

van Duyne, Petrus C. "Organizing Cigarette Smuggling and Policy Making, Ending up in Smoke." *Crime, Law and Social Change* 39, no. 3 (2003): 285–317.

van Duyne, Petrus C., Klaus von Lampe, and Nikos Passas, eds. *Upperworld and Underworld in Cross-Border Crime*. Nijmegen: Wolf Legal Publishers, 2002.

Van Heuckelom, Carlo. "The Counterfeiting Phenomenon and Its Scale." Presented at the Towards a more effective criminal enforcement of Intellectual Property Rights, Brussels, November 30, 2010.

von Lampe, Klaus. "Assessing Organized Crime: Provisional Situation Report on Trafficking in Contraband Cigarettes." *Trends in Organized Crime* 9, no. 2 (December 2005): 8–15.

von Lampe, Klaus. "Explaining the Emergence of the Cigarette Black Market in Germany." In *The Organised Crime Economy: Managing Crime Markets in Europe*, edited by Petrus C. van

Duyne, Klaus von Lampe, Maarten van Dijck, and James L. Newell, 209–229. Nijmegen: Wolf Legal Publishers, 2005.

von Lampe, Klaus. "The Cigarette Black Market in Germany and in the United Kingdom." *Journal of Financial Crime* 13, no. 2 (2006): 235–254.

von Lampe, Klaus. "The Illegal Cigarette Trade." In *International Crime and Justice*, edited by Mangai Natarajan, 148–154. Cambdirge: Cambridge University Press, 2011.

von Lampe, Klaus. "The Trafficking in Untaxed Cigarettes in Germany: A Case Study of the Social Embeddedness of Illegal Markets." In *Upperworld and Underworld in Cross-Border Crime*, edited by Petrus C. van Duyne, Klaus von Lampe, and Nikos Passas, 141–161. Nijmegen: Wolf Legal Publishers, 2002.

WHO. "WHO Report on the Global Tobacco Epidemic, 2011, Country Profile Italy," 2011. http://www.who.int/tobacco/surveillance/policy/country_profile/ita.pdf

Wiltshire, Susan, Angus Bancroft, Amanda Amos, and Odette Parry. "'They're Doing People a Service' Qualitative Study of Smoking, Smuggling, and Social Deprivation." *BMJ* 323, no. 7306 (July 28, 2001): 203–207.

Zatonski, Witold. "Democracy and Health: Tobacco Control in Poland." In *Tobacco Control Policy. Strategies, Successes and Setbacks*, edited by Joy de Beyer and Linda Waverley, 97–120. Washington, DC: The World Bank, 2003.

Estimating the size of the loan sharking market in Italy

Attilio Scaglione

Juridical, Social and Sport Sciences, University of Palermo, Palermo, Italy

In the current economic crisis, the risk is so high that entrepreneurs, commercial activities and even families may turn to the illegal market to obtain liquidity. This article proposes an estimate of the size of the usury credit market in Italy. The estimate is based on the assumption, provided by Guiso[1], that before coming to a moneylender the borrower seeks to obtain credit through official channels. The results of our estimates confirm the seriousness of the problem, but provide much lower data than those reported periodically by the media. It is estimated that 372,000 economic activities may have been potentially involved in the usury market in 2012. The volume of loans disbursed in the illegal market would have amounted to €18 billion. The profits of loan sharks would be between a minimum of €3 billion and a maximum of about €6.1 billion.

1. Introduction

Among crimes, usury is an illegal activity which is often underestimated in its consequences and sometimes even tolerated and not recognised by the victims themselves. Nevertheless, it receives intermittent attention from the public opinion. Media coverage is high only when particularly serious events occur but, in a few days, when the spotlights fade, attention recedes, returning to prior arrangements and prior levels of general disinterest. Even in the scientific community the debate is lacking: there are no official statistics, and the available data are poorly reliable. The few published reports address the phenomenon with scarce rigour, lacking transparency in the adopted methodology and often producing unrealistic estimates.[2] These accounts contribute to increase the attention on the phenomenon, but do not contribute to decrease the confusion over a crime, already in itself, submerged and hardly recognisable. The effects of the financial crisis, unemployment, the loss of purchasing power of wages and salaries along with the spread of consumerist lifestyles have dramatically increased the risk of taking money from the illegal market. Moreover, loan sharking appears to be gradually linked to other economic crimes, with the involvement of the mafias. Criminal groups aim at laundering the proceeds of criminal activities and at extending the control on the economic structure of the territory. Criminal groups have the availability of illicit funds that are currently required to compensate for the productive activities of the whole country, and the effects of an economic crisis that produces increasing job losses and failures. During the last years the mafias may have increasing opportunities to invest the proceeds of crimes into the legal economy, including through usury, due to the economic difficulties of households and enterprises.[3] Loan sharking affects broad categories of victims: enterprises, commercial activities and families. To counteract usury, good policies should start from the knowledge of actors, structures, dynamics and consequences of this illegal activity. Only on this basis is it possible to think of an effective policy to prevent loan sharking. Furthermore, in a period in which resources are limited, it is necessary to determine precisely where to allocate them and for which purposes. It is not enough to know if a policy is effective, but it is important to estimate the benefits obtained through a given measure with the cost of the reduction obtained. Evaluating the benefits of fighting crime requires information on costs that would have incurred if it had been carried out in one way or another.

This article will initially review existing empirical evidence on loan sharking and methods to estimate its revenues; subsequently, it will propose an alternative estimate[4] of the usury credit market in Italy.[5] There are at least two aspects which require to be pointed out. As is known, the Italian scenario is highly characterised by the presence of different mafia organisations. The Sicilian Cosa nostra, the Neapolitan Camorra and the Calabrian 'Ndrangheta are the widest and most rooted organisations in the Italian "Mezzogiorno"'.[6] However, settlements of these three major organisations are today established also in Northern Italy.[7] A second matter of interest, connected to the first, is the typical dichotomy between the North and South of the country. From unification of Italy, the most prominent face of the duality has been economic. For several reasons, Southern regions are always lagging behind Northern regions. The typical North–South gap between Italian regions has remained evident through time in many respects. Per capita value added in the North has always been higher than in the South.[8] In the light of these general considerations, it was decided, therefore, to deal exclusively with the Italian literature – perhaps more suitable to frame the specifics of this complex scenario – and in particularly with some of the major studies published over the last 20 years.

The rest of the article is organised as follows. Section 2 contains a brief historical evolution of the activity of lending money at usurious interest. Section 3 provides an analysis of the functioning of the usury market in Italy, on the side of supply and demand. Particular attention is given to the role of mafias that increasingly use these activities with the purpose of money laundering. Section 4 describes the main estimates that have been developed over the years. Section 5 presents the methodology and the data used. Section 6 discusses the results and the limits of the estimates proposed.

2. The usury phenomenon

The word 'usury' denotes a loan with a high interest rate usually given to a person in economic difficulties. The origin of the term is, however, ancient, derived from the Latin word 'usus', which refers to the profit which is granted to the debtor by the lender in addition to the return of the money received. Usury therefore has its roots in history. The earliest records are contained in the Old Testament, which prohibits the use of usurious loan to the members of the Jewish community: 'If you lend money to any of my people, to the poor man that is with you, you do not behave as an usurer'[9]; 'do not lend him your money at interest, nor give him your food at usury'[10]; 'do not do interest loans to your brother, nor money or provisions, nor anything that lends at interest'.[11] The problem of loan sharking, although already present in the Holy Scriptures, however, emerges in all its relevance only from the Middle Ages, with the resumption of commercial activities and the proliferation of different monetary systems. The Church does not hesitate to represent the moneylender as the sinner par excellence. Usury is, not surprisingly, one of the most recurring themes in the tales, so-called '*exempla*', which are recited on the occasion of religious sermons. Also the Italian poet Dante, a keen observer of his time, places loan sharks into Hell, in the group of sinners against nature, in company of sodomites.[12] The prevailing view is synthesised in medieval times by the Latin phrase, attributed to Thomas

Aquinas, 'Nummus non parit nummos', according to which the money itself is a medium that cannot be reproduced in an autonomous way.[13] Charging an interest on a loan is in fact equivalent to committing a theft, 'the moneylender is a lazy, who not earns with the sweat of his brow, but just being inert to wait for his money grow'.[14] Despite the moral condemnation of the institutions, the growing importance of loans to finance the emerging capitalist economy leads to the separation of the concept of 'loan sharking' from that of 'interest', understood as legitimate compensation. In other words, two different financial markets begin to emerge: one, formally legal, in the hands of the great bankers of the time; and the other, illegal and clandestine, populated by individuals belonging to every stratum of society and subject to abuses of each type. In this scenario, with the work of the Franciscans, the first mortgage institutions arise (the so-called Pawnshops), with the intention, not so hidden, to remove the Jewish monopoly from the usury market.[15]

In Italy, 'loan sharking' was not considered a crime until 1930. In a socio-economic context, such as that of the second half of the nineteenth century, marked to the principles of traditional liberalism, the crime of usury could not exist. It is clear, however, that such an option of legislative policy could not survive the decline of the idea that inspired it. The crime of usury was introduced only in 1931 with the promulgation of the Rocco Code (Article 644 and 644-bis of the Criminal Code), which regulated this matter until the early 1990s. In 1996, the enactment of law 108 introduced some changes. In particular, it created a solidarity and prevention fund[16] for the victims of usury, and it revised the limit above which interest was considered illegal.[17] Article 644 of the Criminal Code describes usurer as someone who 'gives or promises, for himself or for others, in respect of the provision of money or other benefits, usurious interest or other benefits'.[18] The usurer is severely punished with imprisonment from 2 to 10 years and a fine of €5000 to €30,000. The law states the limit above which interest is considered illegal. This is established as the average rate recorded in the last survey published in the Official Gazette in relation to the category of transactions in which credit is included, increased by half. The average effective interest rate is fixed every three months by the Ministry of the Economy and in consultation with the Bank of Italy. In this regard, there is no connection with the economic circumstances of the crime victims.[19] Before the reform, the state of need was one of the constituent elements of the offense. Now, it is only an aggravating circumstance.[20] The Italian legislation, apart from establishing a maximum legal rate of interest, it also establishes the nullity of contracts which contain usurious clauses: an effect that the Tribunal may extend to all related mortgages. This can free the victim of usury from any obligation to pay interests and the differences between loan and capital already paid to the moneylender. Since 1999, with the Law n. 44, for the victims of usury and extortion it is possible, with the favourable opinion of the Court and the local Prefect, to suspend creditors' actions to recover debts. The legislation makes it also possible to confiscate loan shark's possessions (or of any straw man) in order to compensate victims for sums already paid.[21]

3. The usury market in Italy

Usury is a complex phenomenon. It is a typical economic crime that cannot be analysed solely by considering its financial aspects because they are linked to legal, social and cultural ones.[22] Usury can be analysed from different scientific perspectives, but the economic approach is particularly relevant, since usury can be considered a real illegal credit market. In general, usury tends to be distinguished from legal credit solely on the basis of the higher rate of interest charged by loan sharks. Masciandaro and Battaglini have highlighted the peculiarity of usurious contracts compared to legal ones. They have shown the inadequacy of the single level of interest rates in discriminating between a legal loan and usury. The element that distinguishes the crime of usury from legal lending money can be found in the discrepancy between the technology for recovering money of the legal creditor (judicial coercion) and that of the usurer (illegal coercion).[23] Loan sharking exists even in the presence of competition and perfect information within the credit markets.[24] This position determines reversal of the traditional approach. The interest rate should not be considered as it is only the endogenous result of the analysis. Scholars also note that an agent may consider it rational to be financed by a loan shark agreeing to pay a higher interest rate. Although banks, in fact, provide generally cheaper credit, if it is necessary to reschedule the debt, they provide lower margins for negotiation. By contrast, in the event of the debtor's illiquidity the moneylender may be more willing to renegotiate the debt. Two main considerations emerge from Battaglini and Masciandaro's analysis: first, concerning the protection of property rights, the advantage of a loan shark comes from the violent methods used for the recovery of credits, more effective than those of the banks. The second is that the inefficiencies of the financial structure more frequently lead to a loss of funding rather than the renegotiation of credit.

These observations confirm the spreading of loan sharking in a context, as evidenced in the Italian case presented here, characterised by a more tenuous protection of property rights and a more backward financial system. Beyond the distinctive features of usury, it is possible to find very different situations in the category of victims of usury (Table 1).[25]

The reasons that may induce an individual to ask for a usurious loan are different, although they all involve a momentary crisis of liquidity and underestimation of the risk of not being able to pay off the debt. In general, two broad categories of usury victims can be distinguished: those who need usury because they are short of money and turn to moneylenders to deal with a situation that otherwise would be hopeless; and those who do not need usury, but are gamblers who require the money to feed their habit.[26] In regard to the first category, the need for usury can originate from both consumption and trade corresponding to two categories: households and entrepreneurs. With reference to the first, Savona has observed that, 'it is common especially in the southern regions, where people face not unexpected expenses but still too much for the family finances (daughter's wedding, baptism or first communion) and therefore resort to usury'.[27] The person who relies on usury is undoubtedly an interesting figure from a psychological point of view. As Savona observed, for these individuals, 'the use of usury is considered an acceptable risk, since the fact that the person that relies on usury, is also in the circuit of gambling which allows him to rely on more possibility to get back the money'.[28] Among entrepreneurs, those most affected are generally small and medium-sized commercial activities, which may encounter more difficulties in obtaining financing or in dealing with a sudden economic downturn.[29] The case of companies is the most interesting from the point of view of the economic analysis because it brings to the fore a number of questions about

Table 1. Actors involved in the demand of illegal credit.

Type	Cause	Victims
Those who do not need usury	–	Gamblers
Those who need usury	Originated from consumption	Households
	Originated from trade	Commercial activities Companies

Source: Author's calculations.

Table 2. Actors involved in the supply of illegal credit.

Category	Type
Unstructured usury	Neighbourhood usury
	District usury
	Suppliers of goods
Structured usury	Local criminal groups
	Mafias

Source: Author's calculations.

the functioning of the credit system, the effectiveness of economic policies and the efficiency of the production system. In regard to the latter, Savona observed that it is 'necessary to distinguish between the incapable entrepreneur, who is undeservedly in the market and has no right to be protected, and the man who found himself in a situation of need, e.g. as a result of the immediate return of the loan granted by the bank'.[30]

The supply of illegal credit can take many forms and involve extremely diverse methods (Table 2). Contrary to popular belief, the usury market is characterised by very different operators. If one considers, for example, the economic base of a usurer, it is possible to distinguish large usurers from low-level ones. Along a temporal dimension, an important distinction is between professionals, who engage in this illicit activity continuously, and occasional moneylenders, who issue usurious loans from time to time. Another indicator is the range of action of the usurer, which can vary on a very large scale from a micro-sized neighbourhood or even an office to an entire city. Another discriminating factor is the type of organisation that uses moneylenders. In theory, this can be, at one extreme, absent, based on just one figure; at the other extreme, it can be a complex crime organisation.[31]

Accordingly, the activities of lenders and loan sharks can be divided into two broad categories: (1) lending to households and micro enterprises in difficulties, where the aim is to derive a parasitic income from the victims; and (2) lending money with the aim of gradually draining the wealth of an individual, usually an entrepreneur or a gambler (structured usury).[32] In the first category, it is possible to find forms of subsistence credit with a family structure. This is a type of traditional, archaic usury based on the authority of the provider, who rarely resorts to violence, and which for this reason arouses little social alarm. The victim and perpetrator have often grown up in the same social environment (the neighbourhood, the city) or are connected by other forms of relationships (they work in the same office or attend the same places). There are certain cultural similarities among them.[33] This category can be divided into three different categories. The first refers to the so-called 'neighbourhood' usury because it is characterised by direct proximity between the victim and the oppressor. It involves short-term loans to working families, but also elderly people who live alone. These loans are small and repeated over time. The second category consists of 'district' usury, which can rely on a greater availability of funds. Also in this case, these are short-term loans, generally, without recourse to violent methods. This category also includes loan among colleagues. The third category instead comprises suppliers of goods to companies or wholesalers, who anticipate money and goods to start a business or pursue it in exchange for the application of usurious rates on the debt.[34] Structured usury refers to the management and operation of the unlawful activity in question through more articulated and consequently dangerous organisational forms. There are two different categories: the first is related to local crime, the second to mafias. In both cases, the usury does not have exclusively parasitic aims, but it is often directed to the acquisition of the assets subject to usury, and in general can be a mean to control the economy of a given area, with negative consequences on the local economy. Also the origin of the capital provided is different compared to the first type of usury. In this case, it is money accumulated through other illicit activities.[35]

As already mentioned, the mafias are involved in the so-called structured usury. In contrast to other illegal activities, usury by criminal gangs is not a constant phenomenon, but rather one of recent emergence.[36] Until the early 1980s, Cosa Nostra, for example, considered usury, along with prostitution and gambling, a reprehensible activity.[37] In recent years, however, investigation has revealed evidence according to which the Sicilian mafia started to be interested in this sector, albeit mediated by a third party.[38] Mafiosi, in fact, have begun to invest a significant portion of their revenues in the profitable business of illicit usury. Investigations have also highlighted an operational strategy aimed, through the provision of usurious loans, at the appropriation of companies and assets in the possession of the usurers. The Camorra, unlike the Sicilian Mafia, has never shown any ethical prejudice against the exercise of usury and this can explain its diffusion in the Campania region.[39] The structured organisation applied to the usury market makes it possible to reach major scale economies, on the one hand, by increasing the number and the quality of contracts, and on the other hand, by reducing the risks of insolvency, thanks to intimidation. Loan sharking is becoming one of the most important criminal activities. In the focus of organised crime today, there are companies and commercial activities which in times of crisis have the urgent need to access credit as to avoid losing orders and thus being cut off from the market. In these cases, criminal organisations are able to move and make available large sums of money in a short time. The sum of loan sharks, which apparently allows an entrepreneur to save his company, enables criminal organisations to gradually take possession of that company. Moreover, the risks of the mafias are minimal because loan sharking is a rarely reported crime. It is often based on the non-perception of the victim to be crushed in an illicit affair, and sometimes leads the entrepreneur to feel a sense of gratitude to the moneylender.[40] Ultimately, usury enables criminal organisations to achieve different purposes. First, as mentioned, it is functional to money laundering. Secondly, through victims' assets stripping, which means that it allows mafias to take possession of companies and control them in the legal economy. Thirdly, usury, which often combines with the extortion racket, has significant importance also for control of the territory.[41]

4. Previous estimates of usury

Estimating the usury market encounters particular difficulties. The dark number (unreported crimes) is particularly large in this context. As a result, the market size of usury, the profit gained by loan sharks and the number of victims are difficult to detect solely on the basis of statistics on criminality and crime. Not surprisingly, most of the attempts in the literature have not made direct estimates but have resorted to indirect methods. Many studies have performed risk ratings, combining proxy variables for social, economic, institutional and cultural conditions, to provide a more realistic representation of the spread of usurious activities.[42] In Italy, the scientific debate on the crime of usury has focused on quantifying the extent of the problem and identifying the areas most at risk. However, the estimates made by associations, organisations, institutions, experts and scholars are highly discordant with each other.[43] In consideration of the peculiarities of the Italian case, the literature review will focus only on some of the most significant works published in Italy in the last 20 years.

Guiso provided an estimate of the potential size of the usury market by adding two values: the share of rationed families multiplied by the total number of households in the population, and the share of rationed companies multiplied by the number of households in which at least one member was a self-employed person.[44] Rationed families and rationed companies are those who have not obtained credit through official channels. The estimate of Guiso is based on the assumption that before resorting to a loan shark the borrower seeks to obtain credit through official channels. Guiso suggested that the average size of the loan requested is equal to the average loan issued in the field of consumer credit and production activities. About 90% of the usury market consisted of loans to businesses, while the remaining 10% was used for consumption purposes. According to Guiso, households that resorted to usurious loans in 1993 numbered 342,000 for a total turnover of around 7595 billion lire (corresponding today to approximately €6.3 billion), while the total volume of annual gross revenues amounted to around 3500 billion lire (€2.9 billion).[45]

Goisis and Parravicini, on the basis of 1995 data, carried out an empirical analysis on the link between interest rates and usurious credit markets at regional level.[46] The two authors identified the variables that affect the determination of interest rates. Among these they identified the ratio of bad debts to credit granted, the number of bank branches on the population, average productivity per worker and the average propensity to save, etc. The first three variables contributed most to explaining the trend of interest rates. There appeared to be a positive correlation between interest rates and the bad debts and indexes of credit risk, whereas the negative correlation was the relationship between the interest rates, the frequency of bank branches and average productivity.

Dalla Pellegrina et al., on behalf of the Ministry of Economy and Finance, drew on official data related to complaints in order to carry out an econometric study which was aimed at obtaining estimates of the incidence of usury in the Italian provinces.[47] The regressions referred to observations made for the period 1999–2002 in all the Italian provinces. The selected variables were indicators of both the supply of and demand for illegal credit (mafia-type associations, the number of banks, the volume of subsidised credit granted, unemployment rate, GDP at provincial level, number of protests, etc.). In the same report, Macis and Masciandaro, on the basis of the above considerations, developed an Index of Global Usury (IGU). The analysis of the data showed that the provinces at high risk of usury were those of Calabria: Reggio Calabria, Catanzaro and Vibo Valentia, followed by the provinces of Caltanissetta, Crotone, Naples, Enna, Palermo, Taranto and Brindisi.

The CNEL has focused its attention on the risk of usury in the Italian provinces in 2005–2006. Noting the unreliability of complaints and criminal proceedings in reconstructing the extent of the phenomenon, the research group developed a model with three variables on the extent of usury.[48] The Usury Risk Quotient (Quoziente Rischio Usura, QRU, in Italian) was defined on the basis of three indices: a statistical penalty, which took account of the number of complaints and prosecutions; an economic–financial variable constructed by combining three parameters (real estate executive procedures, failures and protests); and a final social danger drawn from monitoring operations concerning usury and judicial prosecutions in 2006. Analysis of the QRU individuated the provinces with the highest risk of usury: Pescara, Messina, Syracuse and Catanzaro, but also Reggio Calabria, Naples and Genoa.

Sos Impresa-Confesercenti estimates that about 200,000 Italian commercial activities are involved in usury, on the basis of 2010 data, but the report does not provide any information on the methodology used to arrive at this number.[49] In particular, the most affected regions were Campania (32,000), Lazio (28,000) and Sicily (25,000). The turnover of the illegal credit market was estimated at around €20 billion. Also small business owners were involved, as well as civil servants, workers and pensioners, which together brought to over 600,000 the total number of people involved in usury.

Highlighting the low propensity of victims to report, Eurispes[50] adopted a Usury Risk Index (Indice Rischio Usura, IRU, in Italian). The IRU is based on the analysis of a set of socio-economic variables which are thought to affect the degree of vulnerability/permeability of a territory with respect to loan sharking: the economic framework (GDP, unemployment), the banking system (protests, suffering, interest rates on loans, the value of consumer credit, number of bank branches, etc.), the economic structure (number of individual holdings, sold and registered) and crime (extortion, crimes for criminal associations). The official data relating to each variable context were then aggregated to allow comparisons at a provincial level. The resulting index takes values between 0 and 100 (in increasing function of the degree of vulnerability of the territory).

5. Methodology used to estimate the usury market

The illegal nature of credit at usurious interest rates makes it difficult to quantify the turnover. In order to assess the market size, it is necessary to use some proxy indicators. The estimation of the turnover of the illegal credit market in Italy adapted the methodology used by Guiso.[51] In particular, usury was connected to credit for production and not for consumption because the latter is difficult to quantify, and in any case negligible compared with the former. To estimate the usury market, the groups most at risk must be identified. Loan sharking involves in particular enterprises and commercial activities. Our estimate will focus on companies and commercial activities of retail and wholesale. Table 3 shows the data used for the estimate.

Table 3. Data used to estimate the loan sharking market.

Name	Variable	Disaggregation	Year	Source
Number of companies	Number of companies (manufacturing, service and constructions)	Regional	2012	Istat
Number of commercial activities	Number of commercial activities (retailer, wholesale)	Regional	2012	Observatory of Commerce of the Ministry of Economic Development
Share of rationed enterprises	Percentage of enterprises whose requests for new loans were refused in whole or in part	National (macro-area)	2012	Survey on the balance sheets of enterprises carried out by the Bank of Italy
IRU	Usury Risk Index	Regional	2011	Eurispes
Average amount of loans to enterprises	Average amount of loans to enterprises	National	2012	Periodic survey of loans requested by enterprises from the banking system (CRIF)
Average interest rate for loans to enterprises	Average interest rates for loans applied by banks to funding requests by enterprises	National	2012	Periodic survey by the Bank of Italy

In fact, it is believed that enterprises and commercial activities have more difficulties in accessing credit. The potential size of the usury market was measured starting from identification of the number of economic activities which had been denied credit in the same year. The underlying assumption of the estimate was in fact that, since these entities had not obtained credit through legitimate channels, they might be interested in obtaining it through the illegal market.[52] A relevant factor is also the desire to speed up the procedures for obtaining the loan.[53] The data on the number of companies and commercial activities are on a regional basis. As for the data on the productive structure, the information gathered periodically by the Italian National Institute of Statistics (Istat) were used, while for the commercial activities, we used data published by the National Observatory of Commerce of the Ministry of Economic Development. Based on the assumptions discussed above, the usury market in Italy was estimated for 2012. The number of companies was about 4.4 million, while the number of commercial activities was about 1.4 million. To estimate the number of companies which have been denied credit in the legal market, data originated from surveys on access to credit on investment of manufacturing firms conducted annually by the Bank of Italy. These data are useful to calculate the share of rationed companies in Italy according to the productive sector (manufacturing, service and construction). The number of rationed entrepreneurs is about 612,000 units.[54] To estimate the proportion of commercial activities that were denied credit in the legal market, it was assumed that credit rationing among commercial activities is equal to the average rationing for companies (18.05% Centre–North, South 18.75%).[55] Therefore, the estimate of the number of commercial activities potentially exposed to the usury market was equal to more than 260,000 units. The overall numbers of rationed economic activities, companies and commercial activities are over 873,000 units. Obviously, not all rationed companies and commercial activities resort to usurers for credit.

In the face of rationing in legal channels, access to the illegal market is not automatic and immediate. In other words, some of the entrepreneurs, for example, managed to obtain the money from friends or relatives, others simply gave up. Therefore, to identify the proportion of subjects entering the usury market, it was possible to refer to the above-described usury risk index (IRU) on a regional basis developed by Eurispes (2011).[56] Another assumption of the analysis was that the average size of the loan requested was equal to the average granted in the field of credit for production activities.[57] The evidence on the average amount paid for the forms of credit to companies are periodically collected by the CRIF database.[58] This study refers to the average amount of financing requested by Italian companies in 2012. The value for 2012 was equal to €55,914. For commercial activities, the average loan requested from individual companies was equal to €32,503 in the same period.

The turnover of the usury market Um_{reg} in each region was calculated as follows:

$$Um_{reg} = \overline{Cre}_{nat} \cdot Rat_{reg} \cdot Iru_{reg}$$

where $\overline{Cre}_{nat}$ is the average credit requested by companies and commercial activities; Rat_{reg} is the total of companies and commercial activities to whom credit had been refused (rationed economic actors on regional basis); and Iru_{reg} is the percentage of rationed firms in each region that are actually turning to loan sharks to borrow money.

To calculate the revenue of usurers, the total amount of money circulating in the illegal credit market is multiplied by the average interest rate applied in this type of transaction. This is a problematic point. Usury is, as mentioned, a complex phenomenon. From this point of view, the interest rates charged by moneylenders may vary significantly according to numerous factors, such as the economic activity of the applicant, the area, the size of the loan, the psychological profile, the usurer organisation, etc.[59] Since it was not possible to calculate an average rate of usury, the reference threshold identified by the Bank of Italy was taken in order to define the usurious interest rates. For the purpose of determining the thresholds above which the interest rate is to be considered usurious, the law n.108/96 (with changes from the dl 70/2011) states that the average interest rates have to be increased by a quarter plus a margin of further four percentage points (the difference between the threshold and the average rate cannot exceed 8 percentage points).

The revenue of the usury market in each region (Rum_{reg}) was obtained through the following:

$$Rum_{reg} = Um_{reg} \cdot \overline{Ius}_{nat}$$

where Um_{reg} is the turnover of the usury market, and $\overline{Ius}_{nat}$ is the percentage average interest rate of usury calculated as follows $\overline{Ius}_{nat} = \overline{Tu}_{nat} + 0.1$; whereas is the threshold usury rate, not considered usurious, as established by the Bank of Italy[60] and is defined as follows: $\overline{Tu}_{nat} = \left(\overline{i}_{nat} + \overline{i}_{nat}\frac{1}{4}\right) + 4$ where $\overline{i}_{nat}$ is the percentage average interest rate applied in the legal market in the period considered. In this case, assuming a minimum and a maximum, the minimum value was the threshold usury rate increased by 0.1 point, while the maximum was twice this value.[61]

$$Rum_{reg\ min.} = Um_{reg} \cdot \overline{Ius}_{nat}$$

$$Rum_{reg\ max.} = Um_{reg} \cdot (2\overline{Ius}_{nat})$$

The interest rate threshold on an annual basis in 2012 was equal to 17%.[62] Consequently, the minimum interest rate was 17.1%, whereas the maximum was 34.2%.

6. Results and discussion

In 2012, the turnover of the usury market in Italy amounted to approximately €18 billion (Table 4). The product of the total volume of money and the above-defined usury yielded the total revenue of the usury market. The revenues in Italy from usury were equal to a

Table 4. The estimates of the number of rationed entrepreneurs, entrepreneurs victims of loan sharking, total collected funds and minimum and maximum revenues (year 2012, € millions).

	No. of rationed entrepreneurs	No. of involved entrepreneurs	Market dimension (€ million)	Min revenues (€ million)	Max revenues (€ million)
Companies	612,151	254,492	14,230	2433	4867
Commercial activities	260,854	118,065	3838	656	1311
Total	873,005	372,557	18,067	3090	6178

Source: Author's calculations.

Table 5. The estimates of the number of rationed companies, companies victims of loan sharking, total collected funds and minimum and maximum revenues per region (year 2012).

Region	No. of rationed companies	No. of involved companies	Market dimension (€ million)	Min revenues (€ million)	Max revenues (€ million)
Emilia Romagna	49,030	7649	427.7	73.1	146.3
Friuli V. G.	11,490	2838	158.7	27.1	54.3
Liguria	17,038	7241	404.9	69.2	138.5
Lombardy	107,481	21,389	1195.9	204.5	409.0
Piedmont	44,538	16,835	941.3	161.0	321.9
Trentino A. A.	11,033	11	0.6	0.1	0.2
Valle D'Aosta	1,567	437	24.4	4.2	8.4
Veneto	53,388	10,944	612.0	104.6	209.3
North	295,565	67,344	3765.5	643.9	1287.8
Lazio	56,375	25,312	1415.3	242.0	484.0
Marche	17,398	6907	386.2	66.0	132.1
Tuscany	43,820	13,058	730.2	124.9	249.7
Umbria	9181	3828	214.1	36.6	73.2
Centre	126,774	49,105	2745.7	469.5	939.0
Abruzzo	15,470	8787	491.3	84.0	168.0
Apulia	38,713	26,364	1474.1	252.1	504.1
Basilicata	5388	4305	240.7	41.2	82.3
Calabria	16,883	15,110	844.9	144.5	289.0
Campania	51,848	42,153	2356.9	403.0	806.1
Molise	3288	2354	131.6	22.5	45.0
Sardinia	16,514	10,106	565.1	96.6	193.3
Sicily	41,708	28,862	1613.8	276.0	551.9
South	189,812	138,041	7718.5	1319.9	2639.7
Italy	612,151	254,492	14,229.7	2433.3	4866.6

Source: Author's calculations.

minimum of €3 billion and a maximum of about €6.2 billion. Tables 5 and 6 show the estimates in regard to the usury market, referring to the number of companies and commercial activities involved, the size of the market and its revenues.

The results reveal an overall usury market size, which is lower compared to some estimates made by research institutes and reported by the media in Italy in recent years. Just consider that, in the above-mentioned report of Sos Impresa, released in 2011, the turnover of the illegal credit market, coming from commercial activities, was estimated at around €20 billion.[63] The economic activities involved in usury were 372,557, of which 254,492 in the productive sector and 118,065 in the commercial, less than half of the potential 873,000.

The overall figure for Italy hides regional differences. The regions with the highest number of subjects involved are Campania, Sicily, Apulia, Lazio and Piedmont (Tables 5 and 6). The regions where the phenomenon is more widespread are those of the south (10 billion) and in particular Campania (3.2 billion), Sicily (2.1) and Apulia (1.8). In the first five positions, there are also the major regions of Lazio (1.8) and Lombardy (1.4). The phenomenon appears serious also in Calabria (1.1) and Piedmont (1.2). On the opposite side, the value of Trentino-Alto Adige is possibly an underestimate due to the very low score of the IRU (0.1%). Among the least affected regions by usury, there are the little

Table 6. The estimates of the number of rationed commercial activities, commercial activity victims of loan sharking, total collected funds and minimum and maximum revenues per region (year 2012).

Region	No. of rationed commercial activities	No. of involved commercial activities	Market dimension (€ million)	Min revenues (€ million)	Max revenues (€ million)
Emilia Romagna	18,848	2940	95.6	16.3	32.7
Friuli V. G.	4590	1134	36.9	6.3	12.6
Liguria	7577	3220	104.7	17.9	35.8
Lombardy	37,276	7418	241.1	41.2	82.5
Piedmont	18,560	7015	228	39	78
Trentino A. A.	3695	4	0.1	0.02	0.04
Valle D'Aosta	487	136	4.4	0.8	0.2
Veneto	20,412	4184	136	23.3	46.5
North	111,445	26,051	846.8	144.8	288.2
Lazio	24,101	10,822	351.7	60.2	120.3
Marche	7258	2881	93.7	16	32
Tuscany	16,808	5009	162.8	27.8	55.7
Umbria	4038	1684	54.7	9.4	18.7
Centre	52,205	20,396	662.9	113.4	226.7
Abruzzo	6039	3430	111.5	19.1	38.1
Apulia	18,550	12,633	410.6	70.2	140.4
Basilicata	2536	2026	65.9	11.3	22.5
Calabria	9314	8336	271	46.3	92.7
Campania	30,623	24,897	809.2	138.4	276.8
Molise	1382	989	32.2	5.5	11
Sardinia	7457	4564	148.3	25.4	50.7
Sicily	21,304	14,743	479.2	81.9	163.9
South	97,205	71,618	2327.8	398.1	796.1
Italy	260,854	118,065	3837.5	656.2	1311.1

Source: Author's calculations.

populated regions of Valle d'Aosta (0.03), Molise (0.2) and Friuli Venezia Giulia (0.2). These estimates are consistent with the analyses reported by law enforcement agencies.[64]

The approach adopted in this research has obviously some limitations. First, the estimates, as mentioned, do not take account of the credit for consumption. Although families today are turning more frequently to loan sharks, even for small amounts, it is plausible to assume that this market share is still marginal compared to others. Second, at the foundation of the estimates there is the hypothesis that the actors who resort to usurious loan are those who have previously tried to obtain credit through legal markets. However, this assumption cannot be accepted at all. It is possible to assume that some contractors are requested directly to the market usurer bypassing official channels.

A third limit is the problem of duplication of data. With the data available, the path followed – even approximately – it is perhaps the only practicable. In this way, however, it is almost certain that there is an overestimate of the proportion of the actors who turn to loan sharks. The information used does not take into account the fact that the same individual can own one or more companies and one or more commercial activities. This inevitably leads to a problem of oversized estimates and how to overcome this limitation data based on the number of self-employed who may have been used, in line with

Guiso.[65] However, the results do not differ much, which is why it was preferred to follow the approach adopted in this work. A fourth limit concerns the average amount requested that is based on an existing parameter in the licit market but not directly transferable to the illicit market. A final relevant limit is furthermore constituted by the choice of interest rates. Usurers often apply interest rates of 100 or 200% and over. The choice made in this study significantly reduces these values. The lack of accurate statistics, however, suggests the adoption of a more cautious approach. The usurious rate established by the Bank of Italy, as small compared to other values, represents a value of reference on which it is possible to build a reliable estimate of the market size.[66]

In conclusion, this article has sought to provide an updated estimate of the size of the credit market of usury by following a simple methodology but transparent where all assumptions are made explicit. Even with margins of error, the estimates provide a plausible framework of the extension reached so far by the illegal credit market. The numerous assumptions made, and the difficulty of controlling the validity, do not allow us to establish the degree of reliability of these estimates. It would be useful, as suggested by Guiso,[67] to collect additional information on this phenomenon. One should start from a systematic review of the judicial material. This should allow to collect more accurate data, for example, the average volume of money lent by loan sharks and the interest rates applied.

Notes

1. Guiso, "Quanto è grande il mercato dell'usura".
2. Eurispes, *L'usura: quando il "credito" è nero*; Busà and La Rocca (eds.), *L'Italia incravattata*; and Libera, *Usura, il bot delle mafie*.
3. Direzione Nazionale Antimafia, *Relazione annuale*.
4. The estimates presented in this article should not be considered in an econometric sense. The word 'estimate' is used in this study in a general sense as 'an approximate calculation or judgment of the value, number, quantity, or extent of something' (Oxford English Dictionary).
5. The methodology was developed in a research project awarded by the Italian Ministry of Interior to Transcrime (Joint Research Centre on Transnational Crime of Università Cattolica del Sacro Cuore of Milan and Università di Trento) Transcrime, Progetto PON Sicurezza 2007–2013: Gli investimenti delle mafie. Rapporto Linea 1.
6. Lupo, *Storia della mafia*.
7. Sciarrone, *Mafie vecchie, mafie nuove*.
8. La Spina, *La politica per il Mezzogiorno*.
9. Old Testament, "Exodus", 24:22.
10. Ibid., "Leviticus", 25:37.
11. Ibid., "Deuteronomy", 23:20.
12. Dante Alighieri, *La divina commedia*, Inferno, Canto XVII.
13. Le Goff, *La borsa e la vita: dall'usuraio al banchiere*, 14.
14. Cipriani, *Un mondo alla rovescia nella società medioevale*, 7.
15. Ibid.
16. The Solidarity Fund, introduced by Law 108 of 1996 and modified by Law 512 of 1999, provides financial support to victims of extortion and usury. It allows the provision of zero interest loans in proportion to the amounts paid to the moneylender and to the consequent loss (or loss of earnings). Only individuals who report usury to the police have access to the fund and, after the conviction of the usurer, to the cancellation of mortgages.
17. Bonora, *La nuova legge sull'usura*; Masullo, "A due anni dalla riforma del delitto di usura," 1264; and Manna, *La nuova legge sull'usura*.
18. Art. 644 Italian Criminal Code.
19. Frescura, *L'accertamento dell'usura nei finanziamenti bancari*, 2.
20. To this end, usury means that there are usurious 'interests, even if lower than the limit previously determined, and other advantages or payment, that, considering the concrete mode of the offense and the average rate for similar transactions, are excessive to the provision

of money or other benefits, or the mediation work, where those who gave or promised was is in a state of economic and financial difficulty' (ibid.)
21. Spina and Stefanizzi, *L'usura. Un servizio illegale offerto dalla città legale.*
22. Masciandaro and Battaglini, "Il vantaggio di bussare due volte," 416.
23. Ibid.
24. The literature on credit rationing (Stiglitz and Weiss, "Credit Rationing in Markets with Imperfect Information") is mainly based on the assumption of the existence of information asymmetries between the borrower and the lender (companies and banks). Nowadays this stream of literature is quite ample.
25. Grasso, *Ladri di vita.*
26. Savona and Stefanizzi, *I mercati dell'usura a Milano.*
27. Savona, *Le dinamiche del fenomeno dell'usura*, 4.
28. Ibid., 5.
29. Eurispes, *L'usura: quando il "credito" è nero.*
30. See note 27 above.
31. CNEL, *Usura. Diffusione territoriale, evoluzione e qualità criminale del fenomeno.*
32. Fiasco, *L'usura nelle città*; CNEL, *Usura. Diffusione territoriale, evoluzione e qualità criminale del fenomeno*; Busà and La Rocca (eds.), *L'Italia incravattata*; and Eurispes, *L'usura quando il "credito" è nero.*
33. CNEL, *Usura. Diffusione territoriale, evoluzione e qualità criminale del fenomeno*; and Busà and La Rocca (eds.), *L'Italia incravattata.*
34. CNEL, *Usura. Diffusione territoriale, evoluzione e qualità criminale del fenomeno.*
35. Busà and La Rocca (eds.), *L'Italia incravattata.*
36. Lo Forte, "Criminalità organizzata ed economia illegale".
37. Arlacchi, *Addio Cosa nostra*, 63; and Arlacchi, *Gli uomini del disonore*, 93.
38. Direzione Nazionale Antimafia, *Relazione annuale.*
39. Ibid.
40. Spina and Stefanizzi, *L'usura. Un servizio illegale offerto dalla città legale*, 9.
41. See note 37 above.
42. Guiso, "Quanto è grande il mercato dell'usura"; Fiasco, "L'usura nelle diverse province italiane"; Dalla Pellegrina et al., *Il rischio usura nelle province italiane*; CNEL, *Usura. Diffusione territoriale, evoluzione e qualità criminale del fenomeno*; Busà and La Rocca (eds.), *L'Italia incravattata*; and Eurispes, *L'usura: quando il "credito" è nero.*
43. Guiso, "Quanto è grande il mercato dell'usura"; Dalla Pellegrina et al., Il rischio usura nelle province italiane.
44. See note 1 above.
45. The currency revaluation was carried out on the basis of the FOI index (calculated by the Italian National Institute of Statistics, Istat) – a consumer prices index which measures changes in prices of goods and services bought by families of workers and employees.
46. Goisis and Parravicini, "Tassi di interesse usurari e mercati regionali del credito".
47. Dalla Pellegrina et al., *Il rischio usura nelle province italiane.*
48. See note 42 above.
49. Busà and La Rocca (eds.), *L'Italia incravattata.*
50. Eurispes, *Rapporto Italia 2011.*
51. See note 42 above.
52. Ibid.
53. Dugato, *The Crime Against Businesses in Europe.*
54. Banca d'Italia, "Indagine sulle imprese industriali e dei servizi," 24.
55. Ibid.
56. Eurispes, *Rapporto Italia.* The Research Institute has not replicated the study in the 2012. The choice of the IRU, in comparison to other indices (QRU and IGU), is due to at least two reasons. One is that it has been developed on a most recent dataset of variables. The second is that it includes a wider set of variables. With respect to the supply side, for example, the IRU is built on the crime of mafia type criminal association and the crime of extortion, while the other indexes use only the first indicator. Empirical evidence, however, shows how often the crime of usury is employed by mafia groups to perpetuate extortions. On the other hand, it should also be noted that the results obtained with the other index do not differ greatly from those presented here.
57. See note 42 above.

58. CRIF is an independent company specialised in the field of banking credit information. The company regularly conducts scenario studies on the evolution of the credit to households and companies (www.crif.it).
59. See note 31 above.
60. Banca d'Italia, *Comunicato Stampa*.
61. This choice is suggested by the fact that there are no statistics on the average interest rates applied in the illegal market. The media often report cases of interest rates of 100 and even 200%. These values take into account only the most dramatic investigations. These are the most noticeable events which often emerge as a result of the report of the victims due to their inherent unsustainability. However, there is no evidence enabling generalisation of these data. In the awareness of the limits of this choice, we have decided to set a lower interest rate. It is likely that the results may lead to an underestimation of the true extent of the phenomenon.
62. Ibid.
63. Although the approach adopted in this study may have underestimated the average value of the usury interest rate, it may have overestimated the number of entrepreneurs who actually turn to the illegal market to obtain liquidity. Moreover, there are no data on the proportion of subjects who manage to get the required money from friends or relatives. In addition, there are no data on the risk aversion of rationed entrepreneurs. Most of them could prefer to deal with the economic consequences of their situation rather than take money in the illegal market endangering their own lives and those of their families.
64. Direzione Investigativa Antimafia, *Relazione semestrale*.
65. See note 1 above.
66. In this regard, however, the availability of regional interest rates would have allowed to capture more in deep the Italian dichotomy in the access to credit.
67. Ibid.

Bibliography

Arlacchi, Pino. *Addio Cosa Nostra. La vita di Tommaso Buscetta*. Milano: Rizzoli, 1994.

Arlacchi, Pino. *Gli uomini del disonore*. Milano: Rizzoli, 1992.

Banca d'Italia. *Comunicato Stampa. Diffuso a cura del servizio segreteria particolare*, Roma, 27 settembre 2012.

Banca d'Italia. "Indagine sulle imprese industriali e dei servizi, Anno di riferimento 2011." Supplemento al *Bollettino statistico*, anno XXII, no. 38 (2012). Accessed October 31, 2013. www.bancaditalia.it/statistiche/indcamp/indimpser/boll_stat/sb38_12/suppl_38_12.pdf

Bonora, Claudio. *La nuova legge sull'usura*. Padova: Cedam, 1998.

Busà, Lino, and Bianca La Rocca, eds. *L'Italia incravattata. Diffusione territoriale ed evoluzione del fenomeno usuraio*. Roma: Sos Impresa-Confesercenti, 2010. Accessed October 31, 2013. www.sosimpresa.it/userFiles/File/Documenti5/italia_incravatta_busa-larocca.pdf

Cipriani, Alberto. *Un mondo alla rovescia nella società medioevale. Il prestatore su interesse: da usuraio a professionista*. Roma: Edup, 2005.

Consiglio Nazionale dell'Economia e del Lavoro (CNEL). *Usura. Diffusione territoriale, evoluzione e qualità criminale del fenomeno*, Rapporto finale. Roma, settembre 2008. Accessed October 31, 2013. www.cnel.it/Cnel/view_groups/download?file_path=/shadow_documento_attachment/file_allegatos/000/009/581/Rapporto_20finale_20su_20usura.pdf

Costa, Giacomo. "Storie di usura. Una discussione su un libro di Tano Grasso e Gaetano Savatteri." *Rivista Internazionale di Scienze Sociali* 55, no. 4 (1997): 527–550.

Dalla Pellegrina, Lucia, Giuseppe Macis, Matteo Manera, and Donato Masciandaro, eds. *Il Rischio Usura nelle Province Italiane, Ministero dell'Economia e delle Finanze*. Roma: Istituto Poligrafico e Zecca dello Stato, 2004.

Direzione Nazionale Antimafia (DNA). *Relazione annuale sulle attività svolte dal Procuratore nazionale antimafia e dalla Direzione nazionale antimafia nonché sulle dinamiche e strategie della criminalità organizzata di tipo mafioso nel periodo 1° luglio 2011–30 giugno 2012.* Roma: DNA, 2012.

Direzione Investigativa Antimafia (DIA). *Relazione del Ministro dell'Interno al Parlamento sull'attività svolta e sui risultati conseguiti dalla Direzione Investigativa Antimafia,* II semestre. Roma, 2012.

Dugato, Marco, ed. *The Crime Against Businesses in Europe: A Pilot Survey.* Final report of the project: EU Survey to assess the level and impact of crime against business – Stage 2: Piloting the survey module, Transcrime, Milano, 2013. Accessed December 31, 2013. transcrime.cs.unitn.it/

Eurispes. *L'usura: quando il "credito" è nero.* Milano, 2010. Accessed October 31, 2013. www.eurispes.eu/

Eurispes. *Rapporto Italia 2011.* Milano, 2011. Accessed October 31, 2013. www.eurispes.eu/

Fiasco, Maurizio, ed. *L'usura nelle città. Mercato, crimine e risposta sociale*, febbraio, ciclostilato, 1996.

Fiasco, Maurizio, ed. "L'usura nelle diverse province italiane." Consulta nazionale antiusura, bozza provvisoria, presentata al Convegno "Dieci Anni di Solidarietà", 22 novembre, Roma, 2005.

Frescura, Giovanni. *L'accertamento dell'usura nei finanziamenti bancari*, 2010. Accessed October 30, 2013. www.altalex.com/index.php?idnot=49689

Goisis, Gianandrea, and Paola Parravicini. "Tassi di interesse usurari e mercati regionali del credito: un'analisi in termini di efficienza." *Rivista Internazionale di Scienze Sociali*, gennaio-marzo, no. 1 (1999): 3–30.

Grasso, Tano. *Ladri di vita. Storie di strozzini e disperati.* Milano: Baldini e Castoldi, 1996.

Guiso, Luigi. "Quanto è grande il mercato dell'usura?." *Temi di discussione della Banca d'Italia*, no. 260 (1995): 20–22.

Lasco, Federico, and Sonia Stefanizzi. "I mercati dell'usura a Milano." In *Osservatorio permanente sull'usura e la criminalità economica-Camera di commercio, industria, artigianato e agricoltura di Milano*, Centro nazionale di prevenzione e difesa sociale, dossier n. 4 (1996).

La Spina, Antonio. *La politica per il Mezzogiorno.* Bologna: Il Mulino, 2003.

Le Goff, Jacques. *La borsa e la vita: dall'usuraio al banchiere.* Roma-Bari: Laterza, 1987.

Libera. Associazioni, nomi e numeri contro le mafie. *Usura, il BOT delle mafie. Fotografia di un paese strozzato*, Roma, 30 ottobre 2012.

Lo Forte, Guido. "Criminalità organizzata ed economia illegale." In *I costi dell'illegalità. Mafia ed estorsioni in Sicilia*, edited by A. La Spina, 43–75. Bologna: Il Mulino, 2008.

Lupo, Salvatore. *Storia della mafia. Dalle origini ai nostri giorni.* II edizione. Roma: Donzelli, 1996.

Manna, Adelmo. *La nuova legge sull'usura.* Torino: Utet, 1997.

Masciandaro, Donato. "Shylock era banchiere o usuraio? Una teoria del credito d'usura." *Moneta e Credito* 50 (1997): 167–202.

Masciandaro, Donato. "Economia dell'usura e politica dell'antiusura: l'analisi della legge 108/96." In *La legge sull'usura*, edited by G. Zadra, 67–92. Roma: Bancaria Editrice, 1998.

Masciandaro, Donato, and Angelo Porta. "Il mercato dell'usura: analisi macroeconomica ed alcune evidenze empiriche sull'Italia." In *L'usura in Italia*, edited by D. Masciandaro, and A. Porta, 1–38. Milano: EGEA, 1996.

Masciandaro, Donato, and Angelo Porta, eds. *L'usura in Italia.* Milano: Egea, 1997.

Masciandaro, Donato, and Marco Battaglini. "Il vantaggio di bussare due volte: contratti bancari ed usura, diritti di proprietà, valore della garanzia e della rinegoziazione." *Economia Politica* XVII, no. 3 (2000): 415–443.

Masullo, Maria Novella. "A due anni dalla riforma del delitto di usura: una riflessione sulla nuova scelta strategica." *Cassazione Penale* II (1998): 1264.

Savona, Ernesto Ugo. *Le dinamiche del fenomeno dell'usura.* Transcrime, 1997.

Savona, Ernesto Ugo, and Sonia Stefanizzi, eds. *I mercati dell'usura a Milano.* Milano: Camera di commercio, industria artigianato e agricoltura di Milano, 1998.

Sciarrone, Rocco. *Mafie vecchie, mafie nuove. Radicamento ed espansione.* Roma: Donzelli, 2009.

Spina, Rosario, and Sonia Stefanizzi. *L'usura. Un servizio illegale offerto dalla città legale.* Bruno Milano: Mondadori, 2007.

Stefanizzi, Sonia. "Il credito illegale tra espropriazione e scambio: una lettura sociologica della relazione usuraio-usurato." *Polis* XVI, no. 1 (2002): 35–56.

Stiglitz, Joseph Eugene, and Andrew Weiss. "Credit Rationing in Markets with Imperfect Information." *American Economic Review* 71 (June 1981): 393–410.

Proceeds from extortions: the case of Italian organised crime groups

Maurizio Lisciandra

Department of Economics, Management, Environmental and Quantitative Methods (SEAM), University of Messina, Messina, Italy

This paper provides an estimate of the monetary proceeds from extortion racket accruing to the Italian mafias using two unique data sets: one recording periodic and one-time episodes of extortion from judicial and investigative sources, and another one consisting of a victimisation survey of Italian businesses. The estimate of the revenues at a national level lies between 2760 and 7740 mln euros. The regions with a strong presence of traditional organised crime groups remain the most exposed and provide about 65% of all extorted monetary flows, although some important regions in North Italy show a significant presence of extortion rackets in non-traditional areas. Finally, the most exacted economic activities are wholesale and retail trade that, along with construction, overall account up to 70% of all revenues in the lower-bound scenario.

Extortion is a typical predatory activity of organised crime groups. By means of intimidations and threats, the principal aim is to achieve cash or other utilities, especially from businesses. A more subtle intent is to psychologically and economically enslave the victims. According to existing judicial evidence, the extortion of businesses by Italian mafias consists in the imposition of more or less regular or one-off cash payments or of other types of transactions, such as the supplying of raw materials, services or manpower, by criminal businesses or criminal groups to the victims.

In particular, Sciarrone observes three different extortionary mechanisms of Italian mafias against businesses.[1] The first mechanism is merely intimidating; by means of threats, businesses must comply with the illegal request. The second mechanism is, to a certain extent, cooperative and considers an 'active' involvement of the extorted businesses that may find some advantage by complying with the undue request. The third mechanism includes only infiltrated businesses; as being part of the criminal association, they must divert part of their profits to the organised crime group.

However, the second mechanism, which alludes to a reciprocal advantage similar to a market exchange between demand and supply, appears, at the very least, debatable in the Italian context. The voluntariness of the demand of services, which is at the basis of an exchange, can be considered in the great majority of cases widely inexistent when the supplier of these services is a criminal organisation. Gambetta, and Gambetta and Reuter observe extortion in Sicily in the form of protection racket against ordinary criminals, 'unprofessional' racketeers and other gangs.[2] This view is shared by Chu, Varese and Hill, respectively, for the Hong Kong Triads, the Russian Mafia and the Japanese Yakuza.[3] However, in these circumstances, it is still difficult to perceive voluntariness in the demand of protection of legal businesses. As observed by Schelling, organised crime groups operate as tax authorities but provide no benefit to their victims.[4]

The phenomenon of extortion transcends the borders of organised crime vis-à-vis legal businesses. On the one hand, professionals, simple employees or even common citizens can be subject to extortionary practices. On the other hand, extortion is an activity also involving individual criminals or non-organised crime groups.[5] Nevertheless, as shown by Schelling, organised crime groups tend to generate monopolies in the activities they pursue.[6] In particular, we have no evidence contrasting this view with reference to extortion racket of Italian Mafias against businesses. Therefore, it is reasonable to assume that Italian Mafias would impose a monopoly in this type of rent extraction from businesses.[7]

Extortion can be a very profitable activity for criminal organisations and evaluating the dimension of this phenomenon beyond the number of reported crimes is not just a mere estimation exercise, but it helps to understand how much money is drained away from legal economy and how many resources criminal organisations have at their disposal to invest either in illegal activities or in the legal economy, thereby distorting regular competition. Further, a quantification of the money transfer from the victims to the criminal organisations is also a valid instrument to assess the actual damage suffered by the victims. This is important in terms of security policies when deciding how many human and monetary resources are to be devoted to fight against a range of different crimes.

Therefore, this paper aims to provide an estimate of the monetary proceeds accruing to mafias from this very lucrative – we will see how much – activity. Non-monetary extortions will not be estimated due to their very uncertain nature and the lack of reliable data. The focus is on Italy because, as will be seen below, previous partial estimates are available along with repeatable although improvable methodologies. Further and most importantly, two unique data sets are available and can be used for this estimation. The disaggregation level will be at a regional level (NUTS 2) and, for each vulnerable economic activity, at the national level.[8] The estimates of the withdrawal at regional level will lie within a range of statistical significance. Finally, it is worthwhile noting that the estimates exclude similar crimes committed against individuals, and corruption crimes that can be confused with extortions such as payments for illegal services that facilitate the success in public tenders.

This paper is divided into the following sections. Section 1 presents a literature survey on this topic, which is scanty and sometimes barely informative with very few exceptions. Of course, this criminal phenomenon suffers from the lack of data, hence, this makes our analysis more meaningful. Section 2 describes the data sets and the methodology used to construct the estimates. Section 3 comprises the results and presents a discussion. Section 4 concludes.

1. A literature survey

Very few studies have attempted to estimate the proceeds of extortion accruing to criminal organisations, despite extortion being a common as well as serious crime. The estimation faces two main problems: (1) estimating the pervasiveness of the phenomenon, which is translated into how many and which businesses are extorted, and (2) estimating the actual extortion to businesses, which may consist in either a direct withdrawal of money or an indirect predatory burden, such as the imposition of supplies or labour. Regarding the first estimate, the number of crimes reported to the judicial authorities is not a reliable figure since fear, intimidation and threats are a strong inducement to silence, thereby producing large underreporting. Victimisation surveys can help to mitigate the dark number, although anonymous questionnaires on this topic may still suffer from widespread reticence. The second estimate is more difficult to produce. This is a very intangible and fragmented area that cannot be easily captured since there are no accounting or non-accounting data supporting the money transfer from the business to the organised crime groups, and also judicial evidence is scattered and focused on certain aspects of the criminal procedure and judgement.

As a consequence, the literature on the estimation of the proceeds of extortion rackets is quite poor and uneven. The first available information concerns the criminal organisations of Chicago in the 1930s. On the 21st of September 1932, *The New York Times* reported that the cost of extortion in the city of Chicago amounted to $136 million per year (about $2.2 billion in 2013's prices). Alexander studied the Chicago pasta market during those years, showing that pasta factories were paying up to a quarter of their profits to local criminal gangs.[9]

More recently, Iwai estimated the extortion racket in Japan at around 2% of the GDP, however, with no clear methodology.[10] Smith and Varese reported that in 1988, more than half of about 6000 cases of extortion in the Soviet Union related to regular payments varying between 500 and 1000 roubles.[11] The presence of this criminal phenomenon in Russia was confirmed in a report prepared in 1994 for the Russian president Yeltsin, as noted in an article of *The Economist* on 19 February 1994, which claimed that three-quarters of Russian businesses paid between 10% and 20% of their earnings to local criminal organisations. A study on Colombia showed great variability in the amounts extracted, ranging from $20 per month for butchers to $19 per day for taxi drivers.[12] Even in a country traditionally considered as having a low presence of organised crime as Germany, the results of a questionnaire about the extortion suffered by German restaurateurs across the country showed that, according to their ethnicity, between 2% and 6% of them reported at least one case of extortion racket, while between 15% and 28% claimed to know cases of extortion among colleagues.[13]

Estimates produced with a clearer methodology can be found in the Italian studies by Asmundo and Lisciandra on Sicily, and by Lisciandra on Campania, more precisely on the provinces of Naples and Caserta.[14] These estimates were based on separate analyses of judicial evidence of the last 20 years in the two regions, which helped to build two different data sets of the payments by businesses to mafias. The estimates referred to the direct monetary proceeds of mafias; other types of direct and indirect benefits accruing to mafias could not be estimated. With regard to the number of business units subject to extortion, in the case of Asmundo and Lisciandra, the provinces were distinguished into two types: high mafia intensity province (60% of all local units of enterprises active in vulnerable economic activities) and low mafia intensity province (48% of all local units of enterprises active in vulnerable economic activities).[15] The intensity was calculated by cross-referencing various investigations previously carried out by several research institutes, applied to vulnerable economic activities, in which judicial evidence of extortion was detected.[16] Similarly, Lisciandra distinguished vulnerable activities into two categories, the less affected one with 50% of active business units hit by extortion rackets, and the most affected one with 70% of active business units hit.[17] Asmundo and Lisciandra in Sicily, and Lisciandra in Campania list, respectively, 646 cases and 238 cases.[18] Lisciandra distinguishes between periodic extortion episodes and one-time requests; the former do not consist of a structured form of monthly payment, but rather a periodic cash flow usually exacted in two or three, sometimes four, instalments per year whereas the latter are typical of new business units that are supposed to pay a sort of starting fee.[19] Thus, in the case of Campania, additional one-time revenues from 155 cases are estimated. Finally, while in the Sicilian case, the construction sector is considered within the periodic sampling, in that of Campania, there is a refinement of the estimate by applying a percentage varying from 3% to 5% in construction investment. According to estimates, the total amount of periodic extortions in Sicily per year is about one billion euros, and in a range between 780 and 1120 mln euros all direct monetary extortions both periodic and one-time in the provinces of Naples and Caserta.

Another Italian estimation – but for which it is not possible to know either the methodology or the database used – is conducted annually by SOS-Impresa on behalf of an Italian association of businesses.[20] Its most recent available report in 2012 states that the extortion racket attributable to organised crime in the whole country was worth 8 billion euros. Further investigations have been carried out on the relationship among organised crime, business and security. In particular, two surveys conducted by GFK Eurisko-Confcommercio show that 8% of Italian entrepreneurs have personally received threats and intimidation for extortion purposes.[21] This percentage is much higher in the South, especially in Campania (30%). Another survey, which was carried out by Censis-BNC Foundation, covered only Southern regions, with a sample of 750 companies with fewer than 250 employees, and found that 27.2% of businesses in the South had been the victims of extortion.[22] Finally, Transcrime has conducted a survey, which is also used in this study, with more than 11,000 interviews in the years 2007–2008 on crimes against business in Italy.[23] In a general report on the results of the survey, Mugellini and Caneppele show that only 0.4% of all surveyed businesses are victimised by extortion rackets, and 6.6% of them reported the extortion episodes to the police.[24]

2. Data sets and estimation methodology

The estimation methodology makes use of two main data sets, which are combined to produce an estimation of the overall amount of extorted money per region and per economic activity:

(1) A data set of the extortion episodes is used for estimating the average amount of money extorted. This data set groups the data sets available for Asmundo and Lisciandra, and Lisciandra on several extortion episodes that are geographically confined, respectively, to Sicily and the provinces of Naples and Caserta in Campania.[25]

(2) The victimisation survey of Italian businesses conducted by Transcrime on behalf of the Ministry of the Interior in the years 2007–2008 will serve for calculating the percentage of extorted business units in Italian regions and economic activities.

Table 1 summarises all the data sources used to generate the estimates.

The two data sets of extortion episodes contain an unrepresentative sample of businesses facing an extortion racket, because their detection emerged from investigations or judicial evidence during recent years. They include indication about the economic activity, according to the latest International Standard Industrial Classification (ISIC), the province of the extorted business, the date, the amount, and the frequency of the extortionary episode.

CRIMINAL MARKETS AND MAFIA PROCEEDS

Table 1. Databases used for estimation.

Data	Disaggregation	Years	Source
Data set on extortion episodes	Sicily + Provinces of Naples and Caserta	1988–2009	Fondazione Chinnici
Consumer price index (F.O.I.)	National	1988–2012	Istat
Victimisation survey on crimes against Italian businesses	Regional and by economic activities	2007–2008	Transcrime
Number of active businesses	Regional up to 4-digit level ISIC codes	2012	Infocamere
Number of local units	Regional up to 2-digit level ISIC codes	2007	Asia archive/Istat
Investments in construction industry	National	2010–2012	ANCE
Added value	Regional up to 2-digit level ISIC codes	2009–2011	Istat

The statistical plausibility of these data sets is supported by the following considerations: (1) the purpose of the data sets is limited to quantify an average extortionary episode for a large set of economic activities within an interval of statistical significance; (2) the numerosity of the observations allows, in many circumstances, to apply, to a certain extent, the law of the large numbers such that the estimates obtained from a large number of episodes should be close to the expected value; (3) the data sets collect information on the extortionary episodes from many sources such as victim reports, police investigations, confessions from repentant members and informal accounting of criminal organisations, thereby reducing the bias in the representation of extortion racket in some specific economic activity or business size.

The two data sets have been merged so as to capture the widest variability of the phenomenon in the country and to increase the statistical significance of the estimates. Although the new, larger data set consists of observations collected in a part of the country, the indicators have also been applied to other parts of the country since (1) the Sicilian Mafia (i.e., Cosa Nostra) and the Neapolitan Camorra are also spread in other parts of the country, and along with other mafias, such as 'Ndrangheta and to a lesser extent Sacra Corona Unita, they have the monopoly of extortion racket throughout the country[26]; (2) the data set is not used to estimate indicators about the pervasiveness of this criminal phenomenon both geographically and at a sectorial level, but other data sets and methodologies, as explained below, have been applied.

As shown in Figure 1, observations covered the years from 1988 to 2009. We adopted the consistency of the historical data with the current ones, such that past extortion events are considered as if they took place in 2012. Asmundo and Lisciandra in Sicily, and Lisciandra in Campania applied the same conjecture assuming that the phenomenon of extortion rackets has not changed over 20 years in both its level and distribution by economic activity.[27] This has made it possible to increase both the size of the sample and, as a consequence, the statistical significance of the estimates. Therefore, monetary amounts have been adjusted according to the Italian consumer price index (i.e., F.O.I. 2012). The data set consists of 792 observations of periodic payments and 325 one-time episodes for a total number of observations equal to 1117, excluding the construction industry, as will be seen below. They range from less than 30 euros per month, from a

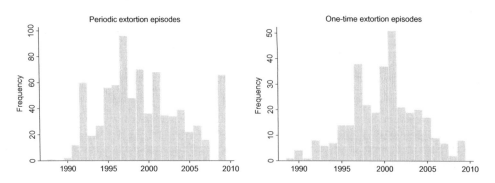

Figure 1. Time profiles of the observed extortion episodes.

small grocery shop or a pizza seller, up to more than 30,000 euros per month for a large wholesale supermarket and even more than 350,000 euros as one-time extortion to a steal company. All periodic episodes of extortion have been annualised.

As anticipated above, another important data set is the victimisation survey of Italian businesses, produced by Transcrime on behalf of the Ministry of the Interior, conducted in 2007–2008. This data set has provided the percentage of business units $(\%E_{ij})$ that are subject to extortion on a regional basis (i) and class of economic activity (j). Obviously, despite the anonymity of the responses, we assumed significant underreporting in the survey, due to the sensitivity of the topic. Consequently, we decided to estimate the actual percentage of extorted businesses by means of the standardisation of the positive percentage responses. We split the estimation of $\%E_{ij}$ into two parts: the estimation of the actual percentage of extorted businesses of region i and the estimation of the actual percentage of extorted businesses of the class of economic activity j at national level. The first estimation attributes 100% to Calabria, the region with the highest percentage of positive responses in the survey. Then, the actual percentage of extorted businesses of region i is equal to the ratio between the percentage of positive responses of region i (i.e., % victimization of region i) and the percentage of positive responses of Calabria (i.e., $\max_i$ (% victimization of region)). In the same fashion, we estimated the actual percentage of extorted businesses by economic activity at national level. 'Construction' is the economic activity with the highest percentage of positive responses in the survey, and thus we attributed 100% to this economic activity. The actual percentage of extorted businesses in the economic activity j is then equal to the ratio between the percentage of positive responses of economic activity j (i.e., % victimization of economic activity j) and the percentage of positive responses of 'Construction' (i.e., $\max_j$ (% victimization of economic activity)). Then, the two percentages have been multiplied in order to provide an estimate of the percentage of extorted business units by class of economic activity and by region, thereby capturing the intensity of the phenomenon in more detail.

$$\%E_{ij} = \frac{\%\text{ victimization of economic activity } j}{\max_j (\%\text{ victimization of economic activity})} \times \frac{\%\text{ victimization of region } i}{\max_i (\%\text{ victimization of region})}$$

Table 2 corroborates judicial and investigative evidence as well as previous rough estimates on the pervasiveness of extortion rackets in the Italian legal economy. Similar to the Calderoni mafia index, the most affected regions are those with the traditional mafia

Table 2. Percentage of estimated extorted business units by economic activity in the most representative Italian regions (%E_{ij}).

	Apulia	Calabria	Campania	Emilia-Romagna	Lazio	Lombardy	Piedmont	Sicily	Tuscany	Veneto
Human health and social work activities	17.66%	44.52%	36.81%	4.24%	5.44%	3.57%	8.47%	24.55%	8.04%	10.33%
Arts, entertainment and recreation + Other service activities	32.14%	81.04%	67.00%	7.71%	9.91%	6.50%	15.43%	44.69%	14.64%	18.80%
Manufacturing + Mining and quarrying	15.61%	39.34%	32.53%	3.74%	4.81%	3.15%	7.49%	21.70%	7.11%	9.13%
Electricity, gas, steam and air conditioning supply + Water supply; sewerage, waste management and remediation activities	6.16%	15.53%	12.84%	1.48%	1.90%	1.24%	2.96%	8.56%	2.81%	3.60%
Construction	39.67%	100.00%	82.69%	9.51%	12.23%	8.02%	19.04%	55.15%	18.07%	23.19%
Wholesale and retail trade; repair of motor vehicles and motorcycles	18.71%	47.17%	39.00%	4.49%	5.77%	3.78%	8.98%	26.01%	8.52%	10.94%
Accommodation and food service activities	16.03%	40.42%	33.42%	3.84%	4.94%	3.24%	7.69%	22.29%	7.30%	9.37%
Transportation and storage	18.14%	45.72%	37.80%	4.35%	5.59%	3.67%	8.70%	25.21%	8.26%	10.60%
Financial and insurance activities	8.65%	21.80%	18.03%	2.07%	2.67%	1.75%	4.15%	12.02%	3.94%	5.06%
Real estate activities + Professional, scientific and technical activities + Administrative and support service activities	14.73%	37.14%	30.71%	3.53%	4.54%	2.98%	7.07%	20.48%	6.71%	8.61%

Source: Our estimates on the victimisation survey of Italian businesses produced by Transcrime on behalf of the Ministry of the Interior in 2008.
Notes: As explained further in the paper, these percentages are applied only to specific subclasses of the economic activities displayed in the table, that is, up to 4-digit level ISIC codes rather than 2-digit level ISIC codes, which are too general and encompass subclasses totally immune to the extortion racket. Consequently, the percentage must not be read as the percentage of extorted businesses with respect to all businesses belonging to the economic activities at 2-digit level ISIC codes, but only with respect to the businesses belonging to the vulnerable subcategories of each economic activity.

presence, such as, in order of severity, Calabria with 'Ndrangheta, Campania with Camorra, Sicily with Cosa Nostra, and Apulia with Sacra Corona Unita.[28] The Northern regions with a worrying presence of extortion rackets are Veneto and Piedmont. The most exposed economic activities are construction, entertainment and recreation, wholesale and retail trade, and transportation.

Given these two main unique data sets, we produced the estimation of the total monetary amount of extortion racket by region and economic activity following three steps. The *first step* produced an estimate, with 90% confidence interval, of the *periodic* average extortion on an annual basis (EP_{ij}) by region and economic activity.[29] This is equal to the product of the arithmetic average, correcting for outliers, of the extortion episodes for each class of economic activity $(\overline{EP}_j)$, and the estimate of the number of local units subject to extortions (NE_{LUij}).[30] In turn, the latter estimate is the product of the following variables:

(1) The number of vulnerable active business units within each class of economic activity for each region (NE_{BUij}). In accordance with Asmundo and Lisciandra for Sicily and Lisciandra for Campania, within the same class of economic activities at 2-digit level ISIC codes, we considered vulnerable those subclasses up to 4-digit level ISIC codes for which the entire judicial and investigative evidence in our possess mentions at least once an extortion episode.[31]

(2) The multiplier of local units by class of economic activity and by region (M_{LUij}). Local units are the actual passive subjects of extortion, as confirmed by judicial evidence and not the business unit itself that may encompass several local units. Since there are no available data on local units at the level of detail required for the year under scrutiny, we constructed a multiplier, which is applied to (NE_{BUij}), by starting from the last available data on local units in 2007.[32]

(3) The percentage of extorted business units by class of economic activity and by region, obtained as described above $(\%E_{ij})$.

Thus, $EP_{ij} = \overline{EP}_j \times NE_{LUij}$ and $NE_{LUij} = NE_{BUij} \times M_{LUij} \times \%E_{ij}$.

The *second step* produced an estimate with 90% confidence interval of *one-time* extortions on an annual basis (EO_{ij}) by region and economic activity, which is equal to the product between the arithmetic mean of one-time extortions per economic activity $(\overline{EO}_j)$ and the estimate of the number of local units subject to extortion (NEO_{LUij}). The latter estimate differs from NE_{LUij} because only local units of new business units (NEO_{BUij}) are considered. All available judicial and investigative evidence recognises one-time extortions as generally prevailing in areas fully controlled by traditional criminal organisations, such as the regions of Sicily, Calabria, Apulia and Campania. Consequently, one-time extortions have been estimated only in those regions. Thus, $NEO_{LUij} = NEO_{BUij} \times M_{LUij} \times \%E_{ij}$, and $EO_{ij} = \overline{EO}_j \times NEO_{LUij}$.

The *third step* of estimation refers to the *construction* industry for which no reliable estimation from the available data sets could be carried out. This is mainly due – on the one hand – to the lack of periodicity of withdrawals and – on the other hand – to the payment method. The latter can be either related to a public tender or to the execution of the public or private work, for these reasons, the notion of one-time extortion is inappropriate. However, judicial evidence shows that a percentage of withdrawal, ranging between 2% and 4%, was typically applied to the value of the construction work.[33] For these reasons, the estimation of the amount extorted to the construction sector by region $(ECOS_i)$ follows a different procedure, which has been already adopted by Lisciandra.[34]

The current estimate considers the product among three factors: (1) the total amount of investments in construction (average 2010–2012) by region (INV_{COSi}),[35] (2) the percentage of extorted business units in the construction sector by the region already presented above $(\%E_{i,cos})$, and (3) the percentage rate $(\%EC)$ ranging from 2% to 4%.[36] However, investment data can be further split into (1) new constructions $(INV\_NEW_{COS_i})$, (2) extraordinary maintenance and restoration work $(INV\_EXT_{COS_i})$, (3) non-residential private constructions $(INV\_PRI_{COS_i})$, and (4) non-residential public constructions $(INV\_PUB_{COS_i})$. In the same fashion as in Lisciandra, with regard to $INV\_EXT_{COS_i}$, only 50% of these investments are considered to be vulnerable to extortion.[37] The estimates will then be the following: $INV_{COS_i} = INV\_NEW_{COS} + 0.5 \cdot INV\_EXT_{COS} + INV\_PRI_{COS} + INV\_PUB_{COS}$, and $ECOS_i = INV_{COS_i} \times \%E_{i,cos} \times \%E$.

Hence, the final estimates of the overall amount of extorted money by region (TE_i) and the overall amount of extorted money by economic activity (TE_j) are the following: $TE_i = \sum_j (EP_{ij} + EO_{ij}) + ECOS_i$, and $TE_j = \sum_i (EP_{ij} + EO_{ij})$ if $j \neq$ construction, otherwise $TE_{construction} = \sum ECOS_i$.

An important validation of our methodology has been carried out by performing a correlation analysis between the number of observed *periodic* extortions by economic activity existing in our data set and $NE_{LU}ij$, that is, the estimate of the number of local units subject to extortions. A high correlation would mean that our apparently unrepresentative sample of periodic extortion episodes by economic activity is actually coherent with the estimated number of local units subject to extortions, which also depends on our estimation of the percentage rates of extorted businesses, $\%E_{ij}$. This further means that our two data sets, one of the extortion episodes and the other on the victimisation of Italian businesses, speak to each other consistently. The correlation analysis has been performed for each region, i. The results are satisfactory and show high correlation indexes for each region, with Sicily having the highest index, 0.968, whereas Trentino Alto Adige shows the lowest index with 0.806.[38] The average among the correlation indexes of all 20 Italian regions is 0.905. The same correlation analysis has been performed for the one-time extortion episodes by economic activity and NEO_{LUij}. As mentioned above, we considered only the regions traditionally influenced by mafias. The results are also satisfactory: Campania shows the highest correlation index, with 0.961, and Apulia shows the lowest, with 0.947.[39]

3. Results and discussion

Table 3 below shows the lower and upper bounds of the sum of periodic and one-time extortion estimates of the revenues from extortion racket, with 90% confidence interval, and the lower and upper bounds of the revenues from extortion racket in the construction sector considering, respectively, the percentage rates of 2% and 4% as described above. Estimates are provided at a regional level.

The estimates of the one-time extortion racket ranging overall from 110 to 850 mln euros are more variable than the periodic extortion racket estimates ranging from 2100 to 5780 mln euros. This is due to the reduced number of observations for each economic activity of the one-time episodes, thereby increasing the standard errors of the mean and frequently cutting to zero the lower endpoints of the 90% confidence interval within each category of economic activity. As previously stated, the revenues from one-time extortion racket are attributed only to the regions with the traditional criminal organisations. The weight of one-time extortion

Table 3. Estimates in 1000 euros of the revenues from extortion rackets in Italy at a regional level.

	Periodic and one-time		Construction		Total	
	Lower	Upper	Lower	Upper	Lower	Upper
Abruzzo	24,317	68,594	7791	15,582	32,108	84,176
Apulia	203,794	660,679	56,290	112,580	260,084	773,259
Basilicata	9928	27,206	3537	7073	13,464	34,279
Calabria	267,249	818,598	55,691	111,381	322,939	929,979
Campania	714,037	2,040,481	107,759	215,517	821,795	2,255,998
Emilia Romagna	49,726	155,492	19,312	38,624	69,038	194,116
Friuli V.G.	16,001	48,085	5949	11,897	21,950	59,982
Lazio	84,903	237,565	31,542	63,084	116,445	300,649
Liguria	24,223	70,587	7834	15,668	32,057	86,255
Lombardy	82,564	271,185	37,212	74,423	119,775	345,608
Marche	45,263	137,007	13,646	27,292	58,909	164,299
Molise	7630	21,105	2327	4654	9957	25,759
Piedmont	96,620	305,952	34,235	68,470	130,855	374,422
Sardinia	15,788	43,299	3914	7828	19,702	51,127
Sicily	329,287	984,196	66,610	133,219	395,897	1,117,416
Tuscany	85,452	267,880	27,831	55,662	113,283	323,542
Trentino A.A.	14,597	42,395	7571	15,141	22,168	57,536
Umbria	10,170	30,485	3912	7824	14,082	38,309
Valle D'Aosta	4288	12,942	3374	6747	7662	19,689
Veneto	122,600	391,972	57,315	114,631	179,916	506,603
ITALY	**2,208,436**	**6,635,705**	**553,650**	**1,107,299**	**2,762,086**	**7,743,004**

Notes: The estimates of periodic and one-time extortions are the lower and upper bounds of the confidence interval at 90% significance level. Specifically, the estimates of the one-time extortion racket refer only to Campania, Calabria, Sicily and Apulia, whose interval estimates in 1000 euros are, respectively, [50,908; 366,627]; [20,698; 171,279]; [19,252; 156,967]; [14,802; 158,816]. The estimates of extortion from construction consider $\%EC = 2\%$ and $\%EC = 4\%$, respectively, for the lower- and upper-bound levels.

racket, with respect to periodic extortion racket in those regions, ranges between 7.5% in the lower bound estimate up to 23.4% in the upper bound estimate.

The region with the largest amount of extortion revenues is Campania (i.e., the region of Naples), with a fork ranging from 820 to 2260 mln euros, which is almost 30% of the total amount exacted from the entire country (i.e., 2760–7740 mln euros). The most victimised regions are Sicily (400–1120 mln euros), Calabria (320–930 mln euros) and Apulia (260–770 mln euros). In particular, there is a certain consistency of the Sicilian estimates with the previous estimates made by Asmundo and Lisciandra of around one billion euros, although unlike the previous investigations, the current estimates take into account an innovative estimation methodology, the confidence intervals, and include the one-time extortion racket.[40] The estimates from Lisciandra, with regard to the provinces of Naples and Caserta as aforementioned, amounting between 780 and 1120 mln euros appear also to be consistent with the current estimates of the entire Naples region.[41] Similar to the current study, the estimation methodology takes into account the one-time extortion episodes and the separate estimate of the revenues from the construction industry, but misses the estimates of the percentage rates of extorted businesses by class of economic activity from the original data set of the victimisation survey of Italian businesses and the statistical significance of the confidence interval.

The regions with the traditional presence of organised crime groups account to about 65% of the total revenues in the country.[42] This means that traditional mafias are still an important constraint for legal businesses in the already sluggish economy of South Italy.

Table 4. Estimates in 1000 euros of the monetary extortions in the most affected economic activities.

	Number of observations		Total estimates	
	Periodic	One-time	Lower	Upper
Manufacture of food products	26	17	78,544	523,609
Construction	–	–	553,650	1,107,299
Wholesale and retail trade and repair of motor vehicles and motorcycles	73	27	137,638	212,731
Wholesale trade, except for motor vehicles and motorcycles	78	32	248,721	376,109
Retail trade, except for motor vehicles and motorcycles	301	117	983,743	1,836,810
Land transport and transport via pipelines	18	10	99,882	293,581
Food and beverage service activities	87	33	186,166	263,819
Sports activities and amusement and recreation activities	33	16	97,947	217,362
Other personal service activities	10	2	153,615	897,719

Notes: In more detail, sports activities and amusement and recreation activities include, for instance, bowling, amusement arcades, football centres, gyms, beach resorts and clubs, movie theatres, etc. Other personal service activities include, for instance, barber shops, hairdressers, beauticians and even burial services.

Nonetheless, an extortion racket appears to be a relevant phenomenon in other parts of the country and especially in the Northern regions such as Veneto, Piedmont and Tuscany, and to a less extent in Lombardy, the richest and most populated Italian region. The figures of the Northern regions stem mainly from the victimisation survey of businesses, showing how the entrepreneurs of these regions are severely affected by extortion rackets, a phenomenon that, a few years ago, was almost unknown in this part of the country.

Table 4 shows the estimates for the most exacted economic activities and their respective number of observations. Wholesale and retail trade sectors are the most affected activities, with an overall burden ranging from 1370 to 2430 mln euros and the largest number of observations. Trade's share of the revenues ranges from 49.6% in the lower bound to 31.3% in the upper bound. Construction is the second most exacted activity, its share of the revenues varies between 20.1% in the lower bound down to 14.3% in the upper bound. It is worthwhile noting that these just mentioned economic activities cover a large share of total revenues in the lower bound (i.e., 69.7%), whereas this share is significantly reduced in the upper bound (i.e., 45.6%). This mainly occurs because of the higher number of observations in the trade sectors, which produce better estimates, thereby making the confidence interval much narrower than other sectors such as manufacture of food products or other personal service activities, whose estimates are based on fewer observations. This occurrence makes the left tail of the confidence interval of the overall amount of monetary revenues from extortion rackets more statistically reliable. Thus, we sense that the actual total figure for Italy leans more towards the lower-bound level such as 2760 mln euros rather than 7740 mln euros, which could possibly represent an overestimation of the actual figure.

4. Conclusion

This empirical investigation has provided an estimate, with 90% confidence interval, of the monetary revenues accruing to Italian mafias from periodic and one-time extortion rackets, including the fixed percentage rates exacted from construction works, as evidenced by investigative and judicial reports. The estimates are also provided by region and by economic activity, up to the second digit of the ISIC classification. The amount of monetary revenues ranges from 0.18% to 0.49% of Italian GDP (2012 prices), which denotes that an extortion racket pulls out a consistent volume of Italian wealth and moves it towards illegal markets or legal markets through laundering.

The regions with a traditional presence of organised crime groups, such as the Southern regions of Campania, Calabria, Sicily and Apulia, confirm to have larger shares of extorted money. However, Veneto, Piedmont, Tuscany and Lombardy in the Northern part of the country contribute significantly to increase cash flows towards the organised crime groups. This indicates the expansion of extortion racket in non-traditional areas or, read differently, the ability of Southern organised crime groups to control and subjugate portions of territories in the Northern regions. The most exacted economic activities are wholesale and retail trades along with construction, which also show the highest victimisation figures along with the entertainment and recreation industry.

The current estimation shows, however, a few limitations due to a biased territorial distribution of the observations on the extortion episodes, which capture only Southern provinces of the country and sometimes are also 20 years old. Further, since estimation is based on the numerosity of the sample for each economic activity, some of the economic activities have very few observations, thereby dilating the confidence intervals, and consequently overweighting these activities in the upper-bound estimates. Hence, future empirical investigations on this topic should move forward a few steps. In particular, improved accuracy of estimates will be achieved by (1) increasing the number of observations of extortion episodes through a wider scale codification of investigative and judicial evidence throughout the country; (2) introducing observations of more recent episodes of extortion – possibly dropping the oldest ones – so as to capture the newest traits of the criminal phenomenon; (3) updating the data set on the victimisation of businesses attempting to reduce the underreporting problem that still exists.

Notes

1. Sciarrone, *Mafie Vecchie, Mafie Nuove*.
2. Gambetta, "Mafia," 158–75; Gambetta, *The Sicilian Mafia*; and Gambetta and Reuter, "Conspiracy Among the Many," 116–35.
3. Chu, *The Triads as Business*; Varese, *The Russian Mafia*; and Hill, *The Japanese Mafia*.
4. Schelling, "What Is the Business," 71–84. In the great majority of the observed cases, the demand for protection or other services (e.g., restriction of competition or the successful completion of credits) is not voluntary or it is surreptitiously elicited by present or future threats. As is well known, the rejection of a protection offer entails risks, threats and harmful consequences for people and goods. As a consequence, an extortion racket hardly identifies a conventional market with demand, supply and prices. The "protection service" appears as an accessory to extortionary activity, and it serves more criminal organisations rather than businesses because it deters incursions by other clans and small-scale criminals.
5. Sometimes, common criminals may even simulate to be real members of some organised crime group. For instance, Gambetta (*The Sicilian Mafia*) and Sciarrone (*Mafie Vecchie, Mafie Nuove*) mention a few cases in Italy, Chu (*The Triads as Business*) mentions some bogus triad members in China.
6. Schelling, "What Is the Business," 71–84.
7. Paoli (*Mafia Brotherhoods*) provides wide illustration of this activity carried out monopolistically by Italian mafias.
8. For details on the nomenclature of territorial units, see http://epp.eurostat.ec.europa.eu/portal/page/portal/nuts_nomenclature/introduction.
9. Alexander, "The Rational Racketeer," 177.

10. Iwai, "Organized Crime in Japan," 203–33.
11. Smith and Varese, "Payment, Protection and Punishment," 376.
12. Moser and McIlwaine, *Urban Poor Perceptions*.
13. Ohlemacher, "Viewing the Crime Wave," 52.
14. Asmundo and Lisciandra, "Un tentativo di stima," 113–36; Asmundo and Lisciandra, "The Cost of Protection," 221–40; and Lisciandra, "Camorra ed estorsioni," 161–84.
15. Asmundo and Lisciandra, "Un tentativo di stima," 129; and Asmundo and Lisciandra, "The Cost of Protection," 238.
16. According to the authors, an economic activity is vulnerable if it is mentioned at least once in the entire judicial evidence and investigative reports.
17. Lisciandra, "Camorra ed estorsioni," 178.
18. Asmundo and Lisciandra, "Un tentativo di stima," 119; Asmundo and Lisciandra, "The Cost of Protection," 224; and Lisciandra, "Camorra ed estorsioni," 168.
19. Lisciandra, "Camorra ed estorsioni," 165.
20. SOS-impresa, *Le mani della criminalità*.
21. Confcommercio-GFK Eurisko, *La mappa della criminalità*; and Confcommercio-GFK Eurisko, *2° Rapporto*.
22. Censis-Fondazione BNC, *Impresa e criminalità*.
23. The sampled businesses were 83,136, the average response rate was about 14%.
24. Mugellini and Caneppele, "Le imprese vittime," 1–2.
25. See note 18 above.
26. The presence throughout the country of the four main Italian mafias has been investigated by Transcrime (*Progetto PON Sicurezza 2007–2013*).
27. See note 18 above.
28. Calderoni, "Where Is the Mafia," 41–69.
29. If a single economic activity shows only one observation, as investigated by Rodríguez ("Confidence Intervals from One Observation"), it is possible to establish a confidence interval through a parametric analysis. The 90% confidence interval for the single observation x results $[x-5|x|, x + 5|x|]$.
30. Local units are intended to be sites or subsidiaries of a business enterprise. A business unit consists of one or more local units.
31. See note 18 above.
32. No data on the local units for agriculture, fishing and aquaculture are available. Consequently, the number of active business units was used instead of local units. However, with regard to agriculture, this number was filtered with the method used by Sotte ("Imprese e non-imprese nell'agricoltura Italiana"), according to which, the agricultural active business units are only those with a minimum turnover of 16 UDE (i.e., Economic Unit Dimension), which is equal to slightly less than 1000 euros.
33. These percentages can be found in several legal cases. For example, the informer of Sicilian Mafia Baldassare Di Maggio in 1993 mentioned 3% as the most common percentage withdrawal rate. In New York, the local mafia imposed a percentage rate of 2% (Gambetta and Reuter, "Conspiracy Among the Many").
34. Lisciandra, "Camorra ed estorsioni," 173–6.
35. Regional data on investments in construction are not available. The national data have been therefore split by region, according to the regional contribution to the national added value of the construction sector as average among three years, i.e., 2009–2011.
36. Our range (i.e., from 2% to 4%) differs from the percentage rates applied to the construction industry in Lisciandra ("Camorra ed estorsioni") (i.e., from 3% to 5%) due to further evidence validating current range, but also to avoid overestimations.
37. The correlation index of Sicily is coherent with the fact that an important share of the observed episodes have been recorded in this region. This is further evidence of the goodness of our estimation methodology.
38. Ibid.
39. Also in this case, the correlation index of Campania confirms the appropriateness of the methodology and the goodness of our data sets in the light of the fact that the observed one-time episodes are mainly recorded in this region.
40. Asmundo and Lisciandra, "Un tentativo di stima," 113–36; and Asmundo and Lisciandra, "The Cost of Protection," 221–40.
41. Lisciandra, "Camorra ed estorsioni," 161–84.

42. Without considering one-time extortion racket, in our estimation only ascribable to the regions with traditional organised crime groups, this percentage decreases to 63.8% in the lower bound and to 61.3% in the upper bound levels of estimation. Thus, a negligible decrease that highlights how traditionally controlled areas still convey many resources to mafias.

Bibliography

Alexander, B. "The Rational Racketeer: Pasta Protection in Depression Era Chicago." *Journal of Law and Economics* 40, no. 1 (1997): 175–202.
Asmundo, A., and M. Lisciandra. "The Cost of Protection Racket in Sicily." *Global Crime* 9, no. 3 (2008): 221–240.
Asmundo, A., and M. Lisciandra. "Un tentativo di stima del costo delle estorsioni sulle imprese a livello regionale: Il caso Sicilia." In *I costi dell'Illegalità – Mafia ed Estorsioni in Sicilia*, edited by A. La Spina, 113–136. Bologna: Il Mulino, 2008.
Calderoni, F. "Where Is the Mafia in Italy? Measuring the Presence of the Mafias Across Italian Provinces." *Global Crime* 12, no. 1 (2011): 41–69.
Censis-Fondazione BNC. *Impresa e criminalità nel Mezzogiorno. Meccanismi illegali di distorsione della concorrenza*. Roma: Gangemi, 2004.
Chu, Y. K. *The Triads as Business*. London: Routledge, 2000.
Confcommercio-GFK Eurisko. *La mappa della criminalità regione per regione*. Palermo: mimeo, 2007.
Confcommercio-GFK Eurisko. *2° Rapporto Confcommercio-GFK Eurisko su sicurezza e criminalità*. Roma: mimeo, 2008. www.governo.it/backoffice/allegati/39765-4845.pdf
Gambetta, D. "Mafia: The Price of Distrust." In *Trust: Making and Breaking Cooperative Relations*, edited by D. Gambetta, 158–175. New York: Basil Blackwell, 1988.
Gambetta, D. *The Sicilian Mafia: The Business of Private Protection*. Cambridge, MA: Harvard University Press, 1993.
Gambetta, D., and P. Reuter. "Conspiracy Among the Many: The Mafia in Legitimate Industries." In *The Economics of Organized Crime*, edited by G. Fiorentini and S. Peltzman, 116–135. Cambridge: Cambridge University Press, 1995.
Hill, P. B. E. *The Japanese Mafia. Yakuza, Law and the State*. Oxford: Oxford University Press, 2003.
Iwai, H. "Organized Crime in Japan." In *Organized Crime: A Global Perspective*, edited by R. J. Kelly, 203–233. Totowa, NJ: Rowman and Littlefield, 1986.
Lisciandra, M. "Camorra ed estorsioni: una stima del costo per le imprese." In *I costi dell'Illegalità – Camorra ed Estorsioni in Campania*, edited by G. Di Gennaro and A. La Spina, 161–184. Bologna: Il Mulino, 2010.
Moser, C., and C. McIlwaine. *Urban Poor Perceptions of Violence and Exclusion in Colombia. Conflict Prevention and Post-Conflict Reconstruction*. Washington, DC: The International Bank for Reconstruction and Development/The World Bank, 2000.
Mugellini, G., and S. Caneppele. "Le imprese vittime di criminalità in Italia." In *Transcrime Report* 16, edited by G. Mugellini. Trento: Università degli Studi di Trento, 2012.
Ohlemacher, T. "Viewing the Crime Wave from the Inside: Perceived Rates of Extortion Among Restaurateurs in Germany." *European Journal on Criminal Policy and Research* 7 (1999): 43–61.
Paoli, L. *Mafia Brotherhoods: Organized Crime, Italian Style*. New York: Oxford University Press, 2003.
Rodríguez, C. C. "Confidence Intervals from One Observation." *Fundamental Theories of Physics* 70 (1996): 175–182.
Schelling, T. C. "What is the Business of Organized Crime?" *The Journal of Public Law* 20, no. 1 (1971): 71–84.
Sciarrone, R. *Mafie Vecchie, Mafie Nuove. Radicamento Ed Espansione*. Roma: Donzelli, 2009.
Smith, A., and F. Varese. "Payment, Protection and Punishment: The Role of Information and Reputation in the Mafia." *Rationality and Society* 13, no. 3 (2001): 349–393.

SOS-impresa. *Le mani della criminalità sulle imprese – XIII rapporto di Sos-impresa.* Reggio Emilia: Aliberti Editore, 2012.
Sotte, F. "Imprese e non-imprese nell'agricoltura Italiana." *Politica agricola internazionale* 1 (2006): 13–30.
Transcrime. *Progetto PON Sicurezza 2007–2013: Gli investimenti delle mafie. Rapporto Linea 1,* 2013. www.investimentioc.it/files/PON-Gli_investimenti_delle_mafie.pdf
Varese, F. *The Russian Mafia: Private Protection in a New Market Economy.* Oxford: Oxford University Press, 2001.

Counterfeiting, illegal firearms, gambling and waste management: an exploratory estimation of four criminal markets

Francesco Calderoni, Serena Favarin, Lorella Garofalo and Federica Sarno

Joint Research Centre on Transnational Crime, Università Cattolica del Sacro Cuore and Transcrime, Largo Gemelli, Milan, Italy

> This article focuses on four different criminal markets: counterfeiting, illegal firearms trafficking, gambling and waste management. Despite recurrent allegations that these markets have a high mafia presence, there is a lack of reliable estimates of their sizes and the revenues that they generate. Figures in reports and media vary significantly, and the methods used to obtain them are often obscure. This study develops four different estimation methodologies with which to estimate the four criminal markets in Italy at the national and regional levels. Considering that these are the first attempts to estimate these markets, the aim of the article is to stimulate debate on how to improve measurement of the crime proceeds from these criminal markets.

1. Introduction

This article describes exploratory methodologies with which to estimate the size and proceeds of four illegal markets: firearms trafficking, counterfeiting, gambling and waste management. Although these activities are very different from each other, there is a substantial lack of reliable estimates of their size in Italy and, frequently, abroad. The few estimates available often lack details on the main assumptions made and the methodologies used. The results are frequently impossible to verify and unreliable. This is particularly surprising because these illegal markets are frequently associated in the media and public opinion with criminal organisations and mafias. The lack of estimates hinders verification of the economic importance of such markets, as well as the claims made by the media and other sources.

Given the lack of reliable methods and transparently calculated estimates for the four illegal markets, this article produces exploratory estimations of the criminal revenues deriving from them in Italy at both the national and regional levels.[1] The purpose is not only to elaborate the first estimates in Italy relative to the mentioned criminal activities, but also, and more importantly, to stimulate a debate on the difficulties and possibilities of measuring criminal markets. In fact, the article proposes four different approaches suited to the specific features of each market and to the data available. The assumptions, data and methods are described in detail so that both replication and improvement are possible.

In the next section, four subsections review current knowledge and estimates on the markets selected, with especial focus on the Italian situation. Section 3 describes the methodologies used to estimate the illegal revenues from each market and discusses their limitations. Section 4 presents and discusses the results. Section 5 concludes.

2. Background on the four criminal market

2.1. *The illegal firearms market*

The most commonly used definition of firearms trafficking is set out in Article 3 of the United Nations Protocol against the Illicit Manufacturing of and Trafficking in Firearms, Their Parts and Components and Ammunition, where it is defined as 'the import, export, acquisition, sale, delivery, movement or transfer of firearms, their parts and components and ammunition from or across the territory of one State Party to that of another State Party if any one of the States Parties concerned does not authorize it in accordance with the terms of this Protocol or if the firearms are not marked in accordance with article 8 of this Protocol'.

There are two frequently overlapping types of illegal firearms markets: the grey one (wherein illegal traffic is carried out by or for governments) and the black one (wherein trades take place outside state control).[2]

Most weapons circulating in the black market come from the legal market and after diversion[3] enter the illegal circuits.[4] Illicit production (mostly by small-scale craftsmen) represents only a small share of the market.[5] Conversely, authorised dealers, pawn shops, trade fairs and straw purchasers play a major role.[6]

The involvement of criminal organisations usually consists in the provision of transport services and the establishment of contacts with international brokers in importing countries.[7] Firearms are distributed both by highly organised criminal networks operating internationally and by criminal entrepreneurs operating on a small scale and at local level.[8]

There are only a few studies on the illegal firearms market, with rough estimates of its size and proceeds, and no details on the methodologies used.[9] This lack of knowledge also implies that there is no common methodology for its estimation. Nevertheless, a number of international studies estimate the illegal firearms market at between 10% and 20% of the legal market.[10]

2.1.1. *The illegal firearms market in Italy*

Italy is a transit country for illegal weapons being trafficked to Northern Europe, and it is located on the route that starts from the former Yugoslavian countries.[11] An investigative report has revealed that 90% of illegal firearms in Rome originate from the Balkans (especially Croatia).[12] Weapons are carried in hidden compartments in cars, vans and trucks. Other supply channels are thefts from apartments or from security guards. An interview with an informant showed that retail prices on the black market vary according to whether the firearm is new or second-hand (Table 1).[13]

Table 1. Retail prices of some firearms circulating on the black market in Rome (prices in euros).

Model	New	Second-hand
9 × 21 mm semi-automatic gun	1700	700
38 mm gun (special and revolver)	1400	700
Rifle	2000	–
Sub-machine gun	3000	2000

Source: See note 12.

The most recent reports by Italian law enforcement agencies emphasise the involvement of both Italian mafias (Cosa Nostra, 'Ndrangheta, Camorra and Sacra Corona Unita) and foreign criminal organisations (Slav, Russian, Albanian and African) in the trafficking of illegal firearms.[14] The Italian mafias operate not only as traffickers but also as buyers to support their illegal activities.

Only two sources provide rough estimates of the involvement of the mafias in the illegal firearms trade in Italy.[15] Eurispes has estimated the 'Ndrangheta's revenues from illegal firearms at €2.9 billion in 2007.[16] SOS Impresa has estimated the revenues for all the major Italian mafias (Cosa Nostra, 'Ndrangheta, Camorra and Sacra Corona Unita) at €5.8 billion.[17] However, the two sources do not provide any details on the estimation methods. Furthermore, they focus only on the Italian mafias, although it is well known that other criminal actors are involved in the market.[18] These features suggest that these figures should be treated with caution.

2.2. The illegal counterfeit market

According to European Union Regulation 1383 of 2003, goods are counterfeits when they bear 'without authorization a trade mark which is identical to a validly registered trade mark, or which cannot be distinguished in its essential aspects from such trade mark'. Drawing a distinction between the concepts of counterfeit and piracy is essential for investigation of the illegal counterfeit market. Counterfeiting concerns the unauthorised use of an unregistered trademark identical to a registered one. Piracy concerns goods that are unauthorised copies of products protected by intellectual property law.[19]

According to the World Customs Organization, the main destinations of seized counterfeits are the United States, Germany, Mexico, France and Japan.[20] The main sources of counterfeits are in Asia, primarily China, Hong Kong and Taiwan.[21] The most frequently seized products according to their value are clothing (16%), cigarettes (11%), sport shoes (10%) and bags, wallets and purses (9%).[22] The sea route is used in 81% of the shipments intercepted at the EU borders.[23]

The role of organised crime in management of the illegal market for counterfeit products is now widely recognised. Interest in this market began in the 1970s with the enlargement of the sphere of illegal activities controlled by these organisations. The demand for illegal products was becoming increasingly diversified, so that mafias were provided with an opportunity to increase their profits through counterfeiting. The products could be easily distributed via the channels already used for other illicit goods such as drugs and cigarettes. Allegedly, the mafias most involved in the counterfeit market are the Chinese Triads, the Japanese Yakuza, the Neapolitan Camorra and the Russian Mafia.[24]

At the international level, a number of studies have been conducted on counterfeiting, piracy and intellectual property protection.[25] A few of these studies have attempted to quantify counterfeiting, mainly by using seizure data.[26] The value of the international market for counterfeit and pirated products in 2005 was estimated at around $200 billion, excluding domestic production for domestic consumption and the volume of pirated digital products distributed via the internet.[27] In 2007, the OECD updated this estimate to $250 billion.[28] The methodology for the estimation was based on seizure data and questionnaires administered to government agencies, customs, industries or business associations.

2.2.1. The illegal market of counterfeit goods in Italy

The illegal market of counterfeit goods in Italy is characterised by a close interaction between Italian and foreign mafias.[29] The criminal groups most involved in this illegal market are the Chinese Triads, the Japanese Yakuza and the Neapolitan Camorra.[30] According to a recent Europol report, the entry and the subsequent distribution of counterfeit goods in Italy is made possible by close cooperation between Chinese criminal groups and Italian mafias, among which the Camorra and the 'Ndrangheta seem to predominate.[31]

The counterfeits market has been estimated at between 5% and 10% of world trade, with a midpoint estimate of around 7%, which is also in line with the WCO, the OECD and the European Commission estimates.[32] The revenues of the Italian counterfeit market are estimated at €7 to €8 billion. Confesercenti states that, in recent years, the volume of the market has almost doubled; more than 50% of the revenues are attributable to clothing and fashion, followed by music, audio-visual and software piracy.[33] There are no details about the methodology of this study, although it appears to have been based on seizures, surveys and other studies. In 2007, Confcommercio carried out a comprehensive data collection project. It used four focus groups to investigate the reasons for purchasing counterfeit products and conducted a survey of 2000 CATI interviews to shed light on the market for counterfeit clothing, accessories and multimedia. It estimated the market at about €3.3 billion (2 for clothing, 1.2 for fashion accessories and 0.13 for multimedia products).[34] Another study estimated the damage suffered by businesses and government revenues in Italy for 2001 by surveying companies from ten sectors at risk of counterfeiting.[35] The damage to businesses was estimated at around €4.2 billion for 2001, while the revenue losses were around €1.5 billion.[36] A study based on seizures by the Guardia di Finanza has estimated the counterfeits market at between €3 and €5 billion.[37] CENSIS estimated a turnover of €7.1 billion in 2008 (domestic market only). The value comprises revenue losses, including direct and indirect taxes, at €5.3 billion.[38] The findings of most recent CENSIS report are consistent with these previous estimates, even if the domestic market has slightly decreased. In addition, it estimated that the legal production of an equal amount of goods would earn additional tax revenues of €1.7 billion, whereas, on considering the induced production, it would be €4.6 billion, or 1.74% of the total state revenues from the relevant taxes.[39]

2.3. The illegal gambling market

'Gambling' includes different wagering systems such as casino games, bets, lotteries and gaming machines. Gambling is also a legal, though heavily regulated, business. Indeed, the literature focuses mostly on legal gambling and the relations with the commission of crimes.[40] There are no studies assessing the proceeds of illegal gambling at the global or national level.

Illegal gambling often reflects the functioning of the legal market. For example, a study on illegal sports bookmakers showed that the illegal businesses were structured like legal ones and operated in a similar manner according to competitive market dynamics.[41]

Illegal gambling is often associated with organised crime, and it is claimed that criminal organisations have control over or monopolise the sector. Reuter and Rubinstein conducted a study to verify this claim by focusing on lotteries, betting and, to a lesser extent, loan sharking in New York.[42] They demonstrated that the sector was in fact not controlled by organised crime. Liddick criticised their results, arguing that the role of organised crime is not so marginal and that there is no sharp distinction between legal and illegal activities, which are often arranged along a continuum of different levels of illegality.[43]

2.3.1. The illegal gambling in Italy

In Italy, the legal gambling market has expanded in recent decades due to the introduction of new games and services. In 2011 it generated a total of €79.8 billion, of which approximately €7–8 billion consisted of taxes. The Autonomous Administration of State Monopolies (AAMS) is the Italian public agency responsible for management of the gambling sector and for the publication of data.

The growth of legal gambling has stimulated greater attention to its illegal side. This includes counterfeit games (such as 'scratch and win' coupons), the management of unauthorised bet collection points, illegal lotteries, illegal gambling houses and the alteration of gaming machines.[44] Various sources have highlighted the role of mafias in this sector. In a 2011 report, the Parliamentary Antimafia Commission analysed mafia infiltration in legal and illegal gambling,[45] finding that mafias manage bingo, clandestine casinos, gaming machines, illegal betting on football matches and horse racing, including online betting.[46] Bets are managed primarily by unauthorised foreign bookmakers. Fake or irregular lotteries are also common means to launder money.[47] In 2010 at least 30 law enforcement operations focused on gambling and organised crime (with arrests and seizures in a number of Italian cities).[48]

Among the various gambling systems, gaming machines are the most important, yielding 50–60% of the total takings from legal gambling.[49] Currently, there are two main types of gaming machines: new slot machines and video lottery terminals (VLT).[50]

Several sources report the involvement of the Italian mafias and foreign criminal groups in illegal gaming machines. In particular, the three most important Italian mafias (Camorra, 'Ndrangheta and Cosa Nostra) have always shown an interest in control of such devices.[51] The mafias control the installation and management of prohibited gaming machines, including the establishment of front companies, and they also force shops and premises to rent machines.[52] Specifically, the National Antimafia Directorate 2011 report states: 'the mafias, without abandoning their traditional gambling halls and organization of *toto nero*, have concentrated on the most lucrative sectors of gaming, and therefore mainly on the management and alteration of machines'.[53] The organisation of gambling is also a typical activity of Chinese criminal organisations, which often use it as an extortion device, in particular towards Chinese nationals.[54]

The 2007 report by the Commissione Grandi[55] estimated the number of illegal slot machines in 2006 at 200,000.[56] The report showed that two-thirds of the gaming machines were disconnected from the control network and achieved a turnover three times greater than that of devices controlled by the State.[57] The Italian government reported that out of 87,050 inspected machines with cash prizes and 13,250 without cash prizes, 12,717 devices (13%) were irregular.[58] However, since the end of 2010, the introduction of new types of gaming machines has led to a drastic reduction in the number of seizures, which in 2011 fell more than six times compared with 2009.[59]

Despite the alleged importance of the sector, there are no reliable estimates of its actual size. According to a dossier compiled by Libera, the turnover of organised crime from illegal gambling amounts to more than €10 billion (€2.5 billion from football betting).[60] Eurispes estimated the total volume of illegal gambling at around €23 billion, equalling 13.1% of the entire turnover of the illegal economy.[61] Sos Impresa gauged the revenues from illegal gambling at more than €4 billion (€3.6 billion directly managed by mafias).[62] The differences among these estimates show that the size of the Italian illegal gambling market is in fact still unknown. Furthermore, the above-mentioned estimates do not give any clear information on the methodology used, so that it is impossible to verify their reliability and accuracy.

2.4. The illegal waste market

Illegal activities related to the waste market are commonly defined as 'any movement of waste which is not in accordance with environmental regulations'.[63] They include the illegal management (i.e. storage, transfer or disposal) of waste, as well as its illegal trafficking.[64] At the same time, these activities may occur both domestically and internationally.[65] The illegal waste market is particularly difficult to measure because, like its legal counterpart, it is characterised by different types of waste and different phases in the management cycle.

The illegal management and the illegal trafficking of waste are associated with several factors. The introduction of stricter regulations and the resulting increase in prices have been emphasised by many scholars,[66] institutions[67] and empirical studies.[68] The demand for illegal waste management and disposal services almost always comes from legitimate businesses.[69] Waste producers seek cheap services to minimise costs and maximise revenues, and the illegal market is able to provide these services.[70] Some estimates have reported that, at the end of the 1980s, the average disposal cost of one ton of hazardous waste was between $100 and $2000 in an OECD country and between $2.5 and $50 in Africa.[71] More recently, Italian sources have suggested that prices in the illegal market are about one-fifth of those charged in the legal market.[72] According to a study from the Netherlands, illegal prices would range between one-third and one-fourth of the legal ones.[73]

This situation has resulted in the waste being transported from industrialised countries for illegal dumping in developing countries. Criminal groups operating the illegal waste trafficking seem to have relatively simple structures. Institutional sources and law enforcement agencies describe small groups of five to ten people, who often have ethnic links with the destination countries.[74] At the same time, it seems that the sector has attracted the growing interest of organised crime groups, owing to the opportunity to make high profits at low risks.[75] However, the actual involvement of traditional organised crime groups in the illegal trafficking of waste is still a matter of debate.[76]

In general, no study has reliably estimated the size of the illegal waste market. Most of the available data refer to the legal movements of waste.[77] Information on the illegal waste market comes primarily from seizures and surveillance efforts, incidents and other forms of crime reporting. However, they are not representative of the actual size of the illegal market and are often of poor quality.[78]

2.4.1. The illegal waste management in Italy

Italy is a rather specific case because of the significant participation of the Italian mafias in the waste market.[79] In particular, the Camorra seems to be directly involved in illegal waste activities. Cosa Nostra and the 'Ndrangheta tend to use their intimidatory power and collusion with public officials to infiltrate the legal market.[80] However, it would be a mistake to consider the illicit waste market in Italy as monopolised by the mafias. Individuals and companies not related with traditional mafias are equally involved in the illegal management and trafficking of waste.[81] In many cases they are 'white collar criminals', in particular entrepreneurs and brokers, but also chemists, engineers and analysts.[82] These actors constitute what the Italian Antimafia Directorate (DNA) has recently called the 'elite of illegal waste trafficking'.[83] Stable partnerships between this 'elite' and the traditional mafias may, or may not, be established. Moreover, the illegal waste market has now extended nationwide and can no longer be considered a localised problem limited to the regions of origin of the mafias.[84]

Owing to these specificities, Italy has become quite sensitive to the issue of 'illegal waste' compared with other European countries.[85] Since 2005, a specific section of the DNA reports has focused on criminal activities related to the illegal management and trafficking of waste. Information on the 'illegal waste cycle' is periodically provided also by the environmental organisation Legambiente as part of its annual report 'Ecomafia'. Despite this attention, reliable estimates of the actual scale of the Italian illegal waste market do not exist. In 2011, Legambiente estimated the turnover from the illegal market of special waste at €3.1 billion.[86] However, this figure should be interpreted with caution since it was calculated on the basis of the price of legal of waste management and disposal services and may thus have been overestimated.[87] In fact, the illegal market can guarantee significant savings compared with the legal one.

3. Methodologies

Owing to the absence of reliable methodologies for the estimation of the four criminal markets, the study reported in what follows developed different solutions for each of them.

3.1. Estimating the revenues from the illegal firearms market

The study calculated the revenues of the illegal firearms market using a supply-based and demand-based approach. Depending on the data available, estimates were calculated for 2010 at both the national and regional levels.

The supply-based approach assumed that firearms seized/confiscated corresponded to 8% of the total market.[88] Owing to the lack of figures on the firearms market, the assumption was based on the incidence of seizures in the volume of the drug market (between 8% and 10%) and of the illicit tobacco market (10% in 2009, 8% in 2010 and 5% in 2011).[89] The national illegal revenues were calculated as follows:

$$\text{Illegal revenues Supply} = \frac{\text{No. of firearms seized/confiscated} \cdot 100}{8} \cdot €1579$$

As regards demand, minimum and maximum values were produced. The demand-based approach assumed the illegal firearms market to be 10% or 20% of the legal market. This amount was determined by the value of exports (foreign demand), imports and the turnover generated by the national market (domestic demand).[90] Estimation was based on the following formulas:

$$\text{Illegal revenues Demand min} = (\text{Export} + \text{Import} + \text{Turnover Italian market}) \cdot 0.1$$

$$\text{Illegal revenues Demand max} = (\text{Export} + \text{Import} + \text{Turnover Italian market}) \cdot 0.2$$

National estimates were divided among the 20 Italian regions in proportion to their resident populations, according to the following formulas[91]:

$$\text{Illegal revenues Supply}_{reg} = \frac{\text{Illegal revenues Supply}_{nat} \cdot \text{Population}_{reg}}{\text{Population}_{nat}}$$

$$\text{Illegal revenues Demand min}_{reg} = \frac{\text{Illegal revenues Demand min}_{nat} \cdot \text{Population}_{reg}}{\text{Population}_{nat}}$$

$$\text{Illegal revenues Demand max}_{reg} = \frac{\text{Illegal revenues Demand max}_{nat} \cdot \text{Population}_{reg}}{\text{Population}_{nat}}$$

The regional revenues thus obtained were then adjusted to take account of the different incidence of the illegal market within each region.[92] For this purpose, the regional illicit revenues were multiplied by the ratio between the rates of firearms seized/confiscated per 100,000 inhabitants at regional and national levels. Estimates were calculated as follows[93]:

$$\frac{\text{Revenues}}{\text{adj\_Supply}_{reg}} = \text{Illegal revenues Supply}_{reg} \cdot \left(\frac{\text{Rate firearms seiz/conf per 100,000 inhab}_{reg}}{\text{Rate firearms seiz/conf per 100,000 inhab}_{nat}} \right)$$

$$\frac{\text{Revenues}}{\text{adj\_Demand}_{reg}} = \text{Illegal revenues Demand}_{reg} \cdot \left(\frac{\text{Rate firearms seiz/conf per 100,000 inhab}_{reg}}{\text{Rate firearms seiz/conf per 100,000 inhab}_{nat}} \right)$$

3.2. Estimating the revenues from the illegal counterfeit market

In general, studies estimating the counterfeit goods market have only calculated revenues based on the goods seized, or they have produced figures without specifying the methodology used. Given the lack of an established methodology in the literature, this study estimates the revenues of the illegal counterfeiting market by taking into account the turnover of companies in the sectors most at risk of counterfeiting and the workforce in those sectors. Estimates are for year 2008 due to the unavailability of more recent data.[94]

The first step was identification of the economic sectors most at risk of counterfeiting in Italy and calculation of their legal annual turnovers. The analysis identified the categories of goods most at risk among those listed in the IPERICO database because they are more likely to be seized. IPERICO collects information on counterfeited goods by commodity macro-categories seized by the Italian law enforcement agencies. Each commodity macro-category listed in the IPERICO database was associated with an ATECO economic sector of the retail market in order to calculate the turnovers of the companies belonging to this economic sector and to estimate the total legal turnover of each sector at national level.[95] Table 2 shows the various macro-categories listed in the IPERICO database, and the ATECO economic sectors that were connected to those categories to calculate the turnover of each sector in 2008.[96] This calculation was performed for all the commodity macro-categories s:

$$\text{Legal Market}_s = \sum \text{Company turnover} \in s$$

Table 2. IPERICO product groups and corresponding ATECO economic sectors.

Product group	Corresponding ATECO sector
Clothing	4771: retail sale of clothing in specialised shops
Accessories of clothing	4772: retail sale of footwear and leather items in specialised shops
Footwear	4782: retail street sale of textiles, clothing and footwear
Electrical equipment	4754: retail sale of electrical equipment in specialised shops
IT equipment	4741: retail sale of computers, peripheral devices, software and office equipment in specialised shops
CD, DVD, tape	4763: retail sale of music and video recordings in specialised shops
Toys	4765: retail sale of toys in specialised shops
Glasses	32504: production of ophthalmic lenses
	32505: production of frames of different types; mass-produced frames of ordinary glasses
Watches and jewels	4777: retail sale of watches and jewels in specialised shops
Perfumes and cosmetics	4775: retail sale of cosmetics, perfumes and herbalist items in specialised shops

The second step consisted in calculating 5% and 10% of the total legal turnover of each sector. Indeed, according to the literature, the counterfeit market has a global value of between 5% and 10% of the total trade. These figures enabled calculation of the minimum and maximum estimates of the total illegal revenues for each commodity macro-category at national level, as the following formulas summarise:

$$\text{Illegal Market max}_s = 0.1 \cdot \text{Legal Market}_s$$

$$\text{Illegal Market min}_s = 0.05 \cdot \text{Legal Market}_s$$

In the third step, the national estimates by commodity macro-category were redistributed among the 20 Italian regions using the number of employees and considering each ATECO economic sector at regional level in 2007. It was assumed that the regions with the highest number of employees also have larger markets, both legal and illegal. Calculation was made of the percentage of the number of employees in each region by commodity macro-category on the total number of employees by category at national level in order to identify which regions have the highest and which the lowest number of employees. The different percentages were then multiplied by the total value of the illegal national market, first according to the lowest estimate of 5% and then according to the maximum estimate of 10%, as shown by the following formulas:

$$\text{Illegal Market max}_{s, reg} = \frac{\text{No. employees}_{s, reg}}{\text{No. employees}_{s, nat}} \cdot \text{Illegal Market max}_s$$

$$\text{Illegal Market min}_{s, reg} = \frac{\text{No. employees}_{s, reg}}{\text{No. employees}_{s, nat}} \cdot \text{Illegal Market min}_s$$

3.3. *Estimating the revenues from the illegal gambling market*

Considering the variety of illegal gambling activities and the lack of data on them, the study opted to focus exclusively on illegal gaming machines. This decision appeared acceptable in various respects. First, in 2011 gaming machines generated a turnover of €44.8 billion, which was more than 56% of the total turnover from legal gambling (€79.8 billion). Lotteries followed at a distance, with €10.1 billion.[97] Second, the DNA has recently stressed the crucial role of revenues from new slot machines and VLT machines for criminal organisations, suggesting that this may become the largest portion of the illicit gambling market.[98] Finally, data on gaming machines are periodically published by AAMS. Given that the gambling supply is constantly changing, it was considered appropriate to limit the estimate to 2011, the most recent year for which data were complete. The choice of that year also made it possible to estimate the illicit market after the introduction of the new gaming machines: 2011 was the first year in which, in addition to new slot machines, also VLT machines were introduced.

Estimation of the revenues from illegal gambling machines in 2011 moved through various stages. First calculated were the regional takings for new slot machines and VLTs. The national legal takings (total cash collected) from gaming machines of each type were distributed among the 20 Italian regions according to the ratio between the total regional takings and the total national takings[99]:

$$\text{Takings new slots}_{reg} = \frac{\text{Takings new slots}_{nat} \cdot \text{Total takings}_{reg}}{\text{Total Takings}_{nat}}$$

$$\text{Takings VLTs}_{reg} = \frac{\text{Takings VLTs}_{nat} \cdot \text{Total takings}_{reg}}{\text{Total Takings}_{nat}}$$

Second, the study calculated the infringement rate. This was given by the ratio between the number of not merely formal infringements and the number of machines inspected.[100]

$$\text{Infringement rate}_{reg} = \frac{\text{not merely formal infringements}_{reg}}{\text{inspected machines}_{reg}}$$

Third, the product of the infringement rate and the regional takings provided the regional illicit takings.[101] The turnover was calculated in a differentiated way for new slot machines and VLTs.

$$\text{Illegal Takings new slots}_{reg} = \text{Infringement rate}_{reg} \cdot \text{Takings new slots}_{reg}$$

$$\text{Illegal Takings VLTs}_{reg} = \text{Infringement rate}_{reg} \cdot \text{Takings VLTs}_{reg}$$

Fourth, the illegal revenues were derived from illegal takings. This derivation was based on a minimum and maximum hypothesis on the subdivision of the takings. In the legal market, takings from gaming machines are distributed as follows: payouts are determined by law (75% of takings for new slot machines and 85% for VLTs); 0.8% equal to the concession fee; state taxation (between 4% and 13% of takings); the rest is divided among distributors, managers, and retailers on the basis of private contracts.[102] The minimum estimate hypothesised that illegal machines may evade only part of the taxation and/or that a part of the takings would be distributed among retailers and distributors. Accordingly, it assumed that revenues amount to 20% for new slot machines and 10% for VLTs. The maximum estimate assumed that illegal machines pay no taxes, no fees to retailers and distributors, and even have reduced payout rates (not excessively, since it may inhibit the players and be suspicious). In this case, revenues may be as high as 30% of the illegal takings for new slots and 20% for VLTs.

$$\text{Illegal Revenues new slots max}_{reg} = 0.3 \cdot \text{Illegal Takings new slots}_{reg}$$

$$\text{Illegal Revenues new slots min}_{reg} = 0.2 \cdot \text{Illegal Takings new slots}_{reg}$$

$$\text{Illegal Revenues VLTs max}_{reg} = 0.2 \cdot \text{Illegal Takings VLTs}_{reg}$$

$$\text{Illegal Revenues VLTs min}_{reg} = 0.1 \cdot \text{Illegal Takings VLTs}_{reg}$$

The sum of max/min revenues from both types of machines yielded the maximum and minimum revenues from the illegal gaming machines market.

$$\text{Total Ill Rev max}_{reg} = \text{Ill Rev new slots max}_{reg} + \text{Ill Rev VLTs max}_{reg}$$

$$\text{Total Ill Rev min}_{reg} = \text{Ill Rev new slots min}_{reg} + \text{Ill Rev VLTs min}_{reg}$$

3.4. *Estimating the revenues from the illegal special waste market*[103]

The methodology used to estimate the illegal waste market drew in part on the approach developed by Legambiente, and it focused on the difference between legal waste production and management, assuming that this difference may be imputable to the illegal market. The estimation was limited to special waste and did not consider municipal waste, mostly entrusted to public companies, but also frequently infiltrated by the mafias (e.g. the infamous waste emergencies in Naples and Palermo).[104] This methodological choice was made for various reasons. First, in 2010 (last available year) special waste represented more than 80% of the total waste produced in Italy. Municipal waste, by contrast, accounted for less than 20%.[105] Second, the illegal management of special waste seems to be particularly attractive to criminal operators since it guarantees higher profits than the municipal waste.[106] Finally, data on the production and management of special waste are periodically released by the Italian Institute for Environment Protection and Research (ISPRA).[107]

The study estimated the volume and revenues of the illegal market of special waste for the period 2007–2010 (mean of the four years). The estimates were performed at both the national and regional levels, and they distinguished between hazardous and non-hazardous waste. The estimation consisted of various steps.

First calculated was the legal management at regional level, i.e. the amount of special waste managed by legitimate facilities in each region (LM_{reg}). The legal management was calculated as the sum of the special waste subject to final operations of recovery and disposal and the stock. The stock was the difference between stored waste in a given year and stored waste in the previous year[108]:

$$LM_{reg_t} = \text{Final Manag}_{reg_t} + \text{Stock}_{reg_t}$$

$$\text{Stock}_{reg_t} = \text{Stored waste}_{reg_t} - \text{Stored waste}_{reg_{t-1}}$$

Second, the legal management was adjusted on the basis of the amount of waste produced in each region (LMadj$_{reg}$.).[109] Two different coefficients were used depending on the type of waste (hazardous/non-hazardous). For non-hazardous waste, the geographical macro-area (Northern, Central and Southern Italy) was considered.[110] With regard to hazardous waste, the national figure was used.[111]

$$\text{LMadj(Non-haz)}_{reg} = \text{Legal Prod}_{reg} \cdot \frac{\text{LM}_{macro\text{-}area}}{\text{Legal Prod}_{macro-area}}$$

$$\text{LMadj (Haz)}_{reg} = \text{Legal Prod}_{reg} \cdot \frac{\text{LM}_{nat}}{\text{Legal Prod}_{nat}}$$

The volume of the illegal market (IM$_{reg}$) was then estimated as the difference between legal production and legal management adjusted.

$$\text{IM(Non-haz)}_{reg} = \text{Legal Prod}_{reg} - \text{LMadj (Non-haz)}_{reg}$$

$$\text{IM(Haz)}_{reg} = \text{Legal Prod}_{reg} - \text{LMadj(Haz)}_{reg}$$

Fourth, multiplying the illegal market by the average price of the legal services of waste management yielded the revenues of the illegal market at legal prices (Rev LPr) for both types of waste (hazardous/non-hazardous).[112]

$$\text{Rev LPr(Non-haz)}_{reg} = \text{IM(Non-haz)}_{reg} \cdot €90.5$$

$$\text{Rev LPr(Haz)}_{reg} = \text{IM(Haz)}_{reg} \cdot €305$$

The sum of the two yielded the revenues of the illegal special waste market at legal prices.

$$\text{Rev LPr TOT}_{reg} = \text{Rev LPr(Non-haz)}_{reg} + \text{Rev LPr(Haz)}_{reg}$$

However, the literature suggests that the illegal market can guarantee significant savings. In particular, it seems that prices in the illegal market are between one-third and one-fifth of the legal ones. The revenues of the illegal market at legal prices were therefore divided by 3 (maximum value) and by 5 (minimum value) to calculate the revenues of the illegal waste market (Rev IM).

$$\text{Rev IM max}_{reg} = \frac{\text{Rev LPr TOT}_{reg}}{3}$$

$$\text{Rev IM min}_{reg} = \frac{\text{Rev LPr TOT}_{reg}}{5}$$

The maximum and minimum estimates were calculated for non-hazardous waste, hazardous waste and the total.

3.5. *Limitations*

Given the lack of previous estimations in the literature, the estimates of the four illegal markets should be considered as exploratory and, as such, treated with particular caution. Indeed, they have a number of limitations.

First, owing to the lack of previous research, in some cases it was necessary to adopt assumptions and hypotheses without adequate empirical bases.[113]

Data availability and reliability was a second major issue. The retrieval, interpretation and analysis of data generated numerous difficulties and problems. Available data were scarce, and it is for this reason that some estimates date back to 2010 (firearms), 2008 (counterfeiting) and 2007–2010 (waste).

Third, the scarcity of data sometimes required the use of data on seizures and confiscations. These sources are particularly problematic since they may frequently represent proxies for law enforcement activity/efficiency rather than for the illegal activities. Whenever possible, inspection was made of the distribution of such data to verify whether they were excessively biased towards measurement of law enforcement performance. For example, data on seized counterfeit goods were excluded from the analysis because they were more representative of the trend in controls than in counterfeiting itself.

For the above reasons, estimation of the revenues from the four illegal markets was conducted with particular caution, and it always included a minimum and maximum estimate.

Overall, these considerations suggest that the estimates should be treated as first attempts to measure a particularly obscure set of criminal activities. Future estimations will have to refine the methodologies and address the above-mentioned limitations in order to gain better understanding of these illegal markets and provide more precise figures. Data availability and reliability will probably be the greatest challenge. Undoubtedly, new data are greatly needed to raise the accuracy of the estimations to the levels of those on other illegal activities.

4. Results and discussion

The estimated revenues from the illegal firearms market ranged between €46 million and €141 million in 2010 (Table 3). The minimum estimate is the result of the supply-based approach, while the demand-based approach provided higher values (between €70 and €141 million, see also Table A1). In both cases, these figures are significantly lower than the estimates provided by previous studies, which have assessed the revenues of the illegal firearms market at between €2.9 and €5.8 billion (see Section 1.1). This remarkable discrepancy is difficult to explain in the absence of any information concerning the sources, methodologies and data used for the previous estimations. These figures appear to grossly overestimate the Italian illicit firearms market. As already mentioned, the total turnover of Italian firearms production (including ammunitions) was approximately €468 million in 2010, of which only €115 million came from the domestic market. If correct, the estimations from the above-mentioned sources would make the illegal market approximately 25–50 times larger than the legal one. This consideration suggests that the previous sources may have merely reported such figures with no verification of their reliability.

As regards the regional figures, the highest values are recorded among the most populated regions, which are also characterised by remarkable ratios of firearms seizures and confiscations (Figure 1). This is due to the methodological approach adopted for the estimation, which was based on the assumption that the illicit market is larger where there

Table 3. Minimum and maximum estimates of the revenues of the markets for illegal firearms (year 2010), counterfeit goods (year 2008), gaming machines (year 2011) and special waste (years 2007–2010) (million €).

	Firearms		Counterfeiting		Gambling		Waste	
	Min	Max	Min	Max	Min	Max	Min	Max
Abruzzo	1.02	2.51	65.9	131.9	2.00	3.20	5.83	9.72
Basilicata	0.72	1.99	22.3	44.5	6.62	10.58	2.65	4.41
Calabria	2.58	7.78	79.7	159.4	21.15	33.83	4.65	7.76
Campania	5.89	16.26	283.6	567.2	47.07	75.28	17.26	28.77
Emilia-Romagna	2.68	6.81	248.5	497.1	4.41	7.06	22.12	36.87
Friuli-V.G.	1.00	2.60	80.9	161.9	6.57	10.50	7.97	13.29
Lazio	2.32	13.03	289.5	579.1	22.02	35.22	25.17	41.95
Liguria	2.05	5.31	82.5	165.1	0.38	0.60	6.51	10.84
Lombardy	3.57	11.01	514.3	1028.6	12.78	20.44	37.86	63.10
Marche	1.05	3.00	68.6	137.1	2.13	3.41	12.42	20.71
Molise	0.35	0.93	12.6	25.1	0.50	0.80	2.32	3.87
Piedmont	2.41	7.67	197.2	394.5	44.85	71.72	17.13	28.54
Apulia	4.16	15.85	171.2	342.4	40.60	64.92	24.95	41.58
Sardinia	1.04	3.14	67.3	134.6	39.75	63.57	11.27	18.78
Sicily	4.17	10.75	205.0	410.1	64.16	102.61	21.72	36.20
Tuscany	4.36	12.11	189.2	378.4	6.46	10.32	37.92	63.19
Trentino-A.A.	0.24	1.79	52.9	105.9	0.3	0.4	8.28	13.80
Umbria	1.62	4.77	40.3	80.7	1.44	2.30	8.40	14.00
Valle d'Aosta	0.03	0.12	5.3	10.7	1.20	1.92	0.53	0.88
Veneto	4.78	13.46	350.5	700.9	2.60	4.16	29.05	48.42
Italy	46.07	140.87	3027.5	6055.0	326.69	522.44	304.01	506.68

Source: Authors' elaboration.

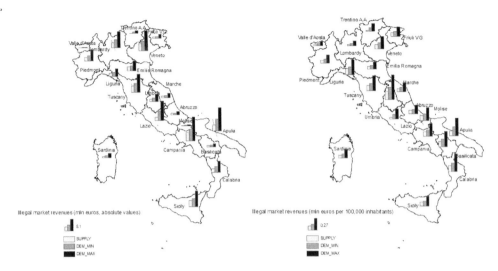

Figure 1. Estimates of the revenues from the illegal firearms market by region (million €). Year 2010. Absolute values and rate per 100,000 inhabitants.

Source: Authors' elaboration.

are more inhabitants and more firearms seized/confiscated. This may have determined only a rough representation of the actual revenues of the illegal firearms market across the Italian regions. Future studies should seek to improve this representation, possibly by gathering better empirical evidence on the concentration of the illicit firearms trade at the regional level. As already argued (see Section 2.5), data availability and reliability will raise the greatest challenges.

The revenues of the market of counterfeit goods range between €3028 million (minimum) and €6055 million (maximum) in 2008 (Table 3). Overall, the figures are broadly comparable with previous estimates. The results are lower than the assessments by Confesercenti and CENSIS (€7000–€8000 million), whereas they are almost in line with those of a study by the Guardia di Finanza, which evaluated the counterfeit market at between €3000 and €5000 million. It is difficult to explain the differences among these estimates owing to the lack of detailed information on the methodologies used by the previous studies. Despite these differences, in accordance with the findings in the literature, the sector yielding the highest illicit revenues is clothing, accessories and footwear, with a minimum estimate of €1854 million and a maximum estimate of € 3708 million (Table A1).

The regional figures seem to confirm that the illegal counterfeit market in Italy is widespread across the country. Taking the absolute values into account, the regions recording the highest estimates are Lombardy, Veneto, Campania and Lazio, whereas according to the rate per 100,000 inhabitants the phenomenon is widespread across the entire country (Figure 2). In part, these results may be biased by the assumptions made for the estimation procedure. The regional figures are based on the number of employees in each sector and region, assuming that regions with the highest number of employees in one sector may also have a more prosperous and larger market in that sector, both legal and illegal. Further research should improve the distribution of the illicit revenues across regions, with better identification of the variables that can affect the counterfeit market at the local level.

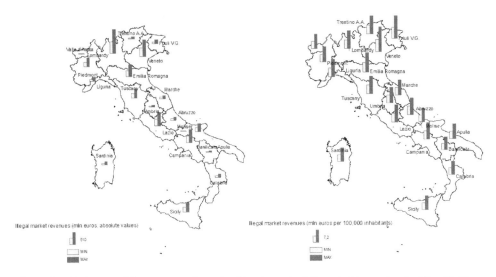

Figure 2. Estimates of the revenues from the illegal counterfeit market by region (million €). Year 2008. Absolute values and rate per 100,000 inhabitants.
Source: Authors' elaboration.

The estimated revenues from illegal gambling machines ranged between €326 and €522 million in 2011 (Table 3). The figures are remarkably below the alleged revenues reported by other sources, which covered the entire illegal gambling sector (see Section 1.3). The difference may be due to a number of factors. 2011 was the first year in which a significant number of VLT machines were operational. These devices had better control systems and were more difficult to tamper with. Analysis of controls and seizures suggests that irregularities have decreased with VLTs, and the estimated illegal revenues may have been higher in previous years. Moreover, the limited information on the methodology used by other sources suggests that these may have been based mostly on heterogeneous law enforcement and institutional material. Finally, the present study has only focused on a specific type of illegal gambling, excluding other potentially profitable subsectors (e.g. illegal football betting).

In regard to the regional distribution, Southern regions, Piedmont and Valle d'Aosta have the highest rates, due to higher violations/controls ratios (Figure 3). For some traditional mafia regions, this may be due to the presence of organised crime. The figure is more surprising in the case of Sardinia, which ranks first for illegal revenues (with a remarkably high violations/controls ratio, second only to Sicily). Further analyses should focus on these regions in order to identify and verify possible causes of the higher prevalence of illegal gambling.

The estimated national revenues from the illegal market of special waste range between €304 and €507 million (Table 3). The bulk of these revenues (between €279 and €466 million) is attributable to non-hazardous waste. Conversely, hazardous waste generated illegal revenues amounting to between €25 and €41 million (see Table A1). This disproportion reflects the methodological approach adopted for the estimation, which focused on the difference between legal waste production and management. Non-hazardous waste represented much the largest amount (around 92%) of the

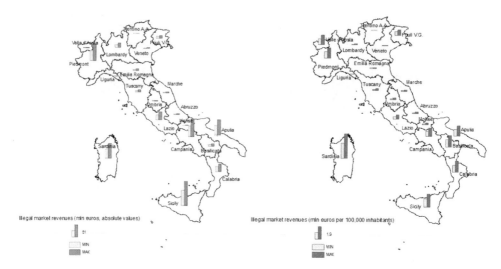

Figure 3. Estimates of the revenues from illegal gaming machines by region (million €). Year 2011. Absolute values and rate per 100,000 inhabitants.

Source: Authors' elaboration.

special waste produced in Italy in the time period considered. Accordingly, the corresponding revenues are higher than those from hazardous waste.

The national figures are significantly lower than the estimates provided by previous studies (see Section 1.4). This discrepancy may be due to the fact that the previous estimates were based on legal prices of waste management and disposal. However, these prices are generally higher than those charged by the illegal market. At the same time, the illegal management and disposal of waste do not incur the same operating expenses as their legal counterparts.[114] It can therefore be argued that large part of the estimated revenues from the illegal waste market result in direct profits for the illegal actors. Unfortunately, the actual scale of these profits is difficult to estimate owing to the lack of reliable data.

The regional figures seem to confirm that the illegal waste market in Italy has extended nationwide (Figure 4). However, the estimation process 'levelled out' the regional values on the basis of those in the macro-area or at national level, depending on the type of waste (see Section 2.4). This may have resulted in a poor representation of the actual levels of the illegal waste market across the Italian regions. Future research should address the limitations of the present study in order to provide better understanding of the regional distribution of illegal waste activities, as well as a first evaluation of the profits associated with this market. Also for this illicit market, the greatest challenges will probably be data availability and reliability.

5. Conclusions

This article has explored the possibilities of estimating four illegal markets, with the focus on Italy. Considering the lack of previous reliable assessments on any of these four criminal activities, this study should be treated as exploratory. Its goal has been to stimulate debate, at the international and national levels, on the frequently overestimated

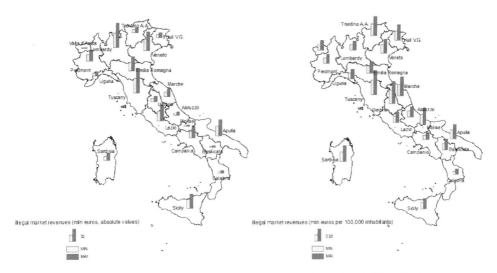

Figure 4. Estimates of the revenues from illegal waste market by region (million €). Average years 2007–2010. Absolute values and rate per 100,000 inhabitants.
Source: Authors' elaboration.

figures recurrently publicised by the media, and on the various ways to produce more reliable estimations.

Despite the clear differences among the four markets analysed in this study, there are common features in regard to estimation of their revenues. First, there is a remarkable absence of reliable data. The availability of seizure data does not solve the problem since these data are not optimal for the measurement of criminal activities across different regions. They may depend more on the performance of, or the resources available to, the law enforcement agencies, or on the entry points of illicit products. For this reason, the estimations excluded seizures and confiscations when estimating the total revenues for all four activities, except for the supply-based approach in the illicit firearms market. In some cases, seizures were used to distribute the criminal revenues at the regional level. Besides seizure data, there is a lack of yearly available and reliable data enabling measurement of the size of the illicit markets, with the possible exception of the tobacco industry's empty pack surveys. Improvement of data collection is crucial for better and replicable estimates of the criminal markets. It is a necessary condition for monitoring their trends and measuring the efficiency of preventive and repressive policies.

Second, despite the dearth of data, a number of different estimates of the four markets circulate in official reports and in the media. All these assessments lack details about the methodologies and the data used. This makes it very difficult to verify and compare these figures with the results of new studies. Furthermore, it raises suspicions as to their reliability, especially when the figures clearly overestimate the proceeds of these crimes. These figures are interesting examples of mythical numbers (i.e. overestimations of a social phenomenon with no empirical support, gaining authority due to repetition).[115] In the criminal markets of this study, these numbers may be created not only by public agencies (e.g. law enforcement agencies seeking additional resources), but also by the legal industries (e.g. to get increased police attention and inflate the value of their brand). Particularly in the case of firearms and waste, the previous figures appear to be gross over-calculations of the sizes of the markets. For example, the alleged yearly revenues from illicit firearms trafficking would be between 25 and 50 times the national demand for firearms and ammunition from the legitimate market. This trend in the diffusion of unreliable estimates is problematic because it contributes to the dissemination of stereotypes on the mafias. Like the lack of information, also the diffusion of wrong figures may jeopardise public and private action against the mafias and impair the allocation of law enforcement resources.

In conclusion, while not claiming to provide definitive estimates, this study has adopted carefully described and replicable methodologies with which to measure the revenues of the illicit markets for firearms, counterfeits, gaming machines and special waste. This is a necessary step towards improving knowledge on these frequently debated, but rarely measured, criminal activities.

Notes

1. Preliminary versions of the methodologies presented in this article were developed in a research project awarded by the Italian Ministry of Interior to Transcrime (*Joint Research Centre on Transnational Crime* of Università Cattolica del Sacro Cuore of Milan and Università di Trento). See Transcrime, *Progetto PON Sicurezza 2007–2013*.
2. Marsh, "Two Sides of the Same Coin?"; ISPAC, *Trafficking*. Considered here is only the black market. The distinction depends on four factors: the status of the buyer, the status of the seller, the status of the weapon and the status of the transaction. See Ruggiero, "Criminals and Service Providers," 32–3; and Cukier, *Illicit Trade in Small Arms*, 1.
3. 'Diversion' is the transfer of arms from the legal market to the illegal one. Stohl, "Fighting the Illicit Trafficking," 61.
4. Spapens, "Trafficking in Illicit Firearms."
5. Cukier, *Illicit Trade in Small Arms*.
6. 'Straw purchasers' are individuals eligible to buy firearms. They buy weapons on behalf of third parties (usually representatives of criminals or intermediaries) in return for money. See Kleck, "BATF Gun Trace Data and the Role"; Koper, *Crime Gun Risk Factors*; GAO, *Firearms Trafficking*; UNODC, *Globalization of Crime*; and Feinstein, Schumer, and Whitehouse, *Halting U.S Firearms Trafficking*.
7. Ruggiero, "Criminals and Service Providers," 33.
8. Rainelli, "Le Armi Leggere Nel Mondo," 9.
9. For instance, the UN Office on Drugs and Crime estimates that the global value of the illegal firearms market is from $170 million to $320 million annually, UNODC, *Globalization of Crime*. As regards the illegal traffic from the United States to Mexico, the UNODC evaluates it at around 20,000 pieces a year for a value of $20 million, UNODC, *Globalization of Crime*. There are around 1.6 million weapons in Central America, of which 500,000 are legally registered (UNODC 2007). This figure is substantially confirmed by the Small Arms Survey report of 2002, according to which there are about 800,000 unregistered weapons in the region. See Small Arms Survey, Small Arms Survey 2002. In Africa, it is estimated that illegal weapons amount to about 2 million, for a value in the destination countries of $167 million, UNODC, *Transnational Trafficking and the Rule of Law*. The firearms trade from Eastern European countries to the rest of the world has an annual volume of about 40,000 Kalashnikovs, for a value of US$33 million, UNODC, *Globalization of Crime*.
10. Marsh, "Two Sides of the Same Coin?," 220; Cukier, *Illicit Trade in Small Arms*, 3; and UNODC, *Globalization of Crime*, 129.
11. Sagramoso, *Proliferation of Illegal Small Arms and Light Weapons*.
12. Angeli, "Pistole, Kalashnikov, Persino Un Missile Grandi Affari Al Supermarket Dei 'Ferri'."
13. Ibid.
14. DIA, *Relazione del Ministro dell'Interno al Parlamentosull'attività svolta e sui risultati conseguiti dalla Direzione Investigativa Antimafia: Secondo semestre 2011;* and DNA, *Relazione annuale 2011*.
15. Eurispes, *'Ndrangheta holding*; and SOS Impresa, *Le mani della criminalità sulle imprese*, 2012.
16. Eurispes, *'Ndrangheta holding*.

17. This estimate is based on data contained in the 2008 report of the Parliamentary Anti-Mafia Commission. SOS Impresa, *Le mani della criminalità sulle imprese*.
18. DNA, *Relazione annuale 2011*; DNA, *Relazione annuale 2010*; DIA, *Relazione del Ministro dell'Interno al Parlamento sull'attività svolta e sui risultati conseguiti dalla Direzione Investigativa Antimafia: Secondo semestre 2011*; and DNA, *Relazione del Ministro dell'Interno al Parlamento sull'attività svolta e sui risultati conseguiti dalla Direzione Investigativa Antimafia: Secondo semestre 2010*.
19. The TRIPs Agreement, created by the World Trade Organization (WTO), in a note to article 51 defines the concept of counterfeiting in terms of counterfeit trademark goods, and piracy in those of pirated copyright goods. Numerous studies use this distinction because, at international level, the concepts of counterfeiting and piracy are often considered as connected with the issue of infringement of intellectual property rights. Among them: Transcrime, *Anti-Brand Counterfeiting in the EU*; OECD, *Economic Impact of Counterfeiting and Piracy*; and UNICRI, *Contraffazione*.
20. WCO, *Customs and IPR Report 2010*.
21. China has acquired a leading role in the production of counterfeits in the past 10 years. According to the World Customs Organization, 58% of seized shipments originate from China, 19% from Taiwan, followed by India and the United Arab Emirates (Ibid.). These figures are confirmed by the EU, which identifies China as the main country of origin of counterfeited goods. European Commission, *Report on EU Customs Enforcement*.
22. European Commission, *Report on EU Customs Enforcement*.
23. Ibid.
24. UNICRI, *Contraffazione*.
25. Transcrime, *Anti-Brand Counterfeiting in the EU*; UNODC, *Globalization of Crime*; and UNICRI, *Contraffazione*.
26. Frontier Economics, *Estimating the Global Economic and Social Impacts*; WCO, *Customs and IPR Report 2010*; European Commission, *Report on EU Customs Enforcement*; OECD, "Magnitude of Conuterfeiting and Piracy"; and OECD, *Economic Impact of Counterfeiting and Piracy*.
27. OECD, *Economic Impact of Counterfeiting and Piracy*.
28. OECD, "Magnitude of Counterfeiting and Piracy".
29. DNA, *Relazione annuale 2011*.
30. DNA, *Relazione annuale 2010*; and Union des Fabricants, *Counterfeiting and Organized Crime Report*.
31. Europol, *OCTA 2011*.
32. KPMG, *La Contraffazione in Italia*.
33. Confesercenti, *Contraffazione e criminalità informatica*.
34. Istituto Piepoli, *La Contraffazione in Italia*.
35. The economic sectors analysed were: audio-visual equipment and pay TV, music, software and video games, books and fashion field.
36. See note 32 above.
37. di Finanza, *Guardia Di Finanza's Fight*.
38. CENSIS, "Comunicati stampa – CENSIS."
39. CENSIS, *L'impatto della contraffazione sul sistema-Paese*.
40. Cornish, *Gambling*; Gazel, Rickman, and Thompson, "Casino Gambling and Crime"; and Ferentzy and Turner, "Gambling and Organized Crime."
41. Strumpf, *Illegal Sports Bookmakers*.
42. Reuter and Rubinstein, *Illegal Gambling in New York*.
43. Liddick, "Enterprise 'model' of Organized Crime."
44. CPA, *Relazione sul fenomeno delle infiltrazioni*; DNA, *Relazione annuale 2011*; and Libera, *Azzardopoli, il paese del gioco d'azzardo*.
45. CPA, *Relazione sul fenomeno delle infiltrazioni*.
46. DNA, *Relazione annuale 2000*; and DNA, *Relazione annuale 2011*.
47. See note 29 above.
48. LibPie, *Il gioco d'azzardo tra legale ed illegale*.
49. Data are periodically published on the AAMS website (http://www.aams.gov.it).
50. New slot machines [regulated by paragraph 6a of Article 110 of the public security law (TULPS)] are controlled by an electronic card or smart card. In these devices, the cost of the

game cannot be more than €1 and the payout may not exceed €100. Moreover, in a cycle of no more than 140,000 games, winnings (i.e. the payout) must not be less than 75% of the stakes.

Video lottery terminals or VLT (regulated by paragraph 6b of the above mentioned law) are directly connected to the server of the licenced dealer from which games are downloaded. In practice, the game software is not in the machine but is installed on the computer network operated by the licenced dealer. The cost of a game can be up to €10 and winnings up to €5000, or €500,000 in the case of a jackpot. The payout must not be less than 85% of the stakes. VLTs, introduced by the 2006 budget law, were in fact brought into service in late 2010. They cannot be installed in bars, but only in premises specifically dedicated to gambling. DNA, *Relazione annuale 2011*.

51. DNA, *Relazione annuale 2006*.
52. DNA, *Relazione annuale 2000*; DNA, *Relazione annuale 2008;* and DNA, *Relazione annuale 2011*.
53. DNA, *Relazione annuale 2011*, 297.
54. See note 51 above.
55. Commission of inquiry to verify the regularity and transparency of procedures for granting authorisations regarding entertainment equipment and devices, to analyse the functioning of processes, also technological, ensuring that games take place lawfully.
56. See note 45 above.
57. Menduini and Sansa, "Videopoker, 100 miliardi non riscossi."
58. See note 48 above.
59. Twelve thousand five hundred and fifty-four seizures in 2009 vs. 1806 in 2011 (data from AAMS).
60. See note 48 above.
61. Eurispes, *L'Italia in gioco: percorsi*.
62. SOS Impresa, *Le mani della criminalità sulle imprese*.
63. Tompson and Chainey, "Profiling Illegal Waste Activity," 180.
64. Ibid., and Fröhlich, *Organised Environmental Crime*.
65. Liddick, "Traffic in Garbage and Hazardous Wastes"; and Tompson and Chainey, "Profiling Illegal Waste Activity."
66. Massari and Monzini, "Dirty Businesses in Italy"; Vander Beken and Balcaen, "Crime Opportunities Provided"; Vander Beken, *European Waste Industry and Crime Vulnerabilities*; Dorn, Van Daele, and Vander Beken, "Reducing Vulnerabilities to Crime"; Liddick, "Traffic in Garbage and Hazardous Wastes"; Liddick, *Crimes Against Nature;* and Tompson and Chainey, "Profiling Illegal Waste Activity."
67. See, for example, Hayman and Brack, *International Environmental Crime*.
68. See, among others, Sigman, "Midnight Dumping"; and Kim, Chang, and Kelleher, "Unit Pricing."
69. Abele-Nomos, Legambiente, and GEPEC-EC, *Illegal Trafficking in Hazardous Waste*, 24.
70. Elliott, "Fighting Transnational Environmental Crime," 91.
71. Hayman and Brack, *International Environmental Crime*, 13.
72. Legambiente, *Rifiuti Spa*, 12; Abele-Nomos, Legambiente, and GEPEC-EC, *Illegal Trafficking in Hazardous Waste*, 22; and Massari and Monzini, "Dirty Businesses in Italy," 292.
73. Dorn, Van Daele, and Vander Beken, "Reducing Vulnerabilities to Crime," 27–8.
74. Europol, *OCTA 2011*, 40; and UNODC, *Transnational Trafficking and the Rule of Law*, 58.
75. Europol, *OCTA 2011*, 40.
76. Albrecht, "Extent of Organized Environmental Crime," 100; and UNODC, *Transnational Trafficking and the Rule of Law*, 58.
77. Wielenga, *Waste Without Frontiers*.
78. For example, EU Member States must report cases of illegal shipments of waste to the EU Commission every year. However, not all the States report regularly, and many of the reported cases lack information on the amount of waste illegally shipped. See ETC/RWM, *Transboundary Shipments of Waste*.
79. Of particular importance is that in 2010 competence to investigate the offence of "Organized activities for the illegal trafficking of waste" was moved from the Prosecutor's offices to the Anti-mafia Directorates.

CRIMINAL MARKETS AND MAFIA PROCEEDS

80. DNA, *Relazione annuale sulle attività svolte*.
81. Albrecht, "Extent of Organized Environmental Crime," 97.
82. Massari and Monzini, "Dirty Businesses in Italy," 299; and Abele-Nomos, Legambiente, and GEPEC-EC, *Illegal Trafficking in Hazardous Waste*, 24.
83. DNA, *Relazione annuale 2011*; and DNA, *Relazione annuale sulle attività svolte dal procuratore nazionale antimafia e dalla Direzione nazionale antimafia nonché sulle dinamiche e strategie della criminalità organizzata di tipo mafioso nel periodo 1° luglio 2011–30 giugno 2012*.
84. Data from the Italian Antimafia District Directorates (DDAs) on criminal proceedings for the offence of "organized activities for the illegal trafficking of waste" (art. 260 Legislative Decree 152/2006) and referring to the period January 2010–June 2012 show that the phenomenon is widespread also in areas without a traditional mafia presence. The districts of Bologna, Brescia, Florence and Venice recorded a number of proceedings similar to and sometimes higher than Southern districts such as Naples, Palermo and Reggio Calabria (DNA, *Relazione annuale sulle attività svolte dal procuratore nazionale antimafia e dalla Direzione nazionale antimafia nonché sulle dinamiche e strategie della criminalità organizzata di tipo mafioso nel periodo 1° luglio 2011–30 giugno 2012*, 325–6).
85. See note 81 above.
86. Legambiente, *Ecomafia 2012*, 68.
87. The methodology used was based on calculation of the so-called *rifiuti scomparsi* (missing waste), that is, the difference between waste produced and waste managed in approved facilities. This missing amount was attributed to the illegal market. Legambiente estimated the revenues of the illegal special waste market on the basis of these data, and prices prevailing in the legal market.
88. Number of firearms seized/confiscated by the province of seizure/confiscation. Data regarding 2009, 2010 and 2011 have been used by calculating the average value. The average number of firearms seized/confiscated in the period 2009–2011 has been used because, in many cases, values for each single year were significantly different from those for the other years. It was consequently decided to calculate the average value so as to make it more stable over time. With regard to data on seizures and confiscations, to be noted is that the reasons for the seizure/confiscation of a weapon cannot be attributed only to illicit trafficking or related activities but to all provisions contained in the Italian law on firearms. Therefore, figures should be considered as rounded up. Data have been provided by the Italian police force database SDI (Sistema D'Indagine).
89. Transcrime, *Progetto PON Sicurezza 2007–2013*, 310–14 and 342.
90. These estimates are based on the findings in the literature, namely the calculation that the illegal traffic amounts to between 10% and 20% of the legal one. Data on imports and exports refer to the total monetary value of imported/exported firearms from/to Italy (years 2009–2011). The average value of exports was €482,220,636; while that of imports was €106,786,382. These data have been downloaded from the UN Commodity Trade Statistics Database. This variable includes data on 'Arms and ammunition, parts and accessories thereof' (code HS 1992, 93 of the Commodity Trade database). In particular, the following categories have been considered: Air gun pellets, parts of shotgun cartridges; Arms not elsewhere specified or "nes" (spring/air/gas guns, truncheons, etc.); Cartridges nes, parts thereof; Cartridges, shotguns; Munitions of war, ammunition/projectiles and parts; Muzzle-loading firearms; Parts and accessories nes of weapons, nes; Parts and accessories of revolvers or pistols; Parts and accessories of shotguns or rifles, nes; Revolvers and pistols; Rifles, sporting, hunting or target-shooting, nes; Shotgun barrels; Shotguns, shotgun-rifles for sport, hunting or target; Signal pistols, etc., humane killers, etc. The turnover of the Italian companies refers to those companies manufacturing firearms and ammunition belonging to the National Associations of Sportive and Civil Weapons and Ammunition Manufacturers (ANPAM). Estimates have been calculated only for 2010 because data were available only for that year. The total turnover amounted to €486,338,624 while the turnover generated by the national market was equal to €115,347,891. Data from ANPAM include, besides firearms, also parts of weapons, cartridges and ammunitions.
91. It was assumed that the regional market is larger where there are more inhabitants.
92. It was also assumed that revenues are higher where there are more firearms seized/confiscated. For this purpose, data on seizures and confiscations of firearms between 2009 and

93. This formula was applied for both illegal demand at 10% (min) and 20% (max) of the legal one.
94. At first, data on seized goods by region and product category were included in the analysis for the years 2008–2011. The results seemed to be insufficiently representative of the phenomenon of counterfeiting in Italy and for this reason other variables were taken into account.
95. The ATECO classification of the economic sectors is the classification used by the Italian Institute of Statistic (ISTAT) to classify economic activities. Data on turnovers were collected from the I.STAT and AIDA data sets, and the data on employees from I.STAT.
96. Turnovers were calculated for all sectors using the I.STAT database, except for the category 'Watches'. For the latter, I.STAT did not provide a sufficient level of disaggregation, so that the AIDA database was used. Unfortunately, AIDA provides only the turnover of the last available year. To compensate for this characteristic of AIDA, it was decided to include the enterprises' turnover from 2004 to 2011. The purpose was to avoid the loss of information of companies that had not provided more updated data.
97. Data periodically provided by AAMS at http://www.aams.gov.it/?id=5320.
98. See note 29 above.
99. Data from AAMS website (www.amms.gov.it).
100. Data provided by AAMS.
101. The infringement rate for Trentino-Alto Adige was 0.0, a figure that would have invalidated the following operations. For this reason, Trentino-Alto Adige was assigned the value of 0.17, i.e. the lowest rate among other regions (Liguria).
102. Information based on regulations in force and interviews with AAMS staff.
103. *Special waste* is the waste *generated by production activities. Conversely, municipal waste is the 'waste from households, as well as other waste which, because of its nature or composition, is similar to waste from household'*(The Council of the European Union, *Council Directive 1999/31/EC on the Landfill of Waste*).
104. In some Italian regions, the inefficiencies of the public administration in managing municipal waste have been exploited by the mafias, which have entered the waste market. This is particularly the case of the Camorra in Campania. There, the Neapolitan mafia has specialised in criminal activities related to the waste disposal cycle (Savona, "Italian Mafias' Asymmetries," 10).
105. Based on ISPRA data (see ISPRA, *Rapporto Rifiuti Urbani 2012*; and ISPRA, *Rapporto Rifiuti Speciali. Edizione 2012*).
106. Massari and Monzini, "Dirty Businesses in Italy," 297; and Fröhlich, *Organised Environmental Crime*, 22.
107. ISPRA also provides data on the production, separate collection and management of municipal waste. However, these data did not have the level of detail required for the analysis.
108. This calculation was necessary because the stored waste may remain in the storage facilities for a time and be disposed of/recovered at a later date; or it may be disposed of/recovered in the same year. The inclusion of the stored waste in legal management would have led to overestimation of the amount of waste managed in a year, while its exclusion would have resulted in an underestimation (ISPRA, *Rapporto Rifiuti Speciali. Edizione 2011*, 63–4. Data were derived from ISPRA reports on special waste (*Rapporto Rifiuti 2008*; *Rapporto Rifiuti Speciali. Edizione 2010*; *Rapporto Rifiuti Speciali. Edizione 2011*, 2012; *Rapporto Rifiuti Speciali. Edizione 2012*) and referred to the years 2007, 2008, 2009 and 2010. Within the reports the operations of final management are identified by the codes *R1* to *R11* (for recovery) and *D1* to *D12* and *D14* (for disposal). Instead, storage operations are identified by the codes *D13*, *D15*, *R12* and *R13*.
109. This redistribution was necessary since, in some Italian regions, the amount of waste managed was larger than the waste produced. Data on the legal production were derived from the same ISPRA reports as above.
110. Northern Italy comprises the regions of Piedmont, Valle d'Aosta, Lombardy, Trentino-Alto Adige, Veneto, Friuli-Venezia Giulia, Liguria and Emilia-Romagna. Central Italy includes

Tuscany, Umbria, Marche and Lazio. Southern Italy includes Abruzzo, Molise, Campania, Apulia, Basilicata, Calabria, Sicily and Sardinia.
111. This was due to the fact that the amount of hazardous waste managed in Southern Italy was larger than the waste produced. Thus, considering the macro-area would have led to a negative value of the illegal market in Southern regions.
112. The average price differed according to the type of waste (hazardous/non-hazardous). Data were obtained by contacting a waste disposal company.
113. For instance, the incidence of seizures/confiscations in the total amount of illegal firearms or the average price for illegal firearms, the commodity macro-categories chosen for the counterfeiting market, or the price of legal management services used for the illegal waste market. In the latter case, the price was obtained from a waste company operating in Northern Italy and it was applied to the entire country. However, some differences among regions or geographical areas may exist.
114. Legambiente and Carabinieri Tutela Ambiente, *"Rifiuti Spa"*, 18.
115. Singer, "Vitality of Mythical Numbers"; and Reuter, "The (continued) Vitality of Mythical Numbers."

Bibliography

Abele-Nomos, Gruppo, Legambiente, and GEPEC-EC. *The Illegal Trafficking in Hazardous Waste in Italy and Spain. Final Report*. Rome: Gruppo Abele-Nomos, Legambiente e Grup d'Estudi i Protecció dels Ecosistemes del Camp-Ecologistes de Catalunya, 2003.

Albrecht, Hans-Jörg. "The Extent of Organized Environmental Crime. A European Perspective." In *Environmental Crime in Europe: Rules of Sanctions*, edited by Françoise Comte and Ludwig Krämer. Groningen: Europa Law Publishing, 2004.

Angeli, Federica. "Pistole, Kalashnikov, Persino Un Missile Grandi Affari Al Supermarket Dei 'Ferri.'" Inchieste – La Repubblica. 2012. http://inchieste.repubblica.it/it/repubblica/rep-roma/2012/02/21/news/pistole_kalashnikov_persino_un_missile_grandi_affari_al_supermarket_dei_ferri-30261014/.

CENSIS. "Comunicati stampa – CENSIS." 2009. http://www.censis.it/10?resource_50=5717&relational_resource_51=5717&relational_resource_385=5717&relational_resource_52=5717&relational_resource_381=5717&relational_resource_382=5717&relational_resource_383=5717&relational_resource_384=5717.

CENSIS. *L'impatto della contraffazione sul sistema-Paese: dimensioni, caratteristiche e approfondimenti*. Roma: Ministero dello Sviluppo Economico, 2012.

Confesercenti. *Contraffazione e criminalità informatica: i danni all'economia e alle imprese*. Roma: Confesercenti, 2007.

Cornish, Derek Blaikie. *Gambling: A Review of the Literature and Its Implications for Policy and Research*. London: Home Office, 1978.

CPA. *Relazione sul fenomeno delle infiltrazioni mafiose nel gioco lecito ed illecito*. Roma: Commissione parlamentare d'inchiesta sul fenomeno della mafia e sulle altre associazioni criminali, anche straniere, 2011.

The Council of the European Union. *Council Directive 1999/31/EC on the Landfill of Waste*. Luxembourg: The Council of the European Union, 1999.

Cukier, Wendy. *The Illicit Trade in Small Arms: Addressing the Problem of Diversion*. Waterloo: Small Arms Working Group, 2008. http://www.muntr.org/v4/wp-content/uploads/2012/02/ADDRESSING-THE-PROBLEM-OF-DIVERSION.pdf.

di Finanza, Guardia. *Guardia Di Finanza's Fight Against Counterfeiting and Products Piracy*. Brussels: Guardia di Finanza, 2003.

DIA. *Relazione del Ministro dell'Interno al Parlamento sull'attività svolta e sui risultati conseguiti dalla Direzione Investigativa Antimafia: Secondo semestre 2010*. Roma: Direzione Investigativa Antimafia, 2010.

DIA. *Relazione del Ministro dell'Interno al Parlamento sull'attività svolta e sui risultati conseguiti dalla Direzione Investigativa Antimafia: Secondo semestre 2011*. Roma: Direzione Investigativa Antimafia, 2011. http://www.interno.it/dip_ps/dia/semestrali/sem/2011/1sem2011.pdf.

DNA. *Relazione annuale sulle attività svolte dal Procuratore nazionale antimafia e dalla Direzione nazionale antimafia nonché sulle dinamiche e strategie della criminalità organizzata di tipo mafioso nel periodo 1° luglio 1999–30 giugno 2000*. Roma: Direzione Nazionale Antimafia, 2000.

DNA. *Relazione annuale sulle attività svolte dal Procuratore nazionale antimafia e dalla Direzione nazionale antimafia nonché sulle dinamiche e strategie della criminalità organizzata di tipo mafioso nel periodo 1° luglio 2005–30 giugno 2006*. Roma: Direzione Nazionale Antimafia, 2006.

DNA. *Relazione annuale sulle attività svolte dal Procuratore nazionale antimafia e dalla Direzione nazionale antimafia nonché sulle dinamiche e strategie della criminalità organizzata di tipo mafioso nel periodo 1° luglio 2007–30 giugno 2008*. Roma: Direzione Nazionale Antimafia, 2008.

DNA. *Relazione annuale sulle attività svolte dal Procuratore nazionale antimafia e dalla Direzione nazionale antimafia nonché sulle dinamiche e strategie della criminalità organizzata di tipo mafioso nel periodo 1° luglio 2009–30 giugno 2010*. Roma: Direzione Nazionale Antimafia, 2010.

DNA. *Relazione annuale sulle attività svolte dal Procuratore nazionale antimafia e dalla Direzione nazionale antimafia nonché sulle dinamiche e strategie della criminalità organizzata di tipo mafioso nel periodo 1° luglio 2010–30 giugno 2011*. Roma: Direzione Nazionale Antimafia, 2011.

DNA. *Relazione annuale sulle attività svolte dal procuratore nazionale antimafia e dalla Direzione nazionale antimafia nonché sulle dinamiche e strategie della criminalità organizzata di tipo mafioso nel periodo 1° luglio 2011–30 giugno 2012*. Roma: Direzione Nazionale Antimafia, 2012.

Dorn, Nicholas, Stijn Van Daele, and Tom Vander Beken. "Reducing Vulnerabilities to Crime of the European Waste Management Industry: The Research Base and the Prospects for Policy." *European Journal of Crime, Criminal Law and Criminal Justice* 15, no. 1 (2007): 23–36.

Elliott, Lorraine. "Fighting Transnational Environmental Crime." *Journal of International Affairs* 66, no. 1 (2012): 87–104.

ETC/RWM. *Transboundary Shipments of Waste in the EU. Developments 1995–2005 and Possible Drivers. Technical Report*. Copenhagen: European Topic Centre on Resource and Waste Management, 2008.

Eurispes. *L'Italia in gioco: percorsi e numeri della fortuna*. Roma: Istituto di studi politici, economici e sociali, 2009.

Eurispes. *'Ndrangheta holding: Dossier 2008*. Roma: Istituto di studi politici, economici e sociali, 2008. http://www.eurispes.it/index.php?option=com_content&view=article&id=365:ndrangheta-holding-dossier-2008&catid=56:criminalitaesicurezza&Itemid=323.

European Commission. *Report on EU Customs Enforcement of Intellectual Property Rights 2010*. Brussels: European Commission, 2010.

Europol. *OCTA 2011: EU Organised Crime Threat Assessment*. The Hague: European Police Office, 2011. https://www.europol.europa.eu/sites/default/files/publications/octa_2011_1.pdf.

Feinstein, Dianne, Charles Schumer, and Sheldon Whitehouse. *Halting US Firearms Trafficking to Mexico*. Washington, DC: United States Senate Caucus on International Narcotics Control, 2011. http://www.feinstein.senate.gov/public/index.cfm?Fuseaction=Files.View&FileStore_id=beaff893-63c1-4941-9903-67a0dc739b9d.

Ferentzy, Peter, and Nigel Turner. "Gambling and Organized Crime – A Review of the Literature." *Journal of Gambling Issues* 23 (2009): 111–155.

Frontier Economics. *Estimating the Global Economic and Social Impacts of Counterfeiting and Piracy*. London: Business Action to Stop Counterfeiting and Piracy, 2011. http://www.iccwbo.org/uploadedFiles/BASCAP/Pages/Global%20Impacts%20-%20Final.pdf.

Fröhlich, Tanja. *Organised Environmental Crime in the EU Member States. Final Report*. Kassel: Betreuungsgesellschaft für Umweltfragen, 2003. http://ec.europa.eu/environment/legal/crime/pdf/organised_member_states.pdf.

GAO. *Firearms Trafficking: US Efforts to Combat Arms Trafficking to Mexico Face Planning and Coordination Challenges*. Washington, DC: Government Accountability Office, 2009. http://www.gao.gov/new.items/d09709.pdf.

Gazel, Ricardo C., Dan S. Rickman, and William N. Thompson. "Casino Gambling and Crime: A Panel Study of Wisconsin Counties." *Managerial and Decision Economics* 22, no. 1/3 (2001): 65–75.

Hayman, Gavin, and Duncan Brack. *International Environmental Crime. The Nature and Control of Environmental Black Markets. Workshop Report*. London: Royal Institute of International Affairs, 2002.

ISPAC. *Trafficking: Networks and Logistics of Transnational Crime and International Terrorism. International Scientific and Professional Advisory Council of the United Crime Prevention and Criminal Justice Programme*, 2002. http://ispac.cnpds.org/publications-16-trafficking-networks-and-logistics-of-transnational-crime-and-international-16.html.

ISPRA. *Rapporto Rifiuti 2008*. Roma: Istituto Superiore per la Protezione e la Ricerca Ambientale, 2009. http://www.reteambiente.it/normativa/11723/.

ISPRA. *Rapporto Rifiuti Speciali. Edizione 2010*. Roma: Istituto Superiore per la Protezione e la Ricerca Ambientale, 2010. http://www.gruppohera.it/binary/hr_ambiente/angolo_scientifico/rap_125_2010Rapporto_rifiuti_speciali2010.1310544396.pdf.

ISPRA. *Rapporto Rifiuti Speciali. Edizione 2011*. Roma: Istituto Superiore per la Protezione e la Ricerca Ambientale, 2012. http://www.isprambiente.gov.it/site/_contentfiles/00011100/11107_rifiuti_spec_2011_rap_155_2011_.pdf.

ISPRA. *Rapporto Rifiuti Speciali. Edizione 2012*. Roma: Istituto Superiore per la Protezione e la Ricerca Ambientale, 2013.

ISPRA. *Rapporto Rifiuti Urbani 2012*. Roma: Istituto Superiore per la Protezione e la Ricerca Ambientale, 2012.

Istituto Piepoli. *La Contraffazione in Italia*. Milano: Confcommercio, 2007. http://www.largoconsumo.info/052008/DOCConfcommercioLacontraffazioneinItalia05-08.pdf.

Kim, Geum-Soo, Young-Jae Chang, and David Kelleher. "Unit Pricing of Municipal Solid Waste and Illegal Dumping: An Empirical Analysis of Korean Experience." *Environmental Economics and Policy Studies* 9, no. 3 (2008): 167–176.

Kleck, Gary. "BATF Gun Trace Data and the Role of Organized Gun Trafficking in Supplying Guns to Criminals." *Saint Louis University Public Law Review* 18 (1999): 23–40.

Koper, Christopher S. *Crime Gun Risk Factors: Buyer, Seller, Firearm and Transaction Characteristics Associated with Gun Trafficking and Criminal Gun*. Philadelphia: Jerry Lee Center of Criminology, University of Pennsylvania, 2007. http://www.ncjrs.gov/pdffiles1/nij/grants/221074.pdf.

KPMG. *La Contraffazione in Italia*. Geneva: American Chamber of Commerce in Italy, 2003.

Legambiente. *Ecomafia 2012. Le storie e i numeri della criminalità ambientale*. Milano: Edizioni Ambiente, 2012.

Legambiente. *Rifiuti Spa,. I traffici illegali di rifiuti in Italia. Le storie, i numeri, le rotte e le responsabilità*. Roma: Legambiente, Gennaio, 2003. http://www.legambienteverona.it/doc/rifiuti/2003-Rifiuti-spa.pdf.

Legambiente, and Carabinieri Tutela Ambiente. *Rifiuti Spa,. Radiografia dei traffici illeciti*. Roma: Osservatorio nazionale ambiente e legalità di Legambiente e Comando Carabinieri per la tutela dell'ambiente, 2005. http://risorse.legambiente.it/docs/rifiuti_spa_2005.0000002011.pdf.

Libera. *Azzardopoli, il paese del gioco d'azzardo, dove quando il gioco si fa duro, le mafie iniziano a giocare*. Roma: Libera associazioni, nomi e numeri contro le mafie, 2012.

LibPie. *Il gioco d'azzardo tra legale ed illegale: un focus sul Piemonte*. Roma: Osservatorio Regionale di Libera Piemonte, 2012.

Liddick, Don, Don. "The Enterprise 'model' of Organized Crime: Assessing Theoretical Propositions." *Justice Quarterly* 16, no. 2 (1999): 403–430.

Liddick. "The Traffic in Garbage and Hazardous Wastes: An Overview." *Trends in Organized Crime* 13, no. 2–3 (2010): 134–146.

Liddick, Donald R. *Crimes Against Nature: Illegal Industries and the Global Environment*. Santa Barbara, CA: ABC-CLIO, 2011.

Marsh, Nicholas. "Two Sides of the Same Coin? The Legal and Illegal Trade in Small Arms." *The Brown Journal of World Affairs* 9 (2002): 217–228.

Massari, Monica, and Paola Monzini. "Dirty Businesses in Italy: A Case-Study of Illegal Trafficking in Hazardous Waste." *Global Crime* 6, no. 3–4 (2004): 285–304.

Menduini, Marco, and Ferruccio Sansa. "Videopoker, 100 miliardi non riscossi dai Monopoli e finiti alla mafia." Il Secolo XIX, 2007. http://www.ilsecoloxix.it/p/italia_e_mondo/2007/05/31/AKDo9t0-videopoker_miliardi_riscossi.shtml#axzz1uXUue08C.

OECD. *The Economic Impact of Counterfeiting and Piracy*. Paris: Organisation for Economic Co-operation and Development, 2008.

OECD. "Magnitude of Counterfeiting and Piracy of Tangible Products: An Update." 2009. http://www.oecd.org/dataoecd/57/27/44088872.pdf.
Rainelli, Sara. "Le Armi Leggere Nel Mondo." *Sistema Informativo a Schede* 1 (2012): 1–23.
Reuter, Peter. "The (continued) Vitality of Mythical Numbers." *The Public Interest* 75 (1984): 135–147.
Reuter, Peter, and Jonathan Rubinstein. *Illegal Gambling in New York: A Case Study in the Operation, Structure, and Regulation of an Illegal Market*. Washington, DC: US Department of Justice, National Institute of Justice, 1982.
Ruggiero, Vincenzo. "Criminals and Service Providers: Cross-National Dirty Economies." *Crime, Law and Social Change* 28, no. 1 (1997): 27–38.
Sagramoso, Domitilla. *The Proliferation of Illegal Small Arms and Light Weapons in and Around the European Union: Instability, Organised Crime and Terrorist Groups*. London: Centre for Defense Studies, Kings College, University of London, 2001. http://www.isn.ethz.ch/isn/Digital-Library/Publications/Detail/?ots591=0c54e3b3-1e9c-be1e-2c24-a6a8c7060233&lng=en&id=10251.
Savona, Ernesto Ugo. "Italian Mafias' Asymmetries." In *Traditional Organized Crime in the Modern World: Responses to Socioeconomic Change*, edited by Dina Siegel and Hank van de Bunt, 3–25. New York: Springer, 2012.
Sigman, Hilary. "Midnight Dumping: Public Policies and Illegal Disposal of Used Oil." *The RAND Journal of Economics* 29, no. 1 (1998): 157–178.
Singer, Max. "The Vitality of Mythical Numbers." *The Public Interest* 23 (1971): 3–9.
Small Arms Survey. *Small Arms Survey 2002: Counting the Human Cost*. Geneva: Graduate Institute of International Studies, 2002. http://www.smallarmssurvey.org/publications/by-type/yearbook/small-arms-survey-2002.html.
SOS Impresa. *Le mani della criminalità sulle imprese*. Roma: Confesercenti, 2011.
SOS Impresa. *Le mani della criminalità sulle imprese*. Roma: Confesercenti, 2012.
Spapens, Toine. "Trafficking in Illicit Firearms for Criminal Purposes within the European Union." *European Journal of Crime, Criminal Law and Criminal Justice* 15, no. 3–4 (2007): 359–381.
Stohl, Rachel J. "Fighting the Illicit Trafficking of Small Arms." *SAIS Review* 25, no. 1 (2005): 59–68.
Strumpf, Koleman. *Illegal Sports Bookmakers*. Department of Economics, University of North Carolina and Chapel Hill, 2003. http://www.unc.edu/~cigar/papers/Bookie4b.pdf.
Tompson, Lisa, and Spencer Chainey. "Profiling Illegal Waste Activity: Using Crime Scripts as a Data Collection and Analytical Strategy." *European Journal on Criminal Policy and Research* 17, no. 3 (2011): 179–201.
Transcrime. *Anti-Brand Counterfeiting in the EU: Report on Best Practices*. Milan: Transcrime, 2010. http://www.gacg.org/Content/Upload/Documents/Transcrime_Report%20Best%20Practices_Project%20FAKES.pdf.
Transcrime. *Anti-Brand Counterfeiting in the EU: Report on International and National Existing Standards*. Milan: Transcrime, 2010. http://www.gacg.org/Content/Upload/Documents/Transcrime_Report%20Existing%20Standards_Project%20FAKES.pdf.
Transcrime. *Progetto PON Sicurezza 2007–2013: Gli investimenti delle mafie. Rapporto Linea 1*. Milano: Ministero dell'Interno, 2013. www.investimentioc.it.
UNICRI. *Contraffazione: Una Diffusione Globale, Una Minaccia Globale*. Torino: United Nations Interregional Crime and Justice Research Institute, 2007. http://counterfeiting.unicri.it/report2008.php.
Union des Fabricants. *Counterfeiting and Organized Crime Report*. Paris: Union des Fabricants, 2003.
UNODC. *Crime and Development in Central America*. Vienna: United Nations Office on Drugs and Crime, 2007. http://www.unodc.org/documents/data-and-analysis/Central-america-study-en.pdf.
UNODC. *The Globalization of Crime: A Transnational Organized Crime Threat Assessment*. Vienna: United Nations Office on Drugs and Crime, 2010. http://www.unodc.org/documents/data-and-analysis/tocta/TOCTA_Report_2010_low_res.pdf.
UNODC. *Transnational Trafficking and the Rule of Law in West Africa. A Threat Assessment*. Vienna: United Nation Office on Drugs and Crime, 2009. http://www.unodc.org/documents/data-and-analysis/Studies/West_Africa_Report_2009.pdf.
Vander Beken, Tom. *The European Waste Industry and Crime Vulnerabilities*. Antwerp-Apeldoorn: Maklu, 2007.

Vander Beken, Tom, and Annelies Balcaen. "Crime Opportunities Provided by Legislation in Market Sectors: Mobile Phones, Waste Disposal, Banking, Pharmaceuticals." *European Journal on Criminal Policy and Research* 12, no. 3–4 (2006): 299–323.

WCO. *Customs and IPR Report 2010*. Brussels: World Customs Organization, 2011. http://www.wcoomd.org/files/1.%20Public%20files/PDFandDocuments/Enforcement/WCO_Customs_IPR_2010_public_en.pdf.

Wielenga, Kees. *Waste Without Frontiers. Global Trends in the Generation of Transboundary Movements of Hazardous Wastes and Other Wastes*. Geneva: Secretariat of the Basel Convention, 2010.

Appendix

Table A1. Minimum and maximum estimates of the revenues of the markets for illegal firearms (year 2010), counterfeit goods (year 2008) and special waste (years 2007–2010) (million €) per type of estimate or product/service.

	Firearms			Counterfeiting																
		Demand		Clothing accessories and footwear		Electrical equipment		Information technology equipment		CDs, DVDs, tapes		Toys		Glasses		Watches and jewellery		Fragrances and beauty		Total	
	Supply	Min	Max	Min	Max	Min	Max	Min	Max	Min	Max	Min	Max	Min	Max	Min	Max	Min	Max	Min	Max
Abruzzo	1.02	1.26	2.51	38.1	76.2	1.3	2.6	5.5	11.1	0.3	0.5	1.0	2.0	5.2	10.5	7.0	14.0	7.5	15.1	65.9	131.9
Basilicata	0.72	0.99	1.99	14.2	28.5	0.8	1.7	2.1	4.1	0.1	0.2	0.7	1.4	0.9	1.8	2.2	4.4	1.2	2.4	22.3	44.5
Calabria	2.58	3.89	7.78	52.4	104.7	2.2	4.3	7.2	14.4	0.3	0.7	1.6	3.1	2.6	5.2	8.0	16.0	5.5	11.0	79.7	159.4
Campania	5.89	8.13	16.26	200.1	400.2	6.3	12.7	18.7	37.5	1.4	2.8	6.9	13.8	7.5	15.0	23.1	46.1	19.6	39.2	283.6	567.2
Emilia-Romagna	2.68	3.41	6.81	138.8	277.5	3.5	6.9	24.0	47.9	1.2	2.4	4.6	9.1	32.8	65.5	16.1	32.2	27.7	55.5	248.5	497.1
Friuli-V.G.	1.00	1.30	2.60	42.5	85.1	1.0	2.0	4.6	9.1	0.4	0.7	1.6	3.1	9.4	18.7	12.0	23.9	9.6	19.2	80.9	161.9
Lazio	2.32	6.51	13.03	183.0	365.9	7.5	14.9	24.1	48.1	1.6	3.1	6.6	13.1	19.1	38.3	25.7	51.3	22.1	44.2	289.5	579.1
Liguria	2.05	2.66	5.31	52.9	105.8	1.5	3.1	4.3	8.6	0.4	0.9	3.0	6.1	5.7	11.5	8.4	16.8	6.2	12.4	82.5	165.1
Lombardy	3.57	5.50	11.01	316.6	633.2	15.6	31.2	25.9	51.7	1.8	3.7	20.4	40.9	57.4	114.7	38.8	77.6	37.9	75.7	514.3	1028.6
Marche	1.05	1.50	3.00	45.9	91.7	1.0	2.1	4.0	7.9	0.3	0.7	1.4	2.9	5.8	11.5	5.5	11.0	4.7	9.3	68.6	137.1
Molise	0.35	0.46	0.93	7.7	15.5	0.5	0.9	1.1	2.3	0.0	0.1	0.4	0.8	0.7	1.4	1.5	3.0	0.6	1.1	12.6	25.1
Piedmont	2.41	3.84	7.67	128.2	256.4	3.2	6.5	14.2	28.5	1.3	2.5	5.0	9.9	16.0	32.0	17.8	35.5	11.6	23.2	197.2	394.5
Apulia	4.16	7.92	15.85	109.4	218.8	5.0	10.0	16.4	32.7	0.7	1.5	4.6	9.2	8.8	17.6	14.0	28.0	12.4	24.8	171.2	342.4
Sardinia	1.04	1.57	3.14	43.3	86.5	1.6	3.1	5.8	11.6	0.2	0.5	1.0	2.0	3.4	6.8	6.8	13.7	5.2	10.4	67.3	134.6
Sicily	4.17	5.37	10.75	134.1	268.1	5.7	11.3	15.6	31.2	0.9	1.7	6.3	12.6	8.0	15.9	20.1	40.3	14.5	29.0	205.0	410.1
Tuscany	4.36	6.06	12.11	120.8	241.7	4.9	9.9	12.8	25.7	1.1	2.3	4.9	9.8	11.7	23.4	18.1	36.2	14.8	29.5	189.2	378.4
Trentino-A.A.	0.24	0.89	1.79	35.3	70.6	1.0	2.1	3.6	7.1	0.2	0.4	1.4	2.8	4.5	9.0	3.7	7.4	3.2	6.4	52.9	105.9
Umbria	1.62	2.38	4.77	27.8	55.6	0.8	1.6	1.8	3.6	0.2	0.4	1.1	2.2	2.9	5.9	3.8	7.6	2.0	3.9	40.3	80.7
Valle d'Aosta	0.03	0.06	0.12	3.7	7.3	0.1	0.2	0.3	0.5	0.1	0.1	0.2	0.4	0.2	0.4	0.5	1.1	0.4	0.8	5.3	10.7
Veneto	4.78	6.73	13.46	159.4	318.8	4.0	8.0	19.0	37.9	1.0	1.9	4.2	8.3	114.9	229.9	19.9	39.8	28.1	56.3	350.5	700.9
Italy	46.07	70.44	140.87	1854.0	3708.0	67.4	134.9	210.8	421.5	13.5	27.1	76.7	153.4	317.5	635.0	252.9	505.9	234.6	469.3	3027.5	6055.0

(*Continued*)

Table A1. (Continued)

	Special waste					
	Non-hazardous		Hazardous		Total	
	Min	Max	Min	Max	Min	Max
Abruzzo	5.59	9.32	0.24	0.40	5.83	9.72
Basilicata	2.49	4.15	0.16	0.26	2.65	4.41
Calabria	4.43	7.38	0.23	0.38	4.65	7.76
Campania	16.49	27.48	0.78	1.30	17.26	28.77
Emilia-Romagna	19.97	33.29	2.15	3.58	22.12	36.87
Friuli-V.G.	7.45	12.42	0.52	0.87	7.97	13.29
Lazio	24.23	40.38	0.94	1.57	25.17	41.95
Liguria	6.05	10.09	0.45	0.76	6.51	10.84
Lombardy	33.18	55.30	4.68	7.81	37.86	63.10
Marche	12.12	20.20	0.30	0.50	12.42	20.71
Molise	2.25	3.75	0.07	0.12	2.32	3.87
Piedmont	15.26	25.43	1.86	3.11	17.13	28.54
Apulia	24.34	40.56	0.61	1.01	24.95	41.58
Sardinia	10.51	17.51	0.76	1.26	11.27	18.78
Sicily	15.02	25.03	6.70	11.17	21.72	36.20
Tuscany	36.85	61.42	1.06	1.77	37.92	63.19
Trentino-A.A.	8.03	13.39	0.25	0.41	8.28	13.80
Umbria	8.12	13.54	0.28	0.46	8.40	14.00
Valle d'Aosta	0.49	0.82	0.03	0.05	0.53	0.88
Veneto	26.49	44.16	2.56	4.26	29.05	48.42
Italy	279.37	465.61	24.64	41.06	304.01	506.68

Source: Authors' elaboration.

Mythical numbers and the proceeds of organised crime: estimating mafia proceeds in Italy

Francesco Calderoni

Università Cattolica del Sacro Cuore and Transcrime, Milan, Italy

Organised crime is a field vulnerable to mythical numbers, i.e. exaggerated estimates lacking empirical support, but acquiring acceptance through repetition. The figures on mafia proceeds in Italy are a striking example of this problem. This study proposes an estimation of mafia proceeds in Italy from nine criminal activities (sexual exploitation of women, illicit firearms trafficking, drug trafficking, counterfeiting, the illicit cigarette trade, illicit gambling, illicit waste disposal, loan sharking, and extortion racketeering) by region and type of mafia (Cosa Nostra, Camorra, 'Ndrangheta, Apulian mafias, and other mafias). The results estimate yearly mafia proceeds at approximately €10.7 bn (0.7% of the Italian GDP), discussing the impact on the regional and national economies and the differences among the types of mafias as to their geographical sources of revenues.

Introduction

Crime has always been the favourite field for the purveyors of mythical numbers. Mythical numbers are estimates of a phenomenon inevitably overstating its size while lacking empirical support. Nevertheless, they gain acceptance by policy-makers, the media, public opinion and, sometimes, scholars due to their repetition 'as gospel numbers that have no real basis in fact'.[1] Indeed, practitioners and academics in the crime field often know very well that 'because an estimate has been used widely by a variety of people who should know what they are talking about, one cannot assume that the estimate is even approximately correct'.[2]

According to Reuter, there are three main reasons for the success of mythical numbers.[3] First, there is no constituency for accurate numbers, while there is interest in keeping figures high. Second, scholars in the field may have no interest in correct estimations. Third, and most importantly, mythical numbers persist because they have almost no impact on policies.

The vitality of mythical numbers is attributable to the increasing importance of quantification for public policies. The advancement of sciences in different domains has improved mankind's capacity to measure natural and social phenomena. Increasingly, figures are the main subject of policy debates, and there is growing demand for evidence-based policies. This generates its own supply of estimates which, 'particularly in newer areas of policy making, are frequently of poor quality and difficult to evaluate'.[4]

Almost 30 years ago, Reuter claimed that such figures have scant impact on actual policies, but he also predicted that the trend would increase further. He also argued that the problem is difficult to prevent, due to governments' need to back up their claims with (any) evidence; the self-driving appetite of public agencies for resources; the difficulty of refuting bad estimates with better ones (particularly in new policy areas); and the uncritical exploitation of mythical numbers by politicians, policy-makers, and stakeholders in general.[5]

Notwithstanding the development of criminology in recent years, it is hard to contend that the above arguments are today devoid of any relevance. Mythical numbers still enjoy great success as new crime threats develop: e.g. consider the frequent alarming claims by public agencies and by private businesses on the threats of cybercrime.[6]

The field of organised crime is even more exposed to mythical numbers. Since its early stages, the public and scholarly debate on organised crime has been affected by unsubstantiated claims devoid of empirical support. The notion of organised crime gained public importance throughout the twentieth century due to political pressures, simplifications, and stereotypes. After the end of WWII, organised crime in the US was depicted as an alien conspiracy by a small number of Sicilian or Italian *mafiosi*, and this stereotype is still very common.[7] Despite the criticisms of scholars, the concept was successfully exported to other countries with strategies of moral panic and securitisation.[8] At the same time, the general understanding of organised crime remained vague, with scholars discussing its social construction, mystique and paradoxes.[9]

The attempts by national and international institutions to address and quantify organised crime met with criticism by academics.[10] Nevertheless, the media and public opinion are still strongly influenced by mythical numbers on organised crime. For example, a 2011 study by the United Nations Office on Drugs and Crime (UNODC) reviewed a number of estimates of money-laundering and identified a consensus share of world GDP equal to US$870 bn in 2009.[11] While the report was cautious about the reliability of the estimates, the figure rapidly became a mythical number. UNODC's Director declared 'We are able to quantify the cost of transnational organized crime, it is US$870 billion, but we cannot calculate the misery and suffering caused to millions of people by these illicit activities'.[12] The UN agency also launched a public awareness campaign which received worldwide media attention.[13]

The persistence of mythical numbers about organised crime shows most of the features already mentioned. A small, but well-organised, constituency of governments, international organisations, and non-governmental agencies has an interest in keeping such numbers high, while the interest in accurate estimates is widespread among citizens.[14] Debunking such mythical numbers is difficult and unrewarding – any criticisms may be perceived as attempts to minimise the issue of organised crime.[15] Policies are only marginally affected by the estimates. Governments are unable to measure the performance of such policies, so that there is limited interest in questioning the mythical numbers about organised crime.

This situation entails several negative consequences. These numbers may disseminate stereotypes in the population, stimulate xenophobia, heighten the fear of crime, and distort perceptions of what the real problems are. They may ultimately affect the establishment of effective and efficient policies to reduce organised crime.

The long-term solution to the problem may be the integration of estimates of organised crime activities into the policy process.[16] However, this requires establishment of a number of preconditions addressing the causes of the persistence of mythical numbers. Data collection on organised crime should improve; estimation methodologies should be transparent; and scholars should participate in the process more actively than they are currently willing. These preconditions may contribute to informing public opinion and making the success of mythical numbers less likely.

Considering that 'it is easy to point to the failings of the first "measurement" but often hard to produce a convincing alternative',[17] this article opts for the hard path. It tackles the problems of estimating the proceeds of organised crime with an attempt to estimate the revenues of the mafias in Italy which uses a specifically designed method. It addresses questions such as the following: What is the income of the mafias in Italy? How is it distributed across Italian regions and types of mafia? The study is inspired by a research project conducted by Transcrime for the Italian Ministry of Interior, which analysed investments by mafias in Italy and abroad.[18] The results estimate yearly mafia proceeds at approximately €10.7 bn (0.7% of the Italian GDP), with extortion racketeering as the main source of income. Camorra and 'Ndrangheta are the mafias with the highest revenues (€3.3 bn and nearly €3 bn, respectively), totalling more than 68% of total mafia proceeds. Also, the 'Ndrangheta has successfully diversified its source of income, with only 28% of the revenues coming from the native region (Calabria).

The other sections of the article are organised as follows: the next section discusses mythical numbers about mafia proceeds in Italy. The 'Methodology' section describes the methodology and its limitations, while the 'Results and discussion' section presents and discusses the results. The last section concludes.

Mafia mythical numbers in Italy

Despite the abundant literature on mafias, in the past decade mythical numbers have gained increasing importance in Italy. While public institutions have traditionally refrained from producing estimates, mythical numbers have developed as a result of the misinterpretation and uncritical repetition of figures developed by a few academic studies and non-governmental organisations.

The most frequently cited mythical numbers on the mafias in Italy are two estimates of their proceeds or revenues. The first mythical number states that mafia revenues amount to approximately €150 bn yearly, and it is frequently attributed to the Bank of Italy, the country's central bank. The second mythical number is €138 bn, which allegedly corresponds to the annual turnover of the so-called 'Mafia Inc.' and was created by *SOS Impresa*, a non-governmental association of entrepreneurs against extortion racketeering. The accounts of the birth and evolution of these figures provides impeccable examples of the problems of mythical numbers.[19]

The €150 bn number, i.e. approximately 10% of Italy's GDP, originated from studies, published in academic journals and in a paper series of the Bank of Italy, measuring the underground and illegal economy by means of econometric models. In 2008, Argentiero et al. estimated the money laundered yearly from 1981 to 2001 at approximately 12% of Italian GDP.[20] In 2012, Ardizzi and colleagues estimated the underground economy from the demand for cash (using the ratio between withdrawals from current accounts and non-cash payments as the dependent variable).[21] For the period 2005–2008, the study estimated the underground and criminal economy at 16.5% and 10.9% of GDP, respectively. Estimation of the criminal economy was based on reported drug trafficking and exploitation of prostitution offences. Whilst the study adopted an interesting macroeconomic approach, the variables for the criminal economy raise questions about their reliability. As well known, official statistics on these offences have a high 'dark' number. Reports mostly depend on the priorities and intensity of activity of the law enforcement agencies and on the more or less prohibitionist stances taken by governments towards drugs and prostitution. Given these considerations, the resulting estimates should have been treated with extreme caution. A subsequent development of the study by the same authors using a different model produced substantially lower estimates (money laundering by the criminal economy was assessed at between 6.6% and 8% of GDP).[22] Nevertheless, the numbers were cited (along with others) by Anna Maria Tarantola, the Deputy Governor of the Bank of Italy, at a hearing of 6 June 2012 before the Parliamentary Antimafia Commission. Tarantola declared that 'evaluations that have used different methodologies must be analyzed with extreme caution; they may suggest the huge economic importance of the phenomenon, but they do not allow accurate calculation'.[23] Notwithstanding Tarantola's cautions, the machine generating a mythical number soon started. The Antimafia Commission classified the total amount of €150 bn as the 'annual turnover of domestic mafias', attributing it to 'the police and various institutions'.[24] Thus the original estimate, which referred to the criminal economy in general, was already being attributed to organised crime alone. In March 2012, the European Commission, on proposing a new EU Directive on proceeds of crime, stated that 'there are no reliable estimates of the size of criminal profits in the European Union, but in Italy the proceeds of organised crime laundered in 2011 have been estimated by the Bank of Italy at €150 bn'.[25] A video produced by the Directorate General Home Affairs of the European Commission stated that 'in Italy organised crime revenues have been estimated at €150 bn'.[26] The international media promptly leapt on the news. The figure enjoyed wide success and was attributed to the UN or the Bank of Italy, or it was just unreferenced.[27]

The €138 bn number comes from the thirteenth edition of the report entitled *The Hands of Criminality on Enterprises* (*Le mani della criminalità sulle imprese*) by *SOS Impresa*, a non-governmental association campaigning against the mafias. In its ninth report of 2006, *SOS Impresa* provocatively coined the expression *Mafia SpA* (i.e. 'Mafia Inc.').[28] The thirteenth report of 2012 estimated Mafia Spa's yearly revenues for 2010 at €138.09 bn, with profits amounting to €104.70 bn and cash assets to €65.64 bn.[29] The report did not clarify its methodology, raising a number of doubts about its reliability. For example, drug trafficking yearly revenues – the prime source of income for the *Mafia SpA* – were estimated at €65 bn. This figure is higher than other national estimates (ranging between €6 bn and €9 bn, in only two cases reaching €23 bn; see the article on drug trafficking by Giommoni in this double special issue) and even higher than the estimates of the European cocaine market (US$35.6 bn in 2009).[30] A study by the UNODC questioned the *SOS Impresa* estimates, arguing that they are 'most probably gross overestimates'.[31] Nevertheless, the results were massively reported in the media, including the international ones.[32] In particular, a particularly successful claim was that, given its liquidity, 'Mafia Inc. is the first bank in Italy'.[33]

Despite the claim by scholars that mythical numbers have no impact on actual policies, the successful careers of the above-mentioned numbers may prove, at least partially, the contrary. For example, the numbers were used by the UN and the European Commission to call for further resources and policy actions in the fight against organised crime. Furthermore, during the campaign for the Italian 2013 parliamentary elections, some parties argued that the financial resources to redress the country's economy should be obtained by confiscating mafia proceeds.[34] This shows that unreliable estimates can be the basis for policies which, in their turn, are likely to fail owing to the untrustworthiness of the initial assumptions.

These considerations suggest that there is a need for better and more consistent estimations of mafia proceeds in Italy. The lack of reliable methodologies is an opportunity for the creation of mythical numbers which may have a significant impact not only on the general perception in the media and public opinion but also on the policies designed to prevent and fight mafias.

Methodology

Given the vitality of unreliable figures on the mafia proceeds, this study undertakes the daunting task of developing a new, transparent, and more reliable methodology with which to estimate mafia revenues. Owing to the lack of previous studies on the revenues of organised crime, the methods and the results of this study do not claim to be the final word on the subject, but rather a first, exploratory attempt whose purpose is to enable better knowledge and better analyses in the future.

This study is inspired by a research project conducted by Transcrime for the Ministry of Interior.[35] One of the main tasks of Transcrime's project was to estimate the proceeds of crime deriving from a number of criminal activities in Italy. This article is based on estimates updated and revised according to most recent available data. The results are in line with those presented in Transcrime's report, with some differences due to the just mentioned updates.

The analysis of mafia proceeds presented in this article took a bottom-up approach similar to the one adopted by the above-mentioned study by Transcrime. Instead of estimating the proceeds of all criminal activities with a common methodology, it was preferred to select a number of criminal activities and markets and develop a specific estimation for each of them. The criminal activities were selected by applying two main criteria. The first was the frequent association in the literature and official sources of a criminal activity with the mafias. The second criterion was the availability of information and data enabling estimation of the revenues generated by each activity in a transparent, reliable, and replicable way. As a result of the selection, the analysis focused on (1) sexual exploitation of women, (2) illicit firearms trafficking, (3) drug trafficking, (4) counterfeiting of goods, (5) illicit cigarette trade, (6) illicit gambling (7) illicit waste disposal, (8) loan sharking, and (9) extortion racketeering. The methodology and estimates are discussed in greater detail in the previous articles of this double-special issue.

The methodology consisted in three steps:

(1) estimation of the proceeds of crime from selected criminal markets and activities;
(2) allocation of a share of the proceeds of crime to mafia proceeds; and
(3) distribution of the mafia proceeds among different types of mafias.

Estimation of the proceeds of crime from nine criminal activities

The illegal revenues for each activity were estimated at both the national and regional level. Each estimation adopted different methodologies according to the specificities of the criminal market, previous evaluations in the literature, and the availability of data.

The analysis considered only the mid-point estimates for each criminal activity (Table 1). Overall, the sum of the revenues from the criminal activities selected amounted to more than €22 bn, equal to approximately 1.5% of Italian GDP (average 2007–2011) or €379 per resident (average 2007–2012). Extortion, loan sharking, sexual exploitation, counterfeiting, and drugs accounted for more than 85% of the criminal revenues.

Table 1. Proceeds of crime by criminal activity in Italy. Mid-point estimates (€ bn) and shares of the total.

	Year	Proceeds of crime	Share of total (%)
Trafficking & sexual exploitation	2004–2005 and 2008–2009	3081.34	12.6
Firearms	2010	93.47	0.4
Drugs	2008–2012	3310.70	13.5
Counterfeiting	2008	4541.27	18.6
Gambling	2011	424.56	1.7
Waste	2007–2010	405.33	1.7
Cigarettes	2012	1139.06	4.7
Loan sharking	2012	4634.22	18.9
Extortion racketeering	2012	5252.55	21.5
Total		22,882.49	

Source: Author's elaboration.

Allocation of a share of the proceeds of crime to the mafias in general

The analysis allocated a share of the proceeds of crime to the mafias (Mafia Proceeds). The allocation was conducted for each criminal activity and region and calculated a minimum and a maximum share. The calculation of Mafia Proceeds was based on the following formulas:

Mafia Proceeds $x_{reg_{max}}$ = Illegal Revenues x_{reg} · Theoretical Share x_{max} · Effective Share$_{reg}$

Mafia proceeds $x_{reg_{min}}$ = Illegal Revenues x_{reg} · Theoretical Share x_{min} · Effective Share$_{reg}$

where x is one of the selected criminal activities. Estimation of the mafia proceeds moved through two phases.

The first phase estimated what part of each illegal activity was theoretically controllable by the mafias (Theoretical Share). Considering the exploratory nature of the analysis, it identified minimum and maximum (theoretical) shares. As far as possible, the shares were differentiated by sub-activities (e.g. for different types of drugs) on the basis of specific considerations regarding control by criminal organisations (Table 2). The main assumption was that mafias are unable to achieve monopoly at the regional level in any criminal activity, with the sole exception of extortion racketeering, which is considered typical of mafias. This assumption was grounded on the findings in the criminological literature on criminal markets. Criminal activities are normally undertaken by a wide array of actors, and it would be incorrect to assume that mafias control or monopolise any of them. Studies have highlighted that, with the exception of extortion racketeering, criminal activities at the national and regional level are not monopolised by mafias. The most significant example is provided by the drugs market. The literature has constantly rejected the hypothesis of monopoly and oligopoly by large structured mafias.[36] These results have been confirmed also in Italy, except for some small areas, e.g. villages or city neighbourhoods, where elements of mafia monopoly have been observed.[37]

The second phase consisted in estimation of the share of each activity effectively controlled by the mafias (Effective Share). It was assumed that, although it is theoretically possible to control a given share of a criminal market, a mafia must have a strong presence

Table 2. Minimum and maximum theoretical share per criminal activity.

Activities	Sub-activities	Min.	Max.
Sexual exploitation		20	40
Firearms		20	40
Drugs	Heroin	40	80
	Cocaine	40	80
	Cannabis	30	50
	Amphetamines	10	30
	Ecstasy	10	30
Counterfeiting		10	50
Gambling		20	80
Illegal waste trade	Non-hazardous waste	20	60
	Hazardous waste	30	80
Illicit tobacco trade		20	80
Loan sharking		40	80
Extortion		100	100

Source: Author's elaboration.

to do so. Therefore, the main assumption was that in regions where mafias have a stronger presence, they are effectively able to control a share of illegal activities equal to the one theoretically controllable. In regions where mafias have a lower presence, by contrast, they do not have the operational capacity and connections to do so, and they may actually control only a fraction of what they could.

Mafia presence was measured by means of the Mafia Presence Index (MPI) developed by Transcrime for the Italian Ministry of the Interior.[38] Design of the MPI was based on previous attempts to measure the presence of mafias across Italian provinces in a reliable though efficient way.[39] The index is the arithmetic mean of five normalised variables (maximum value = 1000):

(1) reported mafia murders and attempted mafia murders, average of annual rates per 10,000 inhabitants, 2004–2011;
(2) people reported for mafia-type criminal association, average of annual rates per 10,000 inhabitants, 2004–2011;
(3) city councils dissolved for mafia infiltration, number of times, 2000 to August 2012;
(4) assets confiscated from criminal organisations, rate per 10,000 inhabitants, 2000–2011; and
(5) groups reported by the Direzione Investigativa Antimafia (Investigative Antimafia Directorate, DIA) and the Direzione Nazionale Antimafia (National Antimafia Directorate, DNA), average reported groups per year, 2000–2011.[40] In total, the analysis covered 24 semi-annual DIA reports (from the first half of 2000 to the second half of 2011), and 11 annual DNA reports (2000–2011).[41] For each report, the study recorded individual criminal groups, the types of criminal organisation, and the area in which they were present (municipality or province).[42]

The MPI measured the presence of mafias in Italy at the municipal level. Aggregation at the provincial and regional level provided synthetically analysable variables (Figure 1 and Table 3).[43] The regional scores of the MPI should be interpreted with caution. The strong mafia presence in a few southern regions – especially Campania, where the Camorra is traditionally characterised by numerous small groups and a very high number of mafia

CRIMINAL MARKETS AND MAFIA PROCEEDS

Figure 1. Mafia Presence Index at the municipal, provincial, and regional levels (2000–2011).
Source: Author's elaboration on Transcrime data.

Table 3. Mafia Presence Index and Effective Share per region.

Region	Mafia Presence Index	Effective Share
Campania	61.21	1
Calabria	41.76	1
Sicily	31.80	1
Apulia	17.84	1
Lazio	16.83	0.8
Liguria	10.44	0.8
Piedmont	6.11	0.8
Basilicata	5.32	0.8
Lombardy	4.17	0.6
Tuscany	2.16	0.6
Umbria	1.68	0.6
Emilia-Romagna	1.44	0.6
Abruzzo	0.74	0.4
Sardinia	0.70	0.4
Marche	0.67	0.4
Valle d'Aosta	0.57	0.4
Friuli Venezia Giulia	0.42	0.2
Veneto	0.41	0.2
Trentino-Alto Adige	0.37	0.2
Molise	0.31	0.2

Source: Author's elaboration on Transcrime data.

murders – leads to a considerable concentration of the MPI values. However, also relatively low values can indicate a significant mafia presence able to influence criminal markets, as well as the legal economy and politics. For this reason, the study divided the 20 Italian regions into quintiles. It assigned to each quintile a parameter (Effective Share) representing the share of illegal activities effectively controlled by mafias in the theoretically controllable share. Therefore, the Effective Share for the first quintile, corresponding to the regions with the highest MPI values, was 100%, 80% for the second, 60% for the third, 40% for the fourth, and 20% for the last quintile (Table 3). The calculation of Mafia Proceeds generated minimum and maximum values corresponding to the hypotheses of low or high mafia control of each a criminal market.

Distribution of mafia proceeds among different types of mafias

The analysis distributed mafia proceeds among the five main types of mafia: Cosa Nostra, Camorra, 'Ndrangheta, Apulian mafias, and other mafias. This estimation was conducted for each criminal activity, region and type of mafia. The calculations were based on the following formulas (example for the proceeds attributable to Cosa Nostra):

$$\text{CN Proceeds } x_{\text{reg}_{\max}} = \text{Mafia Proceeds } x_{\max_{\text{reg}}} \cdot \% \text{ Presence CN}_{\text{reg}}$$

$$\text{CN Proceeds } x_{\text{reg}_{\min}} = \text{Mafia Proceeds } x_{\min_{\text{reg}}} \cdot \% \text{ Presence CN}_{\text{reg}}$$

where x is one of the selected criminal activities and *Mafia Proceeds* are calculated as described in the previous subsection.

Analysis of the distribution of the five types of mafia across Italian regions was based on the number of groups reported by the DIA and the DNA from 2000 to 2011 (variable 5 of the MPI). As displayed in Figure 2, the five types of mafia concentrate in different areas of Italy.

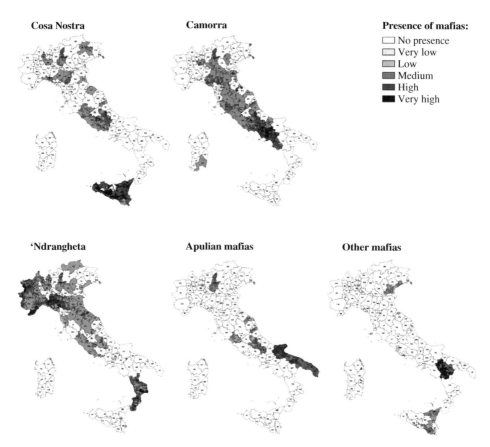

Figure 2. Presence of Cosa Nostra, Camorra, 'Ndrangheta, Apulian mafias, and other criminal organisations in Italy (2000–2011).

Source: Author's elaboration on Transcrime data.

Table 4. Share of mafia presence by type of mafia and region.

Region	Cosa Nostra (%)	Camorra (%)	'Ndrangheta (%)	Apulian OC (%)	Other OC (%)
Abruzzo	8.9	80.6	6.1	4.5	0.0
Basilicata	0.0	0.0	0.6	0.0	99.4
Calabria	0.0	0.1	99.9	0.0	0.0
Campania	0.0	99.8	0.1	0.0	0.0
Emilia R.	8.8	24.4	66.9	0.0	0.0
Friuli-V.G.	73.9	24.3	1.8	0.0	0.0
Lazio	31.0	35.6	30.4	0.7	2.2
Liguria	22.7	7.0	70.3	0.0	0.0
Lombardy	11.6	29.2	53.1	5.0	1.1
Marche	7.0	21.5	54.8	16.7	0.0
Molise	0.2	93.4	2.7	3.7	0.0
Piedmont	2.9	1.1	95.2	0.0	0.8
Apulia	0.0	0.0	0.0	100.0	0.0
Sardinia	0.0	71.0	27.8	0.0	1.3
Sicily	91.1	0.0	0.5	0.0	8.5
Tuscany	5.9	57.7	34.9	1.5	0.0
Trentino A.A.	0.0	0.0	100.0	0.0	0.0
Umbria	5.6	59.1	35.4	0.0	0.0
V. d'Aosta	0.0	0.0	100.0	0.0	0.0
Veneto	5.4	12.5	37.3	0.9	43.9

Note: The sum of the regional shares may differ from 100 because of rounding.
Source: Author's elaboration on Transcrime data.

The relative presence of each type of mafia at the municipal level was calculated as the ratio between the average number of groups of mafia type *i* and the total number of mafia groups (*% Presence CN* in the above formula). The resulting coefficients measured the share attributable to Cosa Nostra, Camorra, 'Ndrangheta, Apulian mafias, and other mafias, respectively. Aggregation at the regional level (weighting each municipal ratio by the resident population 2004–2010) yielded regional scores of mafia presence by type (Table 4).

Limitations

The discussion of mythical numbers and mafias in Italy has highlighted that this field of study has been rather neglected in past years. The lack of serious studies has required development of a new, exploratory methodology which inevitably has a number of limitations.

Estimating the proceeds of crime is a complex task which unavoidably implies assumptions and, not infrequently, simplifications. The analysis reported here used the bottom-up approach adopted in Transcrime's report for the Italian Ministry of the Interior. It selected a limited number of criminal activities according to the frequency of the association in the literature and official reports of each activity with mafias, and the availability of data. This approach entailed that the selection of the activities was crucial in defining the scope of the estimates, and the limited number of activities examined may have underestimated mafia proceeds. For example, the lack of data prevented any exploration of corruption (e.g. public contracts awarded to mafia-related enterprises in exchange for bribes or other favours), sport betting (e.g. match fixing in football championships), and urban waste disposal (e.g. revenues from the illicit disposal of urban waste).

Also the allocation of a share of the proceeds of crime to mafias encountered several difficulties. First, while a number of studies reject the hypothesis that organised crime monopolises criminal markets, there is no research on the actual 'market share' of criminal organisations. This deficiency required adoption of an exploratory approach which assigned to each criminal activity a share which might theoretically be controlled by organised crime (minimum–maximum range). This process was based on various sources and assumptions (e.g. the relevance of a given criminal market for the mafias, technical and operational requirements, and the fragmentation of markets). Unfortunately, it was impossible to establish clear criteria for selection of the above-mentioned shares, and the choices adopted in this study may seem nothing more than informed guesswork. However, compared with the existing mythical numbers, the approach adopted here is more conservative, in that it rejects the idea of a mafia monopoly and identifies a range of mafia market shares. Second, the MPI may be influenced by the reliability and availability of the variables used to calculate it. A previous study in the literature has analysed the reliability of measurement of mafia presence based on four out of the five variables included in the MPI. It also compared the results with another index comprising a larger number of variables, finding a very high and significant correlation.[44] These findings suggest that the MPI is a reliable instrument with which to measure the mafia presence in Italy.

The distribution of criminal proceeds among the different types of mafia also has limitations. First, it is closely dependent on the data extracted by Transcrime from the reports of the DIA and DNA. The analysis may be biased by the law enforcement agencies' perceptions. Nevertheless, both the DIA and the DNA are highly specialised bodies with more than 20 years of experience in the field. Their reports provide a wealth of information and are organised into sections devoted to the different mafias and regions. Transcrime's study analysed tens of thousands of pages recording the groups reported in each municipality and province. The measurement was consistent with the findings in the literature, the media, and other official accounts (Figure 2). In the absence of any better analysis, the breakdown provided by Transcrime appears to be the most reliable proxy of the presence of the various mafias. A second limitation was that it was not possible to differentiate among different types of mafias, and the study assumed that all of them may have the same prevalence in a given criminal market. This was due to a lack of evidence which prevented the drawing of any reliable distinctions.

The above considerations recommend caution in interpreting the result of this study. The aim of the analysis is not to pass final judgement on the topic of mafia proceeds, but rather to explore possible estimation methods taking account of the main results in the literature. The findings should be considered as those of a first attempt to quantify the revenues of the mafias in Italy using a replicable and clearly described methodology. They may provide the basis for future studies using more refined approaches, which will most likely depend on the availability of better data.

Results and discussion

Mafia proceeds

Table 5 reports the yearly estimates of mafia proceeds by activity and region. At national level, the revenues of the mafias from the criminal activities selected range between a minimum of €8.4 bn to a maximum of €13 bn. Compared with the total illegal revenues (mid-point estimate €22.8 bn), those attributable to the mafias may vary between 37% and 57%. They represent between 0.6% and 0.9% of GDP and between €141 and €218 per

Table 5. Mafia proceeds by activity and region. Minimum and maximum estimates (€ mn).

Region		Traff. and sexual expl.	Firearms	Drugs	Counterfeiting	Gambling	Waste	Cigarettes	Loan sharking	Extortion racket	Total
Abruzzo	Min.	6.82	0.14	9.16	3.96	0.21	0.63	2.08	24.74	58.14	105.88
	Max.	13.65	0.28	18.09	19.78	0.83	1.89	8.31	49.48	58.14	170.46
Basilicata	Min.	5.75	0.22	6.70	2.67	1.38	0.58	0.79	25.16	23.87	67.13
	Max.	11.51	0.43	13.23	13.36	5.50	1.73	3.17	50.33	23.87	123.13
Calabria	Min.	8.72	1.04	30.92	11.96	5.50	1.27	2.63	114.48	626.46	802.97
	Max.	17.44	2.07	61.48	59.78	21.99	3.79	10.52	228.97	626.46	1032.49
Campania	Min.	28.64	2.22	137.47	42.54	12.23	4.71	65.18	324.85	1538.90	2156.73
	Max.	57.27	4.43	273.65	212.69	48.94	14.02	260.72	649.69	1538.90	3060.31
Emilia-Romagna	Min.	17.64	0.57	48.87	22.37	0.69	3.71	6.10	32.21	131.58	263.73
	Max.	35.28	1.14	97.15	111.84	2.75	10.96	24.40	64.42	131.58	479.52
Friuli-V.G.	Min.	6.84	0.07	3.11	2.43	0.34	0.44	2.32	4.01	40.97	60.52
	Max.	13.67	0.14	6.14	12.14	1.37	1.30	9.27	8.02	40.97	93.02
Lazio	Min.	83.35	1.23	70.87	34.74	4.58	5.47	10.41	145.04	208.55	564.24
	Max.	166.70	2.46	141.35	173.71	18.32	16.31	41.63	290.08	208.55	1059.10
Liguria	Min.	24.37	0.59	37.30	9.91	0.08	1.44	2.13	41.82	59.16	176.79
	Max.	48.73	1.18	74.18	49.53	0.31	4.26	8.53	83.65	59.16	329.52
Lombardy	Min.	57.46	0.87	133.67	46.29	1.99	6.43	21.08	88.46	232.69	588.96
	Max.	114.92	1.75	268.88	231.44	7.97	18.92	84.33	176.93	232.69	1137.84
Marche	Min.	8.93	0.16	10.72	4.11	0.22	1.34	1.46	19.69	111.60	158.24
	Max.	17.85	0.32	21.10	20.57	0.89	4.01	5.84	39.39	111.60	221.57
Molise	Min.	0.66	0.03	1.34	0.38	0.03	0.13	0.16	3.36	17.86	23.93
	Max.	1.32	0.05	2.66	1.88	0.10	0.38	0.64	6.72	17.86	31.61
Piedmont	Min.	38.35	0.81	76.29	23.67	9.33	3.85	10.30	95.98	252.64	511.21
	Max.	76.70	1.61	150.94	118.34	37.30	11.36	41.20	191.96	252.64	882.05
Apulia	Min.	20.41	2.00	65.41	25.68	10.55	6.73	7.04	193.37	516.67	847.87
	Max.	40.82	4.00	129.99	128.41	42.21	20.12	28.16	386.74	516.67	1297.12
Sardinia	Min.	2.67	0.17	17.81	4.04	4.13	1.24	2.18	29.28	35.41	96.93
	Max.	5.35	0.33	35.47	20.19	16.53	3.69	8.70	58.56	35.41	184.24

(*Continued*)

Table 5. (Continued).

Region		Traff. and sexual expl.	Firearms	Drugs	Counterfeiting	Gambling	Waste	Cigarettes	Loan sharking	Extortion racket	Total
Sicily	Min.	25.31	1.49	66.85	30.76	16.68	6.69	14.58	214.74	756.66	1133.75
	Max.	50.62	2.98	132.87	153.78	66.71	19.16	58.34	429.48	756.66	1670.60
Tuscany	Min.	19.95	0.99	37.73	17.03	1.01	6.15	6.14	54.97	218.41	362.38
	Max.	39.91	1.98	74.47	85.15	4.03	18.37	24.57	109.94	218.41	576.82
Trentino-Alto	Min.	3.86	0.04	3.78	1.59	0.01	0.45	0.59	0.02	39.85	50.19
Adige	Max.	7.73	0.08	7.52	7.94	0.06	1.34	2.36	0.03	39.85	66.90
Umbria	Min.	16.17	0.38	8.29	3.63	0.22	1.37	1.20	16.55	26.20	74.00
	Max.	32.33	0.77	16.33	18.15	0.90	4.08	4.79	33.09	26.20	136.64
Valle d'Aosta	Min.	0.97	0.01	1.56	0.32	0.12	0.06	0.11	1.18	13.68	18.01
	Max.	1.94	0.01	3.12	1.60	0.50	0.17	0.43	2.37	13.68	23.82
Veneto	Min.	10.54	0.36	15.53	10.51	0.14	1.62	4.28	15.35	343.26	401.59
	Max.	21.09	0.73	30.84	52.57	0.54	4.78	17.14	30.70	343.26	501.64
Total Italy	Min.	387.41	13.38	783.38	298.57	69.44	54.31	160.76	1445.27	5252.55	8465.05
	Max.	774.82	26.76	1559.48	1492.85	277.75	160.63	643.04	2890.54	5252.55	13,078.41
	Avg.	581.12	20.07	1171.43	895.71	173.59	107.47	401.90	2167.90	5252.55	10,771.73

Source: Author's elaboration.

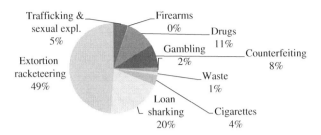

Figure 3. Share of mafia proceeds by criminal activity. Average estimates.
Source: Author's elaboration.

resident. Since the criminal activities considered are only a selection of the sources of revenues for mafias, their magnitude compared with the national economy is significant.

Extortion racketeering is the main source of mafia revenues, yielding more than €5.2 bn, equal to 49% of the total amount (considering the mid-point estimate between the minimum and maximum values). It is followed by loan sharking (20%) and drugs (11%) and counterfeiting (8%) (Figure 3).

These results suggest that closer attention should be paid to extortion racketeering and usury, particularly considering the widespread idea that mafias derive most of their incomes from drugs. These findings receive some support in the literature. One theoretical approach to mafias treats them as suppliers of private protection, an activity where they can exploit their specialisation in the use of violence.[45] While extortion and private protection are different, though sometimes overlapping, concepts, the focus on these activities highlights their key function for mafias instead of other criminal markets, e.g. drug trafficking.[46] Other scholars have demonstrated that criminal markets are not particularly suited to large structured groups like mafias.[47] The frequent assumptions that (1) criminal markets are monopolised by mafias, and that (2) the provision of illicit goods and services is their main activity, have been shown to be paradoxes rather than empirically based facts.[48] While in line with the literature, the particular role of extortion racketeering was one of the main assumptions of the analysis (which attributed 100% of the estimated revenues to mafias) and this inevitably affected its share in total mafia proceeds. Yet the estimated revenues are higher than those deriving from any other of the selected activities. Differently from the Transcrime report, the update of the estimates resulted in extortion revenues higher than those from drugs because of the different years considered (drug consumption may have declined due to economic difficulties) and estimation methodologies used.

Closer attention to extortion racketeering may have significant implications. Indeed, it may partially contribute to explaining the differences in economic performance between Italy and other developed countries. While all the latter record high levels of drug consumption, only Italy has a strong mafia presence on its territory. A number of studies have shown that the mafia impacts on various elements of economic performance, from the general economic structure[49] to regional GDP growth,[50] firms' productivity,[51] and foreign direct investments.[52] All these effects may be associated with the mafias' extortion racketeering, which is likely to affect the local and national economy more than criminal markets like drug trafficking.

Loan sharking may share some of the considerations that apply to extortion racketeering. Violence, threats, and intimidation are important assets for success in the usury

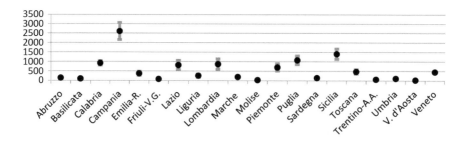

Figure 4. Mafia proceeds by region (absolute values, € mn). Average (point), minimum, and maximum estimates (error bars).

Source: Author's elaboration.

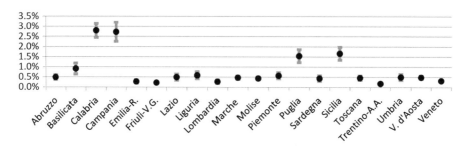

Figure 5. Mafia proceeds as a share of regional GDP (average 2007–2011). Average (point), minimum, and maximum estimates (error bars).

Source: Author's elaboration.

market. While some criminal entrepreneurs may resort to external enforcers, mafias have a reputation which may effectively facilitate the in-house recovery of credit in the case of need. A number of investigations have shown that mafias may use loan sharking as a means to gain control of enterprises and shops with mechanisms that closely resemble extortion racketeering.[53]

At the regional level, the regions of origin of the mafias account for 55% of the mafia proceeds in Italy (Figures 4 and 6). Campania records the highest mafia revenues (average €2.6 bn), followed by Sicily, Apulia, and Calabria (€1.4 bn, €1 bn, and €0.9 bn, respectively). Lazio, Lombardy, and Piedmont (in the Centre and North-West of Italy) also have high values (22%). Besides the methodological assumptions already discussed, possible explanations for these high levels may relate to the large populations of the three regions and the presence in them of the three big cities of Rome, Milan, and Turin. Mafia proceeds from some of the richest and most developed regions in Italy represent an important share of the total, which further confirms that the mafias should be considered a national issue rather than a Southern peculiarity.

The critical impact of the mafias on the economies of the four regions of origin emerges when the values are normalised for the regional GDP (average 2007–2011) (Figure 5). Mafia revenues are equal to nearly 3% of the regional GDP in Calabria and Campania, 1.7% in Sicily, and 1.5% in Apulia. Other regions do not even come close to these figures. These results demonstrate that a strong mafia presence may generate proceeds equal to a substantial share of the regional economy. Given the limited number

CRIMINAL MARKETS AND MAFIA PROCEEDS

Table 6. Mafia proceeds by region. Absolute values (€ mn) and shares of average illegal revenues (minimum, maximum and average estimates).

	Absolute values			Shares of illegal revenues		
	Min.	Max.	Avg.	Min. (%)	Max. (%)	Avg. (%)
Abruzzo	105.9	170.5	138.2	21	34	28
Basilicata	67.1	123.1	95.1	31	58	44
Calabria	803.0	1032.5	917.7	66	85	76
Campania	2156.7	3060.3	2608.5	58	82	70
Emilia R.	263.7	479.5	371.6	24	43	33
Friuli V.G.	60.5	93.0	76.8	12	18	15
Lazio	564.2	1059.1	811.7	28	53	40
Liguria	176.8	329.5	253.2	28	53	41
Lombardy	589.0	1137.8	863.4	21	41	31
Marche	158.2	221.6	189.9	28	39	34
Molise	23.9	31.6	27.8	19	26	23
Piedmont	511.2	882.1	696.6	34	58	46
Apulia	847.9	1297.1	1072.5	51	77	64
Sardinia	96.9	184.2	140.6	17	32	24
Sicily	1133.8	1670.6	1402.2	54	79	66
Tuscany	362.4	576.8	469.6	30	48	39
Trentino A.A.	50.2	66.9	58.5	17	23	20
Umbria	74.0	136.6	105.3	21	38	30
V. d'Aosta	18.0	23.8	20.9	32	43	37
Veneto	401.6	501.6	451.6	24	29	26
TOTAL	8465.05	13,078.41	10,771.73	37	57	47

Source: Author's elaboration.

of activities selected, the figures are probably underestimations. Nevertheless, at these levels, the mafias can easily influence the social, economic, and political dynamics of the regions in which they operate. As already discussed, these considerations receive support from studies that have analysed the negative impact of mafias across the Italian regions.[54]

The regional share of mafia revenues in total illegal revenues varies (Table 6 and Figure 6). Regions with a traditional mafia presence record a share of mafia revenues amounting to between 50% and 80%. Only in four other regions (Basilicata, Lazio, Liguria, and Piedmont) do the maximum mafia revenues equal or slightly exceed 50%. In all other regions, mafia revenues represent less than half of total illegal revenues, indicating that illegal activities are mostly undertaken by people not linked to mafias. Once again, although influenced by the methodological assumptions already discussed, the findings reveal a concentration of mafia activities in a relatively small number of regions, although not exclusively in the South.

Proceeds per type of mafia

The allocation of the proceeds among the different types of mafias provides further information on the sources of income for Italian organised crime groups (Table 7). Overall, Camorra and 'Ndrangheta earn approximately 68% of total mafia revenues (Figure 7). The Camorra earns between a minimum of €3.1 bn and a maximum of €4.7 bn, and the 'Ndrangheta between €2.5 bn and €4 bn. Cosa Nostra follows, with revenues between €1.4 bn and €2.3 bn. The revenues of Apulian mafias vary between €0.9 bn and €1.4 bn.

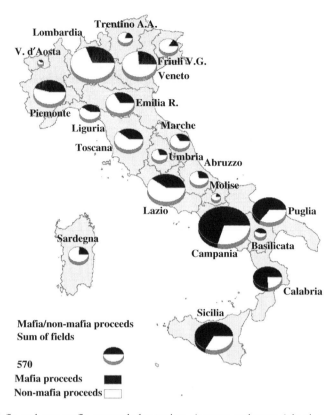

Figure 6. Mafia and non-mafia proceeds by region. Average estimates (pie size = total criminal revenues from selected activities, € mn).

Source: Author's elaboration.

These findings suggest that Cosa Nostra has faced difficulties in recent years due to strong government action since the beginning of the 1990s.[55] Moreover, the majority of Cosa Nostra's revenues come from its native Sicily (approximately 68%, Figure 8). Both the Camorra and the 'Ndrangheta outmatch the revenues of the Sicilian Mafia. While the raw figures for the two types of mafia are similar, there are significant differences in the structure of the organisations and the geographical distribution of their sources of revenue. The Camorra has been traditionally a constellation of different clans and groups, with a prevalently horizontal organisation. With the exception of a few specific periods and groups (e.g. the *Casalesi* group as described in *Gomorrah* by Saviano),[56] there have been no successful attempts to centralise or coordinate the various groups.[57] The high rates of mafia murders in Naples confirm that violent conflicts among these syndicates are frequent. The Camorra groups derive most of their revenues from Campania (66%, Figure 8), their region of origin, and particularly from the provinces of Naples and Caserta (*Casalesi* territory). These findings may indicate that the constantly battling Camorra groups impose an extremely heavy burden on Campania both in terms of violence and insecurity and in terms of criminal revenues. Camorra's concentration in the region may explain the latter's economic difficulties despite the availability of fertile land, an infrastructure endowment above the Italian average, a large city like Naples, and several cultural and natural attractions.

Table 7. Mafia proceeds by region and type of mafia (€ mn). Minimum and maximum estimates.

Region		Cosa Nostra	Camorra	'Ndrangheta	Apulian mafias	Other mafias	Total
Abruzzo	Min.	9.45	85.30	6.41	4.72	0.00	105.88
	Max.	15.21	137.32	10.32	7.61	0.00	170.46
Basilicata	Min.	0.00	0.00	0.38	0.00	66.75	67.13
	Max.	0.00	0.00	0.69	0.00	122.44	123.13
Calabria	Min.	0.05	1.13	801.79	0.00	0.00	802.97
	Max.	0.07	1.46	1030.97	0.00	0.00	1032.49
Campania	Min.	0.39	2152.39	3.12	0.77	0.05	2156.73
	Max.	0.55	3054.16	4.43	1.09	0.08	3060.31
Emilia-Romagna	Min.	23.10	64.23	176.40	0.00	0.00	263.73
	Max.	42.01	116.79	320.72	0.00	0.00	479.52
Friuli-V.G.	Min.	44.72	14.69	1.11	0.00	0.00	60.52
	Max.	68.74	22.57	1.71	0.00	0.00	93.02
Lazio	Min.	175.02	201.01	171.74	3.96	12.50	564.24
	Max.	328.53	377.32	322.36	7.44	23.46	1059.10
Liguria	Min.	40.13	12.40	124.26	0.00	0.00	176.79
	Max.	74.80	23.12	231.61	0.00	0.00	329.52
Lombardy	Min.	68.60	171.76	312.96	29.36	6.27	588.96
	Max.	132.54	331.84	604.63	56.72	12.11	1137.84
Marche	Min.	11.05	33.99	86.79	26.42	0.00	158.24
	Max.	15.48	47.59	121.52	36.99	0.00	221.57
Molise	Min.	0.06	22.34	0.64	0.89	0.00	23.93
	Max.	0.08	29.51	0.85	1.18	0.00	31.61
Piedmont	Min.	14.65	5.41	486.89	0.00	4.26	511.21
	Max.	25.27	9.34	840.09	0.00	7.35	882.05
Apulia	Min.	0.00	0.00	0.00	847.87	0.00	847.87
	Max.	0.00	0.00	0.00	1297.12	0.00	1297.12
Sardinia	Min.	0.00	68.80	26.91	0.00	1.23	96.93
	Max.	0.00	130.76	51.14	0.00	2.34	184.24
Sicily	Min.	1032.42	0.00	5.33	0.00	96.00	1133.75
	Max.	1521.28	0.00	7.86	0.00	141.46	1670.60

(*Continued*)

Table 7. (Continued).

Region		Cosa Nostra	Camorra	'Ndrangheta	Apulian mafias	Other mafias	Total
Tuscany	Min.	21.29	208.99	126.64	5.46	0.00	362.38
	Max.	33.89	332.66	201.58	8.69	0.00	576.82
Trentino-Alto Adige	Min.	0.00	0.00	50.19	0.00	0.00	50.19
	Max.	0.00	0.00	66.90	0.00	0.00	66.90
Umbria	Min.	4.12	43.70	26.18	0.00	0.00	74.00
	Max.	7.61	80.69	48.34	0.00	0.00	136.64
Valle d'Aosta	Min.	0.00	0.00	18.01	0.00	0.00	18.01
	Max.	0.00	0.00	23.82	0.00	0.00	23.82
Veneto	Min.	21.56	50.30	149.85	3.49	176.39	401.59
	Max.	26.93	62.83	187.18	4.35	220.34	501.64
Total Italy	Min.	1466.63	3136.45	2575.59	922.93	363.46	8465.05
	Max.	2292.99	4757.95	4076.72	1421.18	529.57	13,078.41
	Avg.	1879.81	3947.20	3326.15	1172.06	446.52	10,771.73

Source: Author's elaboration.

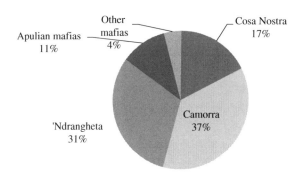

Figure 7. Share of mafia proceeds by type of mafia. Average estimates.
Source: Author's elaboration.

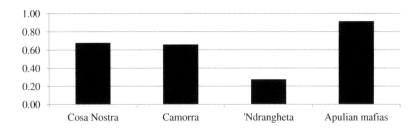

Figure 8. Share of mafia proceeds from the region of origin, by type of mafia. Average estimates.
Source: Author's elaboration.

The case of the 'Ndrangheta is different. This mafia obtains only 28% of its revenues from Calabria, which is a low-populated and relatively underdeveloped region. The 'Ndrangheta has a more composite structure, which has possibly favoured its expansion into other Italian regions and abroad.[58] As shown in Figure 9, Calabria furnishes only

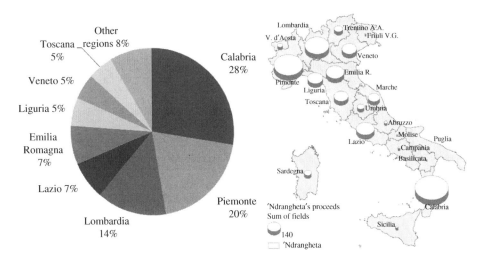

Figure 9. 'Ndrangheta's proceeds by region. Shares of the total and absolute values (€ mn). Average estimates.
Source: Author's elaboration.

28% of the 'Ndrangheta's proceeds. Northern Piedmont and Lombardy provide 20% and 14%, respectively. Emilia-Romagna and Lazio follow with 7% each. The 'Ndrangheta's diversified sources of income highlight its capacity to operate outside its original territory, since almost 50% of its revenues derive from four north-western regions (Lombardy, Piedmont, Emilia-Romagna, and Liguria).

Conclusions

This study is a first attempt to estimate mafia proceeds in Italy. It estimates the total revenues by the mafia between €8.4 bn and €13 bn, numbers which are well below the most popular mythical numbers of €150 bn and €138 bn, widely publicised in the media and public opinion, but based on unclear or imprecise assumptions. Given the lack of previous reliable analyses, the findings reported here must be interpreted with caution. Their purpose is to stimulate public and academic debate on the actual size of mafia-related criminal activities and their impact on the national and local economy.

This study may also prompt further reflection by academics on the persistence of mythical numbers in criminology, particularly in the field of organised crime. These figures have probably also been successful because academics have either belittled estimates or uncritically exploited their sensationalist capacity. Given the shortage of reliable data, scholars have largely refrained from producing estimates. Sometimes, instead of questioning their reliability – with the risk of long technical debates and damage to relations with stakeholders and funders – they have preferred to repeat these figures while citing their sources. As a result, mythical numbers on organised crime have gained power, and governments, international organisations, NGOs, and other stakeholders have found an effective opportunity to support their own agendas. Academics should reverse this attitude, since there is a need for more studies on the revenues of organised crime so that more precise estimations and improved policies can be developed.

In their essays on mythical numbers, both Singer and Reuter expressed pessimism about the possibility of solving the problem. They probably had good reasons for doing so. Indeed, when the results of the study conducted by Transcrime were disseminated, the media and other interested stakeholders were surprised at 'how low' the estimates of mafia proceeds were. However after some discussion and clarification, it was generally recognised that previous estimates were unrealistic and unreliable ('mafias making more than 10% of Italian GDP, i.e. more than the car or tourism industries?!'). Furthermore, when the estimates were discussed with staff of international organisations actively involved in the development of policies against organised crime, an official whispered, 'well, you could have produced higher figures…you know…', suggesting that the estimates were not 'high enough'.

Despite the pessimism, there were also some encouraging signals. For example, a police official praised the study, particularly because 'somebody has finally stopped talking about the 'Ndrangheta's monopoly of the cocaine market'. He then cited an analysis of serious drug cases investigated in the past 2 years in the area around Milan. The data showed than only a minority of the cases involved the 'Ndrangheta, despite constant media attention in the same period. This exchange echoed Reuter's comments on the 'demoralizing impact on lower level officials of having to work with numbers that they know are seriously in error'.[59]

CRIMINAL MARKETS AND MAFIA PROCEEDS

Notes

1. Singer, "Vitality of Mythical Numbers," 6; Reuter, "The (Continued) Vitality of Mythical Numbers"; and Shafer, "The (Ongoing) Vitality of Mythical Numbers."
2. Singer, "Vitality of Mythical Numbers," 6.
3. Reuter, "The (Continued) Vitality of Mythical Numbers," 145–6.
4. Reuter, "Social Costs of the Demand," 807.
5. Ibid., 811.
6. Shafer, "The (Ongoing) Vitality of Mythical Numbers"; Andreas and Greenhill, *Sex, Drugs, and Body Counts*; and Hagan, *Introduction to Criminology*, 442.
7. Woodiwiss, "Transnational Organized Crime"; and Paoli and Fijnaut, "Introduction to Part I."
8. Woodiwiss and Hobbs, "Organized Evil and the Atlantic Alliance"; and Carrapiço, "Chasing Mirages?."
9. Smith, *The Mafia Mystique*; Reuter, *Disorganized Crime*; Paoli, "The Paradoxes of Organized Crime"; and Van Duyne, "Creation of a Threat Image."
10. Von Lampe, "Not a Process of Enlightenment"; Van Duyne, "Introduction: Counting Clouds"; Dorn, "End of Organised Crime"; Van Duyne and Vander Beken, "Incantations of the EU Organised"; and Calderoni, "Definition That Does Not Work."
11. UNODC, *Estimating Illicit Financial Flows*, 34.
12. UNODC, "Transnational Crime Proceeds in Billions."
13. UNODC, "Transnational Organized Crime"; Le monde, "Le crime organisé"; and Reuters, "Cross-border Criminals."
14. Reuter, "Social Costs of the Demand," 810.
15. Ibid., 809; Paoli, "Mafia and Organised Crime in Italy."
16. Reuter, "Mismeasurement of Illegal Drug Markets."
17. See note 14.
18. Transcrime, *Progetto PON Sicurezza 2007–2013*.
19. Singer, "Vitality of Mythical Numbers."
20. Argentiero Bagella, and Busato, "Money Laundering in a Two-sector Model."
21. Ardizzi et al., "Measuring the Underground Economy."
22. Ardizzi et al., "Estimating Money Laundering."
23. Tarantola, *Dimensione Delle Attività Criminali*, 5.
24. CPA, *Relazione sulla prima fase dei*, 15.
25. European Commission, "Proposal for a Directive," 2.
26. European Commission, *Confiscated Assets*.
27. Euronews, "Taking on Organised Crime"; Ruggeri, "Taking a Bite Out"; and Za, "Italy's Crisis Opens Doors."
28. SOS Impresa, *Le mani della criminalità sulle imprese*, 2006.
29. SOS Impresa, *Le mani della criminalità sulle imprese*, 2012, 47–8.
30. UNODC, *Estimating Illicit Financial Flows Resulting*, 61.
31. Ibid., 26.
32. Galullo, "Mafia Spa, in Cassa 65 Miliardi"; Saviano, "Mafie, i Padroni Della"; Sky Tg24, "Sos Impresa"; and Mackenzie, "Mafia Now Italy's No.1 Bank."
33. SOS Impresa, "SOS Impresa."
34. Il Sole 24 ORE, "Le ricette di Ingroia contro la crisi."
35. Transcrime, *Progetto PON Sicurezza 2007–2013*.
36. Reuter and Haaga, *Organization of High-Level Drug Markets*; Pearsons and Hobbs, *Middle Market Drug Distribution*; and Dorn et al., *Literature Review on Upper Level Drug Trafficking*.
37. Becchi, "Italy: 'Mafia-dominated Drug Market'?"; Paoli, *Illegal Drug Markets*; Paoli, "The Paradoxes of Organized Crime"; Paoli, "Illegal Drugs Market"; Varese, "How Mafias Migrate"; and Paoli and Reuter, "Drug Trafficking and Ethnic Minorities."
38. Transcrime, *Progetto PON Sicurezza 2007–2013*.
39. Calderoni, "La misurazione dell'infiltrazione della criminalità organizzata negli appalti"; Calderoni, "Where Is the Mafia in Italy?".
40. The DIA is a national law enforcement agency tasked with the fight against the mafias and organised crime. It is composed of officers from the three main Italian law enforcement agencies, namely the State Police, the Carabinieri and the Guardia di Finanza. The DNA is a national coordinating body consisting of 20 senior prosecutors. Its main task is to coordinate

41. the prosecution of mafia and organised crime cases. To this end, it encourages information sharing and the coordination of investigations among 26 Antimafia District Directorates, these being special bodies established within the prosecutor's offices in cities where a Court of Appeal is based.
41. In regard to the DNA annual reports, it was not possible to find the 2003 report. This document was requested from both the DNA and the library of the Antimafia Parliamentary Commission, but to no avail.
42. The information was entered into two databases at municipal level, one for the DIA and one for the DNA. The following variables were developed from the information extracted for each report: presence of groups in the municipality/province; number of groups in the municipality/province; names of the groups in the municipality/province; and number of groups belonging to each type of mafia organisation in the municipality/province. Finally, the two databases were combined to calculate the sum and the average of the variables listed above. For further details on the methodology, see Transcrime, *Progetto PON Sicurezza 2007–2013*.
43. The aggregation weighted the scores for each municipality in the province/region with the average resident population between 2004 and 2011.
44. Calderoni, "Where Is the Mafia in Italy?"
45. Gambetta, *The Sicilian Mafia*; and Varese, *Mafias on the Move*.
46. Some scholars have criticised this approach mainly because of its alleged incapacity to explain the origin of the demand for private protection (Catanzaro, "La mafia tra mercato e stato"; Santino, *Dalla mafia alle mafie*). Despite these criticisms, the approach has the merit of highlighting the importance of extortion and protection for mafias, thus bringing about a new focus which has been at least partially shared also by the main critics.
47. Reuter, *Disorganized Crime*.
48. Paoli, "Paradoxes of Organized Crime."
49. Lavezzi, "Economic Structure and Vulnerability."
50. Pinotti, *Economic Consequences of Organized Crime*.
51. Albanese and Marinelli, "Organized Crime and Productivity."
52. Daniele and Marani, "Organized Crime."
53. Tribunale di Milano, Ordinanza di applicazione di misura.
54. Pinotti, *Economic Consequences of Organized Crime*; Coniglio, Celi, and Scagliusi, *Organized Crime, Migration and Human Capital Formation*; Centorrino and Ofria, "Criminalità organizzata e produttività del lavoro nel Mezzogiorno"; Daniele and Marani, "Organized Crime, the Quality"; and Lavezzi, "Economic Structure and Vulnerability."
55. Paoli, "Mafia and Organised Crime in Italy."
56. Saviano, *Gomorra*.
57. Behan, *Camorra*; and Allum, *Camorristi, Politicians, and Businessmen*.
58. Paoli, *Mafia Brotherhoods*; Varese, "How Mafias Migrate"; and Calderoni, "Structure of Drug Trafficking Mafias."
59. Reuter, "The (Continued) Vitality of Mythical Numbers," 146 footnote 11.

References

Albanese, Giuseppe, and Giuseppe Marinelli. "Organized Crime and Productivity: Evidence from Firm-level Data." *Rivista Italiana Degli Economisti* 18, no. 3 (2013): 367–394.

Allum, Felia. *Camorristi, Politicians, and Businessmen: The Transformation of Organized Crime in Post-War Naples*, Italian Perspectives 11. Leeds: Northern Universities Press, 2006.

Andreas, Peter, and Kelly M Greenhill, eds. *Sex, Drugs, and Body Counts: The Politics of Numbers in Global Crime and Conflict*. Ithaca, NY: Cornell University Press, 2010.

Ardizzi, Guerino, Carmelo Petraglia, Massimiliano Piacenza, Friedrich Schneider, and Gilberto Turati. "Estimating Money Laundering Through a 'Cash Deposit Demand' Approach." *Pavia*, 2012. http://www-3.unipv.it/websiep/prog2012.htm.

Ardizzi, Guerino, Carmelo Petraglia, Massimiliano Piacenza, and Gilberto Turati. "Measuring the Underground Economy with the Currency Demand Approach: A Reinterpretation of the Methodology, with an Application to Italy." Temi Di Discussione (Working Papers), Banca d'Italia, April 2012.

Argentiero, Amedeo, Michele Bagella, and Francesco Busato. "Money Laundering in a Two-sector Model: Using Theory for Measurement." *European Journal of Law and Economics* 26, no. 3 (2008): 341–359. doi:10.1007/s10657-008-9074-6.

Becchi, Ada. "Italy: 'Mafia-dominated Drug Market'?" In *European Drug Policies and Enforcement*, edited by Nicholas Dorn, Jorgen Jepsen, and Ernesto Ugo Savona, 119–130. Basingstoke: Macmillan, 1996.

Behan, Tom. *The Camorra*. London: Routledge, 1996.

Calderoni, Francesco. "A Definition That Does Not Work: The Impact of the EU Framework Decision on the Fight Against Organized Crime." *Common Market Law Review* 49, no. 4 (2012): 1365–1393.

Calderoni, Francesco. "La misurazione dell'infiltrazione della criminalità organizzata negli appalti." In *La geografia criminale degli appalti: le infiltrazioni della criminalità organizzata negli appalti pubblici nel Sud Italia*, edited by Francesco Calderoni and Stefano Caneppele, 13–31. Milano: Franco Angeli, 2009.

Calderoni, Francesco. "The Structure of Drug Trafficking Mafias: The 'Ndrangheta and Cocaine." *Crime, Law and Social Change* 58, no. 3 (2012): 321–349. doi:10.1007/s10611-012-9387-9.

Calderoni, Francesco. "Where Is the Mafia in Italy? Measuring the Presence of the Mafia Across Italian Provinces." *Global Crime* 12, no. 1 (2011): 41. doi:10.1080/17440572.2011.548962.

CPA. *Relazione sulla prima fase dei lavori della Commissione, con particolare riguardo al condizionamento delle mafie sull'economia, sulla societa' e sulle istituzioni del Mezzogiorno*. Roma: Commissione parlamentare di inchiesta sul fenomeno della mafia e sulle altre associazioni criminali, anche straniere, 2012.

Carrapiço, Helena. "Chasing Mirages? Reflections on Concepts of Security Through the Study of the Securitization of Organized Crime." Paper presented at the annual meeting of the ISA's 49th Annual Convention, Bridging Multiple Divides, San Francisco, CA, March 26, 2008.

Catanzaro, Raimondo. "La mafia tra mercato e stato." In *La mafia, le mafie: Tra vecchi e nuovi paradigmi*, edited by Giovanni Fiandaca and Salvatore Costantino, 177–193. Roma: Laterza, 1994.

Centorrino, Mario, and Ferdinando Ofria. "Criminalità organizzata e produttività del lavoro nel Mezzogiorno: un'applicazione del modello 'Kaldor-Verdoorn'." *Rivista economica del Mezzogiorno* 1/2008 (2008): 163–187. doi:10.1432/27151.

Coniglio, Nicola D., Giuseppe Celi, and Cosimo Scagliusi. *Organized Crime, Migration and Human Capital Formation: Evidence from the South of Italy* (Working Paper). Bari: Southern European Research in Economic Studies Università degli studi di Bari, 2010.

Daniele, Vittorio, and Ugo Marani. "Organized Crime, the Quality of Local Institutions and FDI in Italy: A Panel Data Analysis." *European Journal of Political Economy* 27, no. 1 (2010): 132–142. doi:10.1016/j.ejpoleco.2010.04.003.

Dorn, Nicholas. "The End of Organised Crime in the European Union." *Crime, Law and Social Change* 51 (2009): 283–295.

Dorn, Nicholas, Michael Levi, and Leslie King. *Literature Review on Upper Level Drug Trafficking*. London: Home Office, 2005.

Euronews. "Taking on Organised Crime." *Euronews*, April 4, 2012. http://www.euronews.com/2012/04/01/taking-on-the-mafia/.

European Commission. *Confiscated Assets*, 2012. http://www.youtube.com/watch?v=DUWhIXNPcx4&feature=youtube_gdata_player.

European Commission. "Proposal for a Directive of the European Parliament and of the Council on the Freezing and Confiscation of Proceeds of Crime in the European Union COM (2012) 85 Final," March 12, 2012.

Galullo, Roberto. "Mafia Spa, in Cassa 65 Miliardi." *Il Sole 24 ORE*, January 10, 2012. http://www.ilsole24ore.com/art/economia/2012-01-11/mafia-cassa-miliardi-064340.shtml?uuid=AaSM3fcE.

Gambetta, Diego. *The Sicilian Mafia: The Business of Private Protection*. Cambridge, MA: Harvard University Press, 1996.

Hagan, Frank E. *Introduction to Criminology: Theories, Methods, and Criminal Behavior*. 7th ed. Thousand Oaks, CA: Sage, 2011.

Il Sole 24 ORE. "Le ricette di Ingroia contro la crisi: una banca pubblica e la confisca dei beni agli evasori." *Il Sole 24 ORE*, February 11, 2013. http://www.ilsole24ore.com/art/notizie/2013-02-11/ricette-ingroia-contro-crisi-160121.shtml?uuid=AbeuNKTH.

Lavezzi, Andrea Mario. "Economic Structure and Vulnerability to Organised Crime: Evidence from Sicily." *Global Crime* 9, no. 3 (2008): 198–220.

Le monde. "Le crime organisé, une manne de 870 milliards de dollars annuels." Accessed July 24, 2013. http://www.lemonde.fr/economie/article/2013/07/24/le-crime-organise-une-manne-financiere-de-870-milliards-de-dollars-annuels_3453066_3234.html.

Mackenzie, James. "Mafia Now Italy's No.1 Bank as Crisis Bites: Report." *Reuters*, January 10, 2012. http://www.reuters.com/article/2012/01/10/us-italy-mafia-idUSTRE8091YX20120110.

Paoli, Letizia. *Illegal Drug Markets in Frankfurt and Milan*. Lisbon: European Monitoring Centre for Drugs and Drug Addiction, 2000.

Paoli, Letizia. "The Illegal Drugs Market." *Journal of Modern Italian Studies* 9, no. 2 (2004): 186–207.

Paoli, Letizia. "Mafia and Organised Crime in Italy: The Unacknowledged Successes of Law Enforcement." *West European Politics* 30, no. 4 (2007): 854.

Paoli, Letizia. *Mafia Brotherhoods: Organized Crime Italian Style*. New York: Oxford University Press, 2003. http://books.google.it/books/about/Mafia_brotherhoods.html?hl=it&id=qX5NfHTWzS0C.

Paoli, Letizia. "The Paradoxes of Organized Crime." *Crime, Law and Social Change* 37 (2002): 51–97.

Paoli, Letizia, and Cyrille Fijnaut. "Introduction to Part I: The History of the Concept." In *Organised Crime in Europe: Concepts, Patterns and Control Policies in the European Union and Beyond*, edited by Cyrille Fijnaut and Letizia Paoli, 21–46. Dordrecht: Springer, 2004.

Paoli, Letizia, and Peter Reuter. "Drug Trafficking and Ethnic Minorities in Western Europe." *European Journal of Criminology* 5, no. 1 (2008): 13–37.

Pearsons, Geoffrey, and Dick Hobbs. *Middle Market Drug Distribution*. London: Home Office, 2001.

Pinotti, Paolo. *The Economic Consequences of Organized Crime: Evidence from Southern Italy*. Temi Di Discussione (Working Papers). Roma: Banca d'Italia, 2012.

Reuter, Peter. "The (Continued) Vitality of Mythical Numbers." *The Public Interest* 75 (1984): 135–147.

Reuter, Peter. *Disorganized Crime. The Economics of the Visible Hand*. Cambridge: MIT Press, 1983.

Reuter, Peter. "The Mismeasurement of Illegal Drug Markets: The Implications of Its Irrelevance." In *Exploring the Underground Economy: Studies of Illegal and Unreported Activity*, edited by Susan Pozo, 63–80. Kalamazoo: W.E. Upjohn Institute for Employment Research, 1996.

Reuter, Peter. "The Social Costs of the Demand for Quantification." *Journal of Policy Analysis and Management* 5, no. 4 (1986): 807–812. doi:10.2307/3324886.

Reuter, Peter, and John Haaga. *The Organization of High-Level Drug Markets: An Exploratory Study*. Santa Monica, CA: RAND Corporation, 1989. http://www.rand.org/pubs/notes/N2830.

Reuters. "Cross-border Criminals Make $870 Billion a Year: U.N." Accessed July 12, 2012. http://www.reuters.com/article/2012/07/16/us-crossborder-criminals-idUSBRE86F0DC20120716.

Ruggeri, Amanda. "Taking a Bite Out of Crime in Rome." *The New York Times*, July 4, 2013, sec. Travel. http://www.nytimes.com/2013/07/07/travel/taking-a-bite-out-of-crime-in-rome.html.

Santino, Umberto. *Dalla mafia alle mafie: scienze sociali e crimine organizzato*. Soveria Mannelli: Rubbettino, 2006.

Saviano, Roberto. *Gomorra: viaggio nell'impero economico e nel sogno di dominio della camorra*. Milan: Mondadori, 2006.

Saviano, Roberto. "Mafie, i Padroni Della Crisi Perché i Boss Non Fanno Crac." *Repubblica.it*, August 27, 2012. http://www.repubblica.it/cronaca/2012/08/27/news/saviano_criminalit_padrona_della_finanza-41551075/?ref=search.

Shafer, Jack. "The (Ongoing) Vitality of Mythical Numbers." *Slate*, June 26, 2006. http://www.slate.com/articles/news_and_politics/press_box/2006/06/the_ongoing_vitality_of_mythical_numbers.html.

Singer, Max. "The Vitality of Mythical Numbers." *The Public Interest* 23 (1971): 3–9.

Sky Tg24. "Sos Impresa: 'Mafia Spa è La Prima Banca d'Italia' – Tg24 – Sky.it." Accessed January 10, 2012. http://tg24.sky.it/tg24/economia/2012/01/10/mafia_prima_banca_italia.html.

Smith, Dwight C. *The Mafia Mystique*. New York: Basic Books, 1975.

SOS Impresa. *Le mani della criminalità sulle imprese*. Roma: Confesercenti, 2006.

SOS Impresa. *Le mani della criminalità sulle imprese*. Roma: Confesercenti, 2012.

SOS Impresa. "SOS Impresa: 'Mafia Spa è la prima banca d'Italia'." 2012. Accessed January 27, 2014. http://www.sosimpresa.it/1167/sos-impresa-mafia-spa-e-la-prima-banca-ditalia.html.

Tarantola, Anna Maria. *Dimensione Delle Attività Criminali, Costi Per L'economia, Effetti Della Crisi Economica*. Roma: Commissione parlamentare di inchiesta sul fenomeno della mafia e sulle altre associazioni criminali, anche straniere. Accessed June 6, 2012. http://www.ilsole24ore.com/pdf2010/SoleOnLine5/_Oggetti_Correlati/Documenti/Notizie/2012/06/bankitaliantimafia2012.pdf?uuid=826d0b16-afd4-11e1-b410-28ed72f00729.

Transcrime. *Progetto PON Sicurezza 2007–2013: Gli investimenti delle mafie. Rapporto Linea 1*. Milano: Ministero dell'Interno, 2013. www.investimentioc.it.

Tribunale di Milano. Ordinanza di applicazione di misura coercitiva con mandato di cattura – art. 292 c.p.p. (Operazione Infinito) (Ufficio del giudice per le indagini preliminari 2011).

UNODC. *Estimating Illicit Financial Flows Resulting from Drug Trafficking and Other Transnational Organized Crimes*. Research Report. Vienna: United Nations Office on Drugs and Crime, 2011. http://www.unodc.org/documents/data-and-analysis/Studies/Illicit_financial_flows_2011_web.pdf.

UNODC. "Transnational Crime Proceeds in Billions, Victims in Millions, Says UNODC Chief." 2012. Accessed January 27, 2014. http://www.unodc.org/unodc/en/press/releases/2012/October/transnational-crime-proceeds-in-billions-victims-in-millions-says-unodc-chief.html.

UNODC. "Transnational Organized Crime: Let's Put Them Out of Business." 2012. Accessed January 27, 2014. https://www.unodc.org/toc/.

Van Duyne, Petrus C. "The Creation of a Threat Image: Media, Policy Making and Organised Crime." In *Threats and Phantoms of Organised Crime, Corruption and Terrorism*, edited by Petrus C. van Duyne, Matjaž Jager, Klaus von Lampe, and James L. Newell, 21–50. Nijmegen: Wolf Legal Publishers, 2004.

Van Duyne, Petrus C. "Introduction: Counting Clouds and Measuring Organised Crime." In *The Organisation of Crime for Profit: Conduct, Law and Measurement*, edited by Petrus C. van Duyne, Almir Maljevic, Maarten van Dijck, Klaus von Lampe, and James L. Newell. Nijmegen: Wolf Legal Publishers, 2006.

Van Duyne, Petrus C., and Tom Vander Beken. "The Incantations of the EU Organised Crime Policy Making." *Crime, Law and Social Change* 51 (2009): 261–281.

Varese, Federico. "How Mafias Migrate: The Case of the 'Ndrangheta in Northern Italy." *Law & Society Review* 40, no. 2 (2006): 411–444.

Varese, Federico. *Mafias on the Move: How Organized Crime Conquers New Territories*. Princeton, NJ: Princeton University Press, 2011.

Von Lampe, Klaus. "Not a Process of Enlightenment: The Conceptual History of Organized Crime in Germany and the United States of America." *Forum on Crime and Society* 1, no. 2 (2001): 99–116.

Woodiwiss, Michael. "Transnational Organized Crime: The Strange Career of an American Concept." In *Critical Reflections on Transnational Organized Crime, Money Laundering and Corruption*, edited by Margaret E. Beare, 3–34. Toronto: University of Toronto Press, 2003.

Woodiwiss, Michael, and Dick Hobbs. "Organized Evil and the Atlantic Alliance." *British Journal of Criminology* 49, no. 1 (2009): 106–128.

Za, Valentina. "Italy's Crisis Opens Doors to Cash-rich Mafia." *Reuters*, January 13, 2012. http://www.reuters.com/article/2012/01/13/us-italy-mafia-crisis-idUSTRE80C16320120113.

Index

Note: Figures and illustrations are in *italics*; tables in **bold**.

AAMS (Autonomous Administration of State Monopolies) 112
actors involved in demand and supply of illegal credit **80**, 80–1, **81**
agreement by tobacco companies with EU to fight tobacco counterfeiting 69n19
amphetamine consumption 34–5, **35**

black market prices of firearms **109**

Camorra (mafia) 19, 37, 110, 111, 112, 144–5; and cigarette smuggling 56, 60, 66, 67; and illegal waste 113, 130n104; revenues of 140, *146*, **147**, 153–4, **155**, **156**, *157*; and usury and extortion 78, 82, 97
cannabis consumption 33–4, **34**, **39**, 39–40, 41
cartels of Mexico and Colombia 2
Chicago extortion rackets 95
China and counterfeiting 127n21
cigarette market in Italy 7 *see also* ITTP (illicit trade in tobacco products)
cigarette smuggling and the mafias 56, 66–7
classification of data on organised crime 4
cocaine consumption **32**, 33, 40, 44n45
correlation analysis for extortion by region 101–2, **102**
Cosa Nostra (mafia) 2, 19, 78, 82, 112, 113; and cigarette smuggling 56, 60; revenues of 110, *146*, **147**, 153–4, **155**, **156**, *157*
costs of organised crime 7–8
counterfeiting 6–7, 8, 110–11, 127n19; estimate of market size 115–16, **116**, **121**, 122, *123*, **136** *see also* estimation of mafia revenues
Criminal Code, the 79
criminal groups and sexual exploitation 11–12

Dante 78
data on confiscation of organised crime assets 5
data on organised crime 4–6
demand and supply in the sexual exploitation market 11

demand-side approach to estimate the size of the drug market 30–1
DIA (Investigative Antimafia Directorate) 144, 148, 159n40
discrepancies in estimates of Italian drug consumption 39–41
'district' usury 81
DNA (Italian Antimafia Directorate) 114, 117, 146, 148, 159n40, 160n41–2
drug arrests 41
drug consumption 27–8, 39–41, 44n45; estimate of market size 6, 28–36, **29**, **32**, **34**, **35**, *143*; limitations in measuring 36–7, 42; by region 37–9, **38**

economic activities affected by extortion **103**
ecstasy consumption 35, **35**
EMCDDA (European Monitoring Centre for Drugs and Drug Addiction) 31, **32**, 33, 35, 37, 44n47
EMI (Euromonitor International) 54, 55, 57
EPSs (empty pack surveys) 55, 61–3, *62*, 67–8, 71n80, 71n88–9, 125; and non-domestic packs 57–9, *58*, 60 *see also* ITTP (illicit trade in tobacco products)
estimation of sizes of illegal markets 124–5 *see also* counterfeiting; drug consumption; extortion; firearms trafficking; illegal gambling; illegal waste market; ITTP; sexual trafficking and exploitation; usury
European Parliament report on costs of crime 8
extortion 93–6, 103–4, 104n4; correlation analysis by region 101–3, **102**; economic activities affected by 103, **103**; estimate of market size 96–101, **97**, *98*, 151; impact by region 98–100, **99** *see also* estimation of mafia revenues

figures for organised crime 1–2, 3–4
firearms trafficking **109**, 109–10, 129n88, 129n90–2, 131n113; estimate of market size

165

INDEX

114–15, 120–2, **121**, *122*, 125–6, 126n9, **136** *see also* estimation of mafia revenues
fragmentation of organised crime groups 2
frequency of extortion *98*

gaming machines and illegal gambling *see* illegal gambling
German extortion rackets 95
GPS (General Population Survey) data on drug use 31, 36–7, 41 *see also* Italian drug consumption
groups involved in the illicit tobacco trade 53, 57

heroin use 31–3, **32**, 39, 40

illegal gambling 111–13; estimate of market size 116–18, **121**, 123, *124 see also* estimation of mafia revenues
illegal waste market, the 113; estimate of market size 118–19, **121**, 123–4, *125*, 129n87, **137** *see also* estimation of mafia revenues
illicit trade, concept of 3–7 *see also* ITTP (illicit trade in tobacco products); sexual exploitation
integrating organised crime data figures into the policy process 139–40
intellectual property rights 8, 110, 127n19 *see also* counterfeiting
interest rates and usurious credit 83, 91n61, 91n63
interest rates on loans 79, 80
IPERICO database on counterfeited goods 115–16, **116**
IRU (Usury Risk Index), the 84
Italian Antimafia Parliamentary Commission, the 56
Italian businesses extorted by region 98–100, **99**
ITTP (illicit trade in tobacco products) 51–2, 55–9, *59,* 64, 67–8, 68n12, 69n19; demand and supply 52–3; methodology in estimating size of **60**, 60–4, *62*, 70n41; regional prevalence 64–6, **65**, *66*; size of 53–5, 57, *57*, *58*, 59–60, 71n92 *see also* EPSs (empty pack surveys)

KPMG Star Report into illicit cigarette market 7

law enforcement agencies and crime data 4–5 *see also* DIA (Investigative Antimafia Directorate); DNA (Italian Antimafia Directorate)
legalisation of marijuana debate 2
legislation to control drug trafficking 28
limited knowledge of drug consumption patterns 36
loan sharking 77–8, 79, 151–2 *see also* usury

mafia, the 12, 113; and cigarette smuggling 56, 66–7; and illegal gambling 112; and loan sharking 77–8, 82; presence by region 147, **147**
mafia revenues 140–4, **143**, **144**, 146, 147–8, *151*, 158; and the MPI 144–5, **145**, *145*; by region 148–53, **149–50**, *152*, **153**, *154*; by type of mafia 153–7, **155**, **156**, *157*
'Merlin Law' and prostitution 11
Milan empty cigarette packs survey 61–2, *62*
Milosevic, Slobodan 56
Montenegro and cigarette smuggling 56
MPI (Mafia Presence Index), the 144–5, **145**, *145*, 148
mythical numbers in the estimation of crime, use of 138–9, 140, 158

'Ndrangheta mafia, the 30, 60, 110, 111, 112, 113; revenues of 140, 153, 154, **155**, **156**, *157*, 157–8; and usury and extortion 78, 97
'neighbourhood' usury 81
non-domestic packs in EPSs 57–9, *58*, 60
North-South gap between Italian regions 78

Operation *Primavera* 56
outdoor and indoor sexual exploitation 18–19, **19**
overestimation of data figures for organised crime 139

piracy and intellectual property 110
problems with supply-side approach to estimating the size of the drug market 30–1
Project Star 54–5, 57, 61
prostitution 13, 20n3

quality and limitations of data 7, 18, 120, 125, 147–8, 158 *see also* mythical numbers in the estimation of crime, use of

Rand Europe study of counterfeiting 6
reducing the opportunities for crime 2–3, 8
regional opportunities in sexual exploitation 18–19, **19**, 20
regional prevalence of ITTP 64–6, *66*
revenues from sexual exploitation 13–14, 17–19, **19**
Rocco Code, the 79
Russian extortion rackets 95

Sacra Corona Unita (mafia) 56, 97, 100, 110
Saviano, Roberto 30
seizures of illicit goods 4–5, 28, 30, *59*, 131n113
sexual trafficking and exploitation 10–13, 14–15, 20n3, **143**; estimate of market size 13–14, **15–16**, 15–19, **19**; regional opportunities 18–19, **19**, 20
size of the illicit tobacco market 53–5, 57, *57*, *58*, 59–61, **60**, **143**

INDEX

Solidarity Fund, the 79, 89n16
SOS Impresa 30, 141
St. Thomas Aquinas 78–9
structured usury 81–2

Transcrime study into crime assets 5
TRIPs Agreement, the 127n19

UK prostitution industry, the 13
under-reporting of drug consumption 36
UNODC (UN Office on Drugs and Crime) reports 12–13, 21n35, 126n9, 139

usury 78–82, **80**, **81**, 88–9, 89n16; estimate of market size 82–6, **84**; interest rates charged 83, 91n61, 91n63; regional differences 87–8, **88**; turnover of **86**, 86–7, **87** *see also* loan sharking
Usury Risk Quotient, the 83

VLT (video lottery terminals) machines 112, 117, 123, 128n50

wastewater analysis of cocaine consumption 33, 42